THE INFORMATION SYSTEMS
DEVELOPMENT LIFE CYCLE:
A First Course in Information Systems

INFORMATION SYSTEMS SERIES

Consulting Editors

D. E. AVISON
BA, MSc, PhD, FBCS
Professor of Information Systems,
School of Management,
Southampton University, UK

G. FITZGERALD
BA, MSc, MBCS
Cable & Wireless Professor of
Business Information Systems,
Department of Computer Science,
Birkbeck College, University of London, UK

Editorial Board

This series of student and postgraduate texts covers a wide variety of topics relating to information systems. It is designed to fulfil the needs of the growing number of courses on, and interest in, computing and information systems which do not focus on the purely technological aspects, but seek to relate information systems to their business and organisational contexts.

THE INFORMATION SYSTEMS DEVELOPMENT LIFE CYCLE:

A First Course in Information Systems

D. E. AVISON BA, Msc, PhD, FBCS
Professor of Information Systems
School of Management
Southampton University

H. U. SHAH Bsc, Msc, PhD
Reader in Information Systems
School of Computing
Staffordshire University

The McGRAW-HILL COMPANIES

London ˙ New York ˙ St Louis ˙ San Fransisco ˙ Auckland ˙ Begotá ˙ Caracas ˙ Lisbon ˙ Madrid ˙ Mexico ˙ Milan ˙ Montreal ˙ New Delhi ˙ Panama ˙ Paris ˙ San Juan ˙ São Paulo˙ Singapore ˙ Sydney ˙ Tokyo ˙ Toronto

Published by
McGraw-Hill Book Company Europe
Shoppenhangers Road, Maidenhead, Berkshire, SL6 2QL, England
Telephone 01628 502500
Facsimile 01628 770224

British Library Cataloguing in Publication Data
Avison, D.E.
The Information Systems Development Life Cycle:
A First Course in Information Systems. -
(Information Systems Series)
I. Title II. Shah, H.U. III. Series
004.024658

ISBN 0-07-709244-9

Library of Congress Cataloging-in-Publication Data
The publishers have applied for a listing
Avison, D.E.
The Information Systems Development Life Cycle: a First Course in
Information Systems by D.E. Avison and H.U. Shah
p.cm.
Bibliography: p
Includes index
ISBN 0-07-709244-9
1 System design. 2 system analysis.
I Shah, H.U. (Hanifa) II. Title
1997

11ᴋ09b2-2

Printed and bound in Great Britain by the University Press, Cambridge

To my mother Zohra,
my husband Babar and the
memory of my father Mohammed.
Hanifa Shah

To Peter and June,
Christine and Alain.
David Avison

CONTENTS

7 SYSTEMS DESIGN: A BETTER INFORMATION SYSTEM

8 IMPLEMENTATION: PRODUCING THE GOODS AND GOING LIVE

9 REVIEW AND MAINTENANCE: THE JOB IS NOT YET FINISHED

10 TOOLS

10 TOOLS (CONTINUED)

11 SSADM

12 THE INFORMATION SYSTEMS LIFE CYCLE REVISITED

13 THE TECHNOLOGICAL INFRASTRUCTURE

13 THE TECHNOLOGICAL INFRASTRUCTURE (CONTINUED)

SERIES FOREWORD

The Information Systems Series is a series of student and postgraduate texts covering a wide variety of topics relating to information systems. The focus of the series is the use of computers and the flow of information in business and large organisations. The series is designed to fill the needs of the growing number of courses on information systems and computing which do not focus on purely technical aspects but which rather seek to relate information systems to their commercial and organisational context.

The term 'information systems' has been defined as the effective design, delivery, use and impact of information technology in organisations and society. This broad definition makes it clear that the subject is interdisciplinary. Thus the series seeks to integrate technological disciplines with management and other disciplines, for example, psychology and sociology. These areas do not have a natural home and were until comparatively recently, rarely represented by single departments in universities and colleges. To put such books in a purely computer science or management series restricts potential readership and the benefits that such texts can provide. The series on information systems provides such a home.

The titles are mainly for student use, although certain topics will be covered at greater depth and be more research oriented for postgraduate study.

The series includes the following areas, although this is not an exhaustive list: information systems development methodologies, office information systems, management information systems, decision-support systems, information modelling and databases, systems theory, human aspects and the human-computer interface, application systems, technology strategy, planning and control, expert systems, knowledge acquisition and its representation.

A mention of the books so far published in the series gives a 'flavour' of the richness of the information systems world and of the series. *Information and Data Modelling, second edition* (David Benyon) concerns itself with one very important aspect, the world of data, in some depth; *Information Systems Development: A Database Approach, second edition* (David Avison) provides a coherent methodology which has been widely used to develop adaptable computer systems using databases; *Information Systems Research: Issues, Techniques and Practical Guidelines* (Robert Galliers - Editor) provides a collection of papers on key information systems issues which will be of special interest to researchers; *Multiview: An Exploration in Information Systems Development* (David Avison and Trevor Wood-Harper) looks at an approach to information systems development which combines human and technical considerations; *Relational Database Systems* and *Relational Database Design* (Paul Beynon-Davies) are two books which offer a comprehensive treatment of relational databases; *Business Management and Systems Analysis* (Eddie Moynihan) explores the areas which overlap between business and IT; *Decision Support Systems* (Paul Rhodes) places management decision making in the perspective of decision theory; *Information Systems: An Emerging Discipline?* (John Mingers and Frank Stowell - Editors) debates the practical and philosophical dimensions of the field; *Why Information Systems Fail* (Chris Sauer) looks at the reasons for IS failure and problems of developing IS in organisations; *Human Computer Factors* (Andy Smith) emphasises user-centred design, usability and the role of the users; *Transforming the Business: The IT Contribution* (Robert Moreton and Myrvin Chester) discusses the role that IS/IT can play in organisational change; and the second edition of *Information Systems Development: Methodologies, Techniques and Tools* (David Avison and Guy Fitzgerald), which is a companion text to this book, covers the more advanced methodologies and their techniques and tools.

The Information Systems Life Cycle covers the basic material necessary in a first course in information systems. It is written by authors who have had wide experience teaching in business and computer science departments in both the old and the new universities. It can be used as a 'prequel' to *Information Systems Development: Methodologies, Techniques and Tools* (Avison and Fitzgerald), but can also be used 'stand-alone' where the teaching of IS does not go beyond a first course. The authors provide many examples and diagrams, chapter summaries, exercises and issues to debate, as well as an on-going case study of a typical organisation.

PREFACE

This book is designed to be used as a first course in information systems in colleges and universities. It covers the basic approach to developing information systems. The modern information systems life cycle presented in this text is very different from the 'systems development life cycle' that was presented in texts of the 1970s and 1980s. It draws upon the techniques of structured systems analysis and design, where appropriate, while producing a framework for information systems development as a whole. It also draws on other sources, such as the use of rich pictures in soft systems methodology. It describes how modern software tools, along with the technological infrastructure, can make the job easier.

However, again unlike earlier texts, organisational and people issues are regarded as equally important. Information systems planning and strategy are stressed along with the ways in which information systems can 'fit' into different organisational types. The roles of users are discussed in detail along with the option of end-user development.

Chapter 1 introduces information systems, their nature, examples and types. It introduces the technological, human and organisational aspects. Chapter 2 looks at the domain of information systems, that is, the types or organisations in which they will be implemented. Features of different types of organisation are described along with the processing carried out in them. We also look at the different layers of management.

Chapter 3 introduces the requirements of a methodology to develop information systems and gives an overview of the information systems development life cycle, described in detail in Chapters 4-9, and which is the main content of the book. This chapter also discusses planning and control of the information systems project and introduces software tools to support this. The book emphasises the role of people and information systems in the context of different organisations as much as the role of technology (the emphasis of most books on the subject). The role of the users in information systems development and, in particular, end user computing is also discussed in Chapter 3.

Chapter 4 begins the detailed description of the information systems development life cycle, from feasibility study (Chapter 4), systems investigation (Chapter 5), systems analysis (Chapter 6), systems design

(Chapter 7), implementation (Chapter 8) through finally to review and maintenance (Chapter 9).

In this voyage through the life cycle, we highlight the various steps, techniques, standards, and so on, which are essential in any approach. We also highlight the role of people, technologists, managers and users, in each stage. Techniques are described as they occur in the phase of the life cycle, and therefore they appear in their context, not as theory. As well as giving lots of examples, many illustrated through the copious use of diagrams, there is a continuous case study, set in a video shop. Each chapter ends with a summary, key references, questions, points to debate and a case study for the reader to contemplate, set in a hairdressing salon. Objectives of each phase, problems that occur and ways of solving them are some of the features of each chapter.

Chapter 10 looks at software tools, which support the information systems development process. These include CASE tools, fourth generation languages, database management systems, object-oriented and client-server development tools.

In Chapter 11 we look at a widely used commercial methodology, SSADM, which has many similarities to the 'ideal type' approach discussed in the book.

In Chapter 12, we revisit the information systems development life cycle, looking at potential weaknesses of the approach and responding to those criticisms. We also introduce alternative techniques, tools and methodologies which are the domain of a second-level course in information systems and subject of the companion volume to this: *Information Systems Development: Methodologies, Techniques and Tools* by David Avison and Guy Fitzgerald (2nd edition, 1995, McGraw-Hill).

In many of the previous chapters, we introduce the technology in passing, to illustrate the technological aspects of each phase, but to avoid too much complexity in the development chapters we have reserved Chapter 13 for a more detailed look at the technological infrastructure. Readers may wish to 'dip' into this chapter when appropriate. This includes sections on networks, open systems, client-server, object-oriented systems, AI technologies including neural networks, multimedia and virtual reality systems, workflow computing and data warehouses.

We are grateful to Paul Golder (Aston University) and Janet Blake (Andersen Consulting) for their contribution to the material on the video case study. We would also like to thank Carol Byde (Bass Taverns IT), Bernadette Byrne (Wolverhampton University), Sharon Dingley (University of Central England), Guy Fitzgerald (Birkbeck College), Dave Lawrence (Wolverhampton University), Christine McLean (IBM), Kanchen Shah (BT) and Dave Thomas (RAF Cosford) for their contributions to the book.

Chapter 1

INTRODUCTION

1.1 Domain of information systems

This book is about information systems: what they are, why we need them and, in particular, how we go about developing them. In this chapter we introduce the area by looking at the nature of information systems and some of the issues that concern them. The role of information technology in supporting information systems is discussed. Information systems need to be planned, and information systems strategy and planning are the key concerns of this chapter.

In this first section we look at some of the basics:

- The nature of information systems
- Examples of information systems
- Types of information system
- Types of computer-based information system
- Success and failure of information systems
- 'People' considerations
- Management of the information systems project.

We need first to consider the nature of information systems. A **system** is a grouping of people, objects and processes. An **information system** is such a grouping that provides information about the organisation and its environment. This information should be useful to members and clients of that organisation.

In the example shown in Figure 1.1, the information system is about the processing of sales orders from customers. The **people** include those staff of the company working in sales; the **objects** include records about customers and employees; the **processes** include a check to ensure the customer is creditworthy; and the **information** may be about the customer's creditworthiness, whether the products ordered are in stock, the total cost of the sales order and the profits from those sales. The figure also shows the **environment** which includes important elements outside the organisation. In this example, it includes the firm's competitors as well as its customers.

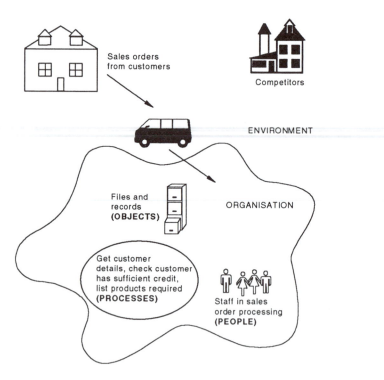

Fig. 1.1: An information system

The **organisation** could be a bank, business, church, hospital, university, and any other group of people trying to achieve a common objective or 'working together'. The information that is provided by the system could relate to its customers, products, suppliers and so on, that is, whatever information is needed to carry out the activities of that organisation.

In Figure 1.2 we see another example, that of a video shop. This is an application that we will return to throughout this text. In order for it to be run efficiently, it will require information about:

- *Video rentals and returns:* for example, who has rented which video and what date is the video due for return.
- *Video reservations:* for example, who has reserved which video for when.
- *Video stocks, orders and suppliers:* for example, which videos do we currently stock, which are on order and who are our suppliers (or potential suppliers).
- *Customers:* for example, who are our customers, what are their profiles (and hence what types of video they might rent) and what are their specific details.
- *Accounts:* for example, what is the daily/weekly/monthly income and expenditure of the business.
- *Trends in rentals:* for example, what are the patterns in video rentals for different times of the day, for different days of the week or seasonal fluctuations.

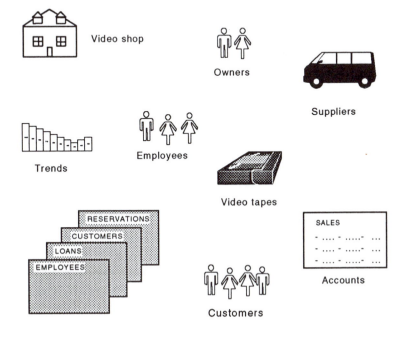

Fig. 1.2: Elements of a video shop information system

- *Employees:* for example, who are the people who work for us, what are their personal details, and what hours and days of the week do they work.

Information of this kind will be required regardless of whether the procedures are manual or computer-assisted. Information systems can be classified into types (see Figure 1.3):

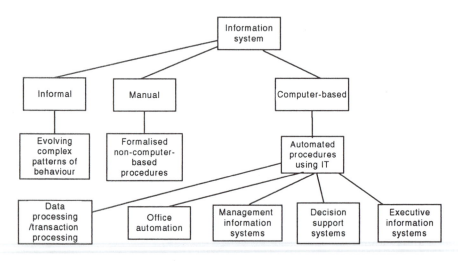

Fig. 1.3: Information systems: a classification

- *Informal information systems:* these are the evolving complex patterns of behaviour within organisations which are never formulated, but which need to be understood by all those involved with the organisation. These informal information systems can be vital to the organisation's effectiveness. It is important that employees communicate effectively, although informal information systems, such as the 'grapevine', may not always be a positive force.
- *Manual information systems:* these are the formalised procedures, which are not computer based, for producing information within an organisation. These were the information systems before the 1960s. It was about that time when computers began to be used by organisations. Most companies had many clerical workers doing the processing, much of which is now done by computer.
- *Computer–based information systems:* these are automated procedures for producing information using information technology, that is, computer hardware, software and telecommunications, to help this process. It is this type of information system with which this text is primarily concerned.

The terms information systems and **information technology (IT)** are sometimes confused. Information systems are the means by which information is delivered from one person to another, while IT is the technology that enables this to happen. The term 'information systems' emphasises the complete system, of which the information technology is only a part, but it is a very important part of most information systems.

We have considered different types of information system and suggested that this book will concern itself in the main on computer-based information systems. There are many types of these, including:

- *Data processing or transaction processing systems:* these involve the use of computers to process the routine transactions of the organisation. Such systems are used, for example, to process accounts, purchasing, product and personnel data.
- *Process control systems:* these involve the use of computers to make routine decisions for controlling some operational process. For example in production control systems, the computer will make decisions automatically for adjusting some production process. Another example is the automatic reordering of stock in an inventory system when stock levels of a particular product reach a certain level.
- *Office automation systems:* these use computers to automate general office tasks. They usually consist of software for typing, processing, storing and retrieving documents electronically; software for managing databases, such as addresses and contacts; software for electronic mailing; software for managing electronic diaries; and software for maintaining and manipulating spreadsheets.
- *Management information systems:* these use data from the data processing system to produce summary information about business performance. A management information system for a chain of supermarkets, for example, might produce aggregate data relating to all its stores.
- *Decision support systems:* these are extended management information systems into which hypothetical information or projections of information can be input to enable 'what if' analysis and hypothesis testing. Thus, for example, users may increase the tax rate in the computer calculations to see the effects of a potential VAT increase. Decision support systems tend to be highly interactive in operation with user inputs playing an important role.
- *Executive information systems:* Designed for top management, these tend to be highly graphical in nature, permitting easy access to a wide range of information. They are expected to have a particularly user-friendly interface.

Although the distinction between data processing systems, office automation systems and the others are clear, the difference between management information systems, decision support systems and executive information systems is more blurred. All three are aimed at supporting management decision making.

There are other ways in which information systems can be classified, Doke and Barrier (1994) discuss this concept in some detail.

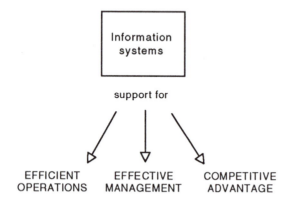

Fig. 1.4: Benefits derived from information systems

Information systems play a crucial role in the success of organisations. As seen in Figure 1.4, they derive benefits from the information that they provide, such as:

- *Efficient operations:* where efficiency is considered to be the maximisation of throughput with respect to the unit of resource input, that is, the organisation obtains maximum benefit with the least waste from the various resources it allocates to tasks.
- *Effective management:* where effectiveness is the ability to produce the intended output in a satisfactory manner. It is one measure, for example, of how well the products and services of an organisation meet customer needs.
- *Competitive advantage:* where, having already used information technology for producing information to make the operational and management activities of the business efficient and effective, the organisation uses information in new and innovative ways to improve business performance, cut costs and to have an advantage in comparison to competitors.

The first two types of benefit are straightforward. Information systems may increase the speed of processing and enable better decision making and thereby increase efficiency and effectiveness respectively. Information systems used as a competitive weapon might be less obvious.

A supplier of DIY products provides an example of an information system used for competitive advantage. This DIY supplier provides terminals placed in the premises of the retailers who stock its goods, from which its catalogues can be accessed. The terminals give the retailer information, such as details of the supplier's products, including prices. It might even allow the retailer to order stock directly from the supplier. This gives the retailer a useful tool. However, from the point of view of the supplier, it gives the retailer easy access to the supplier and by doing so gains competitive advantage because retailers will tend to use that supplier in preference to others without this easy access to catalogues.

Another example might concern a bingo hall chain that networks the computer systems in its halls together so that they all run the same game. This enables the chain to raise the payout and thereby attract more business compared to a bingo hall operating as a single unit.

Using information for competitive advantage involves organisations thinking about their business in a new way. Instead of restricting thought on how organisations can improve their goods and services, thought is turned towards using information systems as a competitive weapon. It means being a leader in the use of new technology.

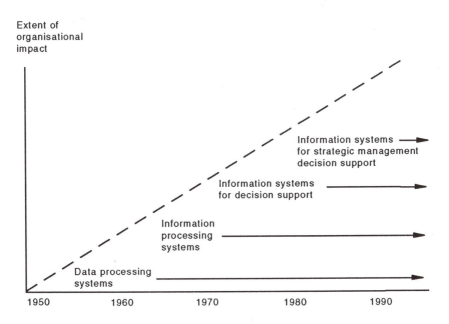

Fig. 1.5: Increasing organisational impact of information systems

Figure 1.5 shows the increasing importance of information systems. The role of information systems has continually expanded and those aspects of the organisation impacted by IS has also grown.

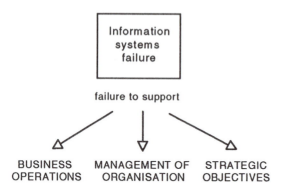

Fig. 1.6: Results of information systems failure

On the other hand, information systems projects can be large and complex, and there is a considerable risk of failure. As seen in Figure 1.6, information systems failure may result in an inability to support:

- *Business operations:* the day-to-day activities of the organisation, such as producing its products or delivering its services, dealing with its customers and suppliers, and so on.
- *Management:* the activities for controlling and monitoring the day-to-day activities of the organisation in the context of its aims and goals.
- *Strategic objectives:* the long-term aims, objectives and goals of the organisation. Goals are broad statements of the end results that the organisation intends to achieve in order to fulfil its purpose (the reasons why it exists). A goal for a certain organisation might be 'to establish ourselves as a leading telecommunications company'. Aims and objectives are specific and tangible measures, for example, 'to achieve product leadership in our core business, in this country and in key foreign markets' or 'to achieve an increase of over 10% in per-share earnings in the next three years'. Strategy represents how the organisation intends to achieve its aims and objectives, for example, 'co-ordinate sales and marketing activities'.

Information systems supporting the business operations and management activities of organisations are well established, but they must also support long-term goals and objectives. For many organisations these will include:

- *Survival:* to ensure the continued existence of the organisation
- *Profitability:* to maximise profits and minimise costs
- *Expansion:* to expand into other market areas and locations
- *Market share:* to improve share of selected markets
- *Customer satisfaction:* to provide customers with the kind of service that they want
- *Employee satisfaction:* to increase the satisfaction and well-being of the workforce.

Many of these may well conflict. This means that there has to be a trade-off between them.

To be able to meet these goals, information systems need to be well designed and cost-effective. There must be a broad framework for information systems development including a strategy for information systems and an allocation of priorities for their development. There also needs to be an agreed approach to develop information systems which follows acceptable standards. The key issue of planning and strategy will be discussed further in Section 1.2 and the systems development life cycle used to develop information systems forms the main theme of this text, and is introduced in Chapter 3.

The success or failure of its information systems can have a significant impact on the survival and success of the organisation as a whole. The development of information systems is a difficult and complex task. There are many failed information systems projects. Some of the difficulties have arisen because information systems projects have been viewed in too simplistic a manner, treating information systems development as merely an issue of technology. It is only recently that the implications of information systems development upon individuals, organisational culture and organisational politics have begun to be explored.

Figure 1.7 shows the five factors which constitute organisations. Changes resulting from information systems development must take account of all five factors and their interdependence. Information systems development therefore, is not simply a technical issue. The reasons for failure very often lie neither on the technical side, though the technology is complex, nor on the economic side, though the cost of these systems can be very high. The reasons for failure are very often due to other problems.

'People' problems, for example, may show themselves through the lack of co-operation when an information system is being developed and a resistance to the changes that occur when the system is implemented.

People may regard the change negatively. They may think that their jobs will be less secure, that they might lose the independence that they previously enjoyed, that their relationships with others will change for the worse and that they might lose status. They may think the change unnecessary or they may simply fear change in itself. In reality, the changes may be positive for the staff, but they may be perceived as negative (there is also the possibility that change will indeed be negative and resistance to change therefore becomes a positive thing).

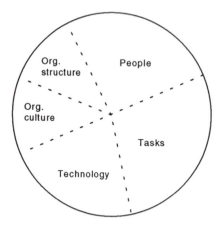

Fig. 1.7: Factors to be considered in information systems development

People fear the unknown and therefore early training, progress reports and user involvement in the change process will help. The work force should be informed of the likely changes in good time. Rumours about impending change will occur anyway, and staff not fully informed are likely to fear the worst. Those who can get jobs will leave, and these are likely to be the staff that the organisation needs to keep most. Further, resistance can be caused by fears which are not based on fact. Education of the workforce: about what computers can and cannot do, is likely to be more important than training in the early stages of the project.

We may be requiring a change in the culture of the organisation. This is a powerful influence on the actions and activities of the people in the organisation, and will be one of the main influences of the attitude to change held by staff. A culture that promotes and encourages change will greatly influence the attitude to change held by staff. However, attempting to change the corporate culture is a very long-term solution (up to ten years) and can be a very difficult period for all involved.

Other difficulties are caused by continual change in technological developments and that of the business and its environment. While systems are being developed over a number of years, the organisation does not stand still but continues to grow, change and evolve. Systems development can be seen as a trade-off between being flexible enough to absorb change and modification, but also rigid enough to ensure that it is not side-tracked or overtaken by events to the extent that nothing ever gets implemented.

Another aspect of information systems development that is important is the effective control and management of the development process itself, commonly referred to as **project management**. Each development project might have its own project development team. This team will normally be headed by a senior systems analyst. Resources, such as systems analysts, programmers, hardware and software, are assigned to the project. An individual project will have its own financial budget and time schedule. The conformance with financial budget should be monitored by regular reports that compare actual costs with budgeted costs. Computer-based software packages are available which can provide support and assistance for project management activities through the regular production of reports and charts, such as Gantt charts and networks.

We have seen the importance of information systems to organisations. In this book we consider how information systems are developed. However, information systems need first to be planned. In the following sections we look at information systems planning and show how we identify projects to be included in the project portfolio. The prioritisation of these projects is also discussed. We explore how an information systems strategy is formulated. We also propose a three-part architecture (data, communications and technology) for developing an information technology (IT) strategy within the context of the overall information systems strategy. Finally, we look at methods to analyse IT investments.

1.2   Information systems planning

An important factor in the success of information systems is planning. Information systems planning is an integral part of organisational planning. Information systems that are necessary for organisational success need to be planned and developed in a systematic and coherent fashion. This will ensure that information systems are aligned to corporate objectives and goals and are an integrated part of the business.

Information systems planning involves formulating policies, objectives and strategies for delivering information services and allocating resources. It also involves studying how the information systems function can contribute to the achievement of the goals of the organisation (possibly contained in a strategic plan). The aim is to plan the development of computer-based information systems which will improve the performance and competitive position of the organisation.

An information systems plan should highlight:

- Types of information systems applications to be developed
- Business functions to be supported
- Resources to be allocated to the information systems function.

In addition to an analysis of the business itself, a strategic information systems plan involves an investigation of the environment of the organisation. This requires an analysis of both the business and technical environments. An important consideration is an analysis of the potential that the organisation has for using IT for competitive advantage.

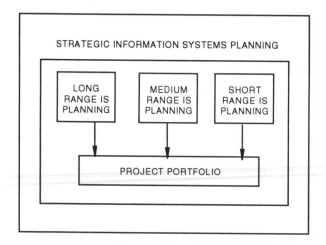

Fig. 1.8: Information systems planning

Information systems planning involves establishing a strategic plan which acts as a framework within which subsequent plans are developed This is illustrated in Figure 1.8. Information systems development requires the following planning:

- *Strategic information systems planning:* this is the process of deciding on objectives for the information systems function, on the resources required to meet these objectives, and on the policies that are to govern the acquisition, use and disposition of resources. It provides the framework for planning over a period of time.
- *Long-range information systems planning:* this deals with meeting the future information requirements of the organisation and with how the information systems are going to be organised to meet those requirements. This type of planning is mainly conceptual and has a time frame of five to ten years.

- *Medium-range information systems planning:* this involves meeting the present information needs of the organisation. This type of planning tends to have a time frame of two to five years.
- *Short-range information systems planning:* this is equivalent to the information systems annual plan. It involves individual computer application development schedules, budget preparation, personnel scheduling and timetables.

Any projects that are identified as being potentially useful to the organisation should be collected together into a **project portfolio**. The portfolio should list all applications that are foreseen in the medium term. The list of projects will be derived from many sources, and the implication is that the organisation has in place an on-going process which scans project possibilities. These projects are likely to belong to the following categories:

- *Applications currently being developed:* those where a need has already been established and which are currently being undertaken.
- *Backlog of applications approved for development but not yet started:* those where a need has already been established and which are currently awaiting development.
- *Projects generated by the long-range plan:* those which will contribute to the achievement of the strategic aims and objectives of the organisation.
- *User requests:* those that arise as a result of users identifying a need for information.
- *Major revisions to existing applications:* those that arise as a result of organisational changes leading to changes in its information needs. As the functions of the organisation change, significant modifications to applications are likely to be required.
- *New opportunities:* those that arise due to changes in legislation or to the cost-effective availability of new technology.

Within any organisation, there will exist a large number of potential information systems projects. Due to limited resources, it is very unlikely that the organisation will be able to develop all projects simultaneously. This means that choices have to be made about the order in which projects are undertaken. **Priorities** have to be established to determine the sequence of implementation. Projects that represent the most effective investment for the organisation will normally be given higher priority.

The **aims** of each information systems project should be reviewed to ensure that:

- It meets an important business need
- It is consistent with corporate strategy
- It leads to the attainment of specific goals and objectives
- It has an acceptable level of risk associated with it.

Risk should be assessed on the following factors:

- Are the requirements of the system well understood?
- What is the extent of the pioneering effort in terms of the technology that is required?
- What is the severity of repercussions on the business if the project fails?

The basic reasons for considering the project in the project portfolio should be identified as these will assist in determining priorities. The prioritisation of projects is discussed in further detail in the next section which discusses ways in which the information systems plan can be realised.

1.3   Information systems strategy

In this section we discuss the development of an information systems strategy and the three main issues to be addressed in its development: business plans and goals; current systems; and opportunities for information systems. We also discuss the development of an appropriate IT strategy within the strategic information systems plan which will provide the planning of the technology for delivering the information systems.

In developing an information systems strategy, it is usual to start at a broad level in order to get some idea of priorities and to put the problems into perspective. In this way it is similar to any information systems development exercise, which is likely to begin with a requirements specification and a top-level design of some sort. It is important to get an overall, directional plan before making any decisions involving technical detail or short-term allocations of available resources. Some consultancy companies use a standard method for analysing the information systems in organisations which involves the use of standard proformas and prompts various analysis procedures. These begin at a broad level, requiring an overview model of the main systems and their inputs and outputs, and later lead to modelling specific systems.

There are three main issues (Figure 1.9) that have to be addressed at the top level of strategy development:

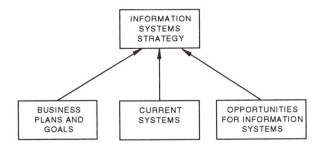

Fig. 1.9: Information systems strategy

- *Business plans and goals:* It is necessary to clarify the objectives of the business and how information systems fit in. This is to ensure that the direction of the information systems function remains in line with business plans. The importance of this cannot be overstated, as it is vital to align investment in information systems with business needs.
- *Current systems:* Some evaluation of current systems is required in order to identify problems, strengths and weaknesses. The examination of current systems may suggest either that some could be better exploited or be built upon to yield added value.
- *Opportunities for information systems:* From what is known about the organisation and its information systems position, through the previous analysis exercises, it should be possible to outline priorities for information systems investment, and areas where new opportunities for information systems exist.

By investigating these three issues individually, it will be possible to develop a long-term directional plan (or information systems strategy) for an organisation. Not all of the methods described are necessarily relevant to all organisations, and there is no definitive method or correct answers. However, there are analysis tools available, and each has relative advantages and disadvantages. We now discuss each of the three main issues in more detail.

Business plans and goals

Usually business plans and goals are not available formally. If they are, they may be ill-defined or difficult to express in terms which are easily translated into information systems needs. The organisation may have a mission statement or similarly expressed goals, but these are rarely specific and are often obscure or bland. Some sort of methodology is therefore required to establish business strategy and derive needs for information systems.

A popular method used to achieve this is the **critical success factors** approach which was pioneered by Bullen and Rockart (1984). This approach is also advocated by Earl (1989) for establishing business plans and goals, as it is easily understood and can cope with varying robustness of business strategies. It provides a workable methodology where business plans are either absent or not specific enough. The steps to this approach are as follows:

* *Identify and agree business objectives for the organisation.* This may be achieved through interviewing key members of the organisation and through studying documents that are produced. It is necessary to include a description of financial and other constraints for information systems in this phase.
* *Identify factors critical to success in achieving the objectives identified.* Again, this will involve interviewing critical staff to obtain their opinions. This might well be easier in a small organisation with less staff as there are less likely to be conflicting opinions.
* *Identify the information systems support which these critical success factors require.* This may be achieved either through the application of technology in products and processes or the development of information systems for the co-ordination and control of activities and for management decision making.

This type of approach is widely used. Daniels (1991) suggests that to evaluate the importance of IT in achieving business objectives, the management of the organisation should identify what it should do to achieve each objective, and grade the importance of information accordingly. If management decides, for example, that to differentiate the company in the market place it must be the lowest cost producer, the organisation needs to ascertain what must be done to achieve that. It requires any department proposing investments in information systems and technology to outline their 'strategic objectives and critical success factors'. This approach is a very flexible one, and may be detailed or in outline form depending on the organisation it is representing.

Establishing the critical success factors is an important step in any organisation as it leads to an explicit statement of goals for information systems, and will inform the direction of further analysis. It can be referred back to at any stage. An essential feature of the process is clarification. Business goals and the potential contribution of information systems must be clarified in order to outline directions, priorities and needs.

Current systems

It is important to evaluate the current state of information systems in the organisation, since information systems strategies are rarely developed from scratch, but must recognise the strengths and weaknesses of applications already in use. Various techniques exist to analyse current systems, but typically organisations commission a survey of current systems, usually called an **audit**. To measure the level of information systems investment necessary, an audit of the information requirements at present and in the future should be undertaken. The exact method will differ according to the needs of the organisation. One way to do this would be to first categorise information systems under headings which might include, for example, manual or computer-integrated. Then it is possible to draw up models of specific systems and note any related information, as well as areas of weakness and potential improvement.

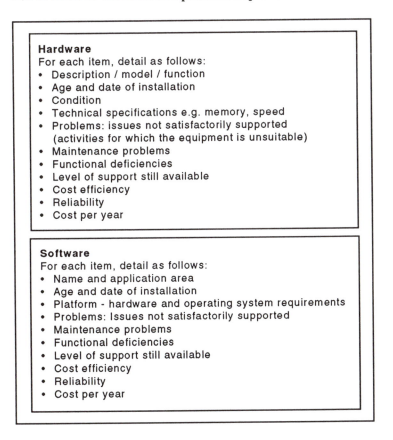

Hardware
For each item, detail as follows:
- Description / model / function
- Age and date of installation
- Condition
- Technical specifications e.g. memory, speed
- Problems: issues not satisfactorily supported
  (activities for which the equipment is unsuitable)
- Maintenance problems
- Functional deficiencies
- Level of support still available
- Cost efficiency
- Reliability
- Cost per year

Software
For each item, detail as follows:
- Name and application area
- Age and date of installation
- Platform - hardware and operating system requirements
- Problems: Issues not satisfactorily supported
- Maintenance problems
- Functional deficiencies
- Level of support still available
- Cost efficiency
- Reliability
- Cost per year

Fig. 1.10: Evaluating hardware and software

Another method, proposed by Earl (1989), whereby the basic coverage of systems is investigated, concerns the mapping of activities, processes and decisions against functions. This is followed by an examination of the business value and technical value. Business value means the value of the system as measured by the users:

- What would happen if it were removed?
- How easy is it to use?
- How often is it used?

Technical value means the technical condition as measured by specialists, in terms of reliability, maintainability and cost efficiency.

In smaller organisations especially, where interfaces are likely to be less complex, it may be just as effective to use a simple checklist to evaluate current hardware and software. Systems and applications are still classified in that each one outlined relates to a specific function within the organisation. Such a checklist is outlined in Figure 1.10. Figure 1.11 shows a simple example of part of a completed checklist.

The checklist should be interpreted as a general guide to evaluation, and can be modified as necessary. Not all factors on the list will necessarily be applicable to all items of hardware and software, but by working through the list for each item it is possible to highlight areas where information systems effort might be concentrated.

```
HARDWARE

DESCRIPTION/MODEL/FUNCTION
IBM compatible PC,  Pentium
AGE AND DATE OF INSTALLATION
1 year
CONDITION
Good
TECHNICAL SPECIFICATION e.g. MEMORY, SPEED
8mb RAM,  1.5gb hard disk drive
PROBLEMS:
MAINTENANCE none
FUNCTIONAL DEFICIENCIES none
LEVEL OF SUPPORT high
COST EFFICIENCY high
RELIABILITY good
COST OF RUNNING electricity .... etc.
```

Fig. 1.11: Hardware checklist

Opportunities for information systems
The purpose of this part of the strategy is to summarise the conclusions drawn from the previous two sections, and to identify opportunities

afforded by information systems which may further serve the aims of the company and create new options. This will include consideration of any plans for future growth or diversification. In large companies various creativity events, such as **think tanks** and **brainstorming groups**, are encouraged to help generate new ideas. Think tanks are groups specifically set up to come up with ideas to do with a specific issue. Brainstorming involves sessions where ideas are put forward and collected (without any validation or evaluation at the time as it might block creativity). These ideas are subsequently subjected to some sort of feasibility and strategic validation.

Studies suggest that innovative use of IT is generally facilitated by individual managers, backed by product 'champions' who become the system's entrepreneurs, and by the promotion of management education and development programmes.

It can be concluded that there are no formal methods whereby new opportunities for information systems can be recognised by management. Indeed, much innovation arises outside the formal planning systems that some organisations adopt. It is of fundamental importance that managers in organisations maintain an external focus, and are aware of the need to identify opportunities for information systems, in particular the requirements of users and customers. Management education could be an important factor, as well as taking advantage of any opportunity to recruit creative people who are likely to promote innovation. Naturally this must be balanced with the need for employees with other skills, such as financial ones. The overriding message is that managers must always be aware of the likely direction of information systems and new technological developments.

1.4   Developing an IT strategy

Information technology has been discussed as part of the information systems strategy. We now focus on IT in particular. The aim of the IT strategy is to develop a framework for the actual technology in the organisation. This is a more detailed plan which involves detailed modelling of the organisation, its specific activities and the role of information and information technology within it.

A commonly used concept at this level is that of an **IT architecture**. This is defined by Earl (1989) as a technology framework which can be used by the managers of the organisation to discuss appropriate information structures and the facilities that are to be provided which will assist in the satisfaction of business information needs. The idea is that a formal framework provides a consistent structure for implementing the information systems needs of the business. It can be used as a basis for resolving and reviewing technology choices over time.

Any architecture is usually divided into its constituent elements which can be analysed separately before being incorporated into an overall framework. Once again, there is no definitive method for either dividing the architecture into its constituent elements or for subsequently analysing these elements. Different situations require different approaches. For many organisations the strategy can be divided into three architecture elements, which are discussed by Earl (1989) and by Daniels (1991), as seen in Figure 1.12:

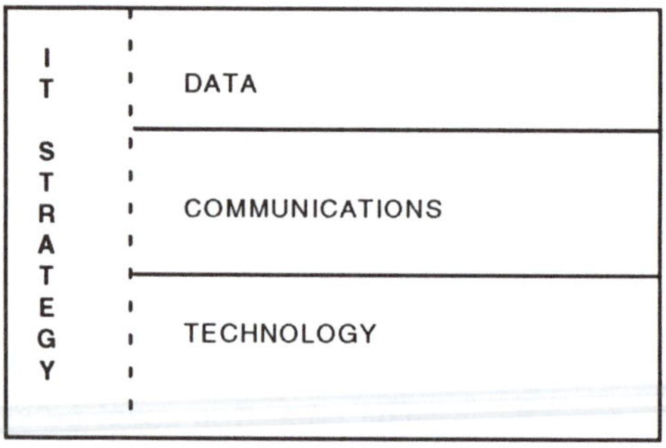

Fig. 1.12: Elements of an IT strategy

- *Data:* the pieces of information a company uses in the course of running its business. This data will have characteristics or attributes. For example, an organisation which manufactures a product will require information about its suppliers. The characteristics or attributes of such information will include, for example, details such as their names and addresses, products supplied, reliability and so on.
- *Communications:* the flow of information within the company. It will include any effort to convey information over distance effectively. This is the most challenging aspect of architecture today, and most companies are still at an immature stage of adopting that technology.
- *Computing technology:* the breakdown of the major technologies covering the activities of the company. This includes the hardware and software supporting the main application systems of the organisation.

One approach that has been suggested for analysing IT requirements is to represent graphically both the structure and processes within a company. This makes it possible to get an overall picture and maintain consistency, since ambiguities and inconsistencies are easily recognised. In larger companies, where there are many more complexities in information systems, a more formal approach may be required, either instead of or as well as graphic models.

Once again, there is no one procedure which can be set forth as being the appropriate method for all organisations. A useful approach would be one where each element is examined in turn and modelled in a consistent manner. Daniels (1991) suggests the following:

- The intention of the data model is to show what information is needed, where and by whom, in order that data may be synchronised. All of the major processes or activities in an organisation are identified along with an outline of the data required for each process and its attributes.
- The communications model shows the major flows of information within the company, thereby building up management's understanding of the importance of various communication flows.
- The technology model should indicate what technology, hardware and software, will provide the information. The aim of this is that implications, constraints and opportunities of the technology for the business should be understood. Where an analysis of current technology has been carried out at information systems strategy level, this will involve linking the systems previously described to the activities outlined in the data model.

The framework can then be used to see where priorities lie, and show how IT decisions will affect the business. The combination of knowledge concerning the strengths and weaknesses of existing hardware and software and the insight into the main activities of the organisation results in a framework which can be used to justify any consequent decisions about IT. For example, top priority would be given to developments which enhance the more important activities of the organisation, especially those that directly contribute to meeting the objectives of the organisation.

It is difficult to know, at this stage, the level of detail necessary. For some companies it may not be absolutely necessary to develop as detailed an information systems strategy and IT strategy as described, although enough detail is included here to enable understanding of the concepts involved. Deciding what methods to use and the way in which they are to be applied, will ultimately be a subjective decision. Developing a framework is an iterative process which should be repeated until the framework cannot be improved upon, and the best guide is experience. Nevertheless, a checklist of factors important in carrying out these exercises has been included as a guide to selecting the appropriate way to develop a strategy in organisations.

Analysis methods, and their results, should be:

- *easily understood:* by both those who are involved in the analysis exercises, and managers in the organisation who will be responsible for the IT;
- *free from ambiguities:* in that they should have only one interpretation;
- *consistent:* in that conclusions should not conflict with one another;
- *thorough:* in that they do not overlook any aspect of the problem;
- *resource limited:* in that they do not require too much time or other resources; and
- *repeatable:* so that new results can be obtained as and when circumstances change.

Any framework developed must also be examined in order to see whether or not it has met its objectives. These are to provide a basis for all IT decisions. The following basic points must be covered somewhere within the strategy development:

- Business objectives and critical success factors
- Awareness of the dependence on IT
- Most important information flows
- Financial and other constraints on IT
- Estimates for growth and diversification.

An IT strategy incorporating these fundamentals will provide a sound basis for the IT structure of an organisation.

1.5   Analysing IT investments

Developing a framework for IT strategy, along with an analysis of IT, allows us to address specific long- and short-term issues within the organisation, in particular, problems that need solving and applications which need attention. However, at this stage of strategy formulation, it is important to make organisational decisions on a course of action which will involve deciding between alternatives. We need a method whereby different investments can be compared. It is not enough for investments to be justified by strategy, they must also be compared with alternatives.

IT is generally regarded as being more difficult to analyse than standard investments due to the difficulty of quantifying the costs and benefits that it may bring. There are both hidden costs and hidden benefits. For example, it is difficult to measure the increase in technology skills required by any information system and to quantify the ease of use of the system relative to alternatives.

Many large organisations have a formal procedure with which proposals for information systems projects can be justified and evaluated by those involved in making the resources available. One example might be to define a common format for IT proposals from different divisions to a senior financial manager. This outlines the existing position of the business, including critical success factors as already mentioned, current problems, and proposed solutions. There should be a full breakdown of costs involved, timings and management issues, along with details of any alternatives that have been considered.

As with most evaluation exercises, there is no correct or universal method for analysing investments. Indeed, it has been found that successful projects in companies which have adopted a formal justification procedure often relied on a champion pushing for the project, and circumventing the formal justification procedure.

In a smaller organisation there is less need for a formal procedure for analysing investments of any sort for the following reasons:

- *There are relatively few people to deal with:* so that factors, such as time spent learning new systems and the impact on people's roles, are easier to judge.
- *Accountability is clear:* as it will usually lie with one or two people and because everyone can see who is driving a project, people are more likely to work to ensure its success.
- *Flexibility is easier:* small organisations are often more flexible as they have less bureaucracy and resources can be used flexibly in order to adapt to changing conditions and thereby to survive.
- *The issues are often (but not always) simpler:* for example, they are likely to involve decisions between a few alternatives whose direct impacts are more evident than the complex systems implemented in larger organisations.

However, the lack of standard procedures could have the following problems:

- *Important issues may get overlooked:* because the fewer people involved and the limits on time may mean an external focus is difficult to maintain.
- *Newer IT products may be overlooked:* as it is not easy to remain up to date with the issues and influences of IT.
- *The first apparently suitable solution to a problem that is uncovered may be chosen:* because of the lack of resources in smaller companies (both in terms of people and time).

- *There is the danger that an investment is chosen on the basis of its appeal to one person:* because the final decision and accountability lies largely with one person and this 'appeal' may take precedence over prospective benefits to the business as a whole.

Consequently, rather than establishing a formal method for analysing investments in smaller companies, a checklist of points to bear in mind when justifying investments is suggested. When used in conjunction with the information systems framework established previously, the checklist aims to provide useful guidelines to future investment decisions so that flexibility is maintained, while the potential problems are avoided. The objective is to strike the right balance between resources spent on analysis and ensuring that analysis is conducted thoroughly, through providing general criteria to determine the quality of information systems. The checklist consists of the following:

- *It is important to consider the human and organisational costs:* as while human IT costs are escalating, hardware costs are falling.
- *All investments contain some element of risk:* so that any evaluation of IT investment should contain some consideration of the risk involved relative to the alternatives.
- *The time scale of likely benefits from any investment must be taken into account:* as many organisations tend to be biased towards projects that will provide quick payoffs (though this may imply reduced gains in the longer term).
- *Intangible costs and benefits must not be neglected:* as these are an important constituent of IT investments, though they are often neglected because they cannot be quantified in money terms.
- *All people affected by the investment must be considered:* so that they are not alienated from the information systems from the start and they should therefore be consulted on the proposed project.

The criteria by which a system is judged should reflect the nature and purposes of that system. Some general criteria for evaluation proposed by Daniels (1991) are:

- *Quality:* in terms of usefulness to the business, its ease of operation, facility for maintenance and so on.
- *Flexibility:* ability to generate changes or respond to *ad hoc* requirements.
- *Importance:* dependence of the business on the system and the level of security required.

- *Scalability:* judgement on how the system will serve future business needs and its expected life relative to the growth prospects of the company.

The idea of a portfolio of information systems and projects has already been introduced. In companies where a large number of alternative investments are being considered at any one time, it is important to ensure that within that portfolio, risk is balanced and spread over a variety of systems. Projects should be planned in order of priority.

Options for prioritising projects specified by Reynolds (1992) include:

- *Give highest priority only to those projects that will assist in meeting critical business needs.* While this is a useful approach because of its low risk, it can lead to the overlooking of strategic opportunities to change the business significantly in the long term.
- *Give highest priority only to those projects that have the highest potential payoff for the firm in terms of costs and benefits.* Again the difficulty with this approach is that projects that try to apply technology in new ways or to new parts of the business may well be overlooked.
- *Give highest priority to those projects that have the lowest risk of failure.* Again, while this is a low risk approach, it does mean that the business following this approach for all its systems development is likely to move forward slowly.

When allocating priorities, therefore, a balanced approach may be more successful in the long run. As with other investments in organisations, it is important that IT investments are analysed and evaluated to ensure the effective use of resources.

1.6   Summary

In this chapter we have broadly defined the nature of information systems. We have identified computer-based information systems to be the concern of this text. Information systems have an important role to play in an success of the organisation and we have identified the benefits that can be derived from them.

Information systems planning, including the development of an information systems strategy, is seen as particularly important. We looked at IT as part of information systems planning, and considered IT investments in particular.

In the next chapter we look in detail at the organisation: its structure and its processes. We also look at the relationship between data and information, and consider the various information needs at different levels of the organisational structure.

Further reading

Ahituv, N., Neumann, S. & Riley, N. H. (1994) *Principles of Information Systems for Management*, 4th edition, B&E Tech, New York, NY.
A detailed and comprehensive text containing amongst other things discussion on decision making and the value of information, models of organisation, strategic information systems and information systems planning. It also contains detailed discussion of planning information systems development and ranking and prioritising projects in the project portfolio.

Barnatt, C. (1996) *Management Strategy and Information Technology Text and Readings*, Thomson, London.
Interesting and easy to read. This categorises information systems and also identifies important trends in computing and new working practices.

Brancheau, J. C., Janz, B. D. & Wetherbe, J. C. (1996), Key issues in information systems management: 1994-95 SIM Delphi Results, *MIS Quarterly*, June 1996, pp. 225-242.
Over the past 15 years, the Society for Information Management (SIM), jointly with the MIS Research Centre at the University of Minnesota, has periodically surveyed its members to determine the most critical issues in IS management. These surveys identify key concerns of the IS community.

Bullen, C. V. & Rockart, J. F. (1984) *A Primer on Critical Success Factors*, Information Systems Working Paper (No. 69), Sloan School of Management, MIT.
The critical success factors approach is discussed in this paper.

Daniels, C. (1991) *The Management Challenge of Information Technology*, Economist and Business International, London.
This explains how evaluation should be carried out including alignment to business objectives. Ideas about an IT architecture in this chapter are based on this text. It also suggests a graphical representation of the structure and processes as a useful way of analysing IT requirements using the IT architecture previously proposed.

Doke, E. R. and Barrier, T. (1994) An assessment of information systems taxonomies: time to re-evaluate?, *Journal of Information Technology*, **9**, pp. 149-157.

Proposes a user-oriented, two-dimensional taxonomy of information systems. This taxonomy utilises user type (institution or individual) and type of system support provided to the user (data, communication, information, or decision).

Earl, M. (1989) *Management Strategies for Information Technology*, Prentice-Hall, Hemel Hempstead.

This book stresses the importance of alignment of IT with business needs. It advocates the use of the critical success factors approach for establishing business goals and plans.

Farbey, F., Land, F. & Targett, D. (1992) Evaluating investments in information technology, *Journal of Information Technology*, **7**, 2, pp. 109-121.

This study finds that successful projects in companies which adopt a formal justification often rely on a champion. It also discusses criteria for evaluating IT investments.

Galliers, R. D., Merali, Y. & Spearing, L. (1994) Coping with information technology? How British executives perceive the key information systems management issues in the mid-1990s, *Journal of Information Technology*, **9**, 3, pp. 223-238.

Reports findings of a survey carried out amongst senior IS and non-IS executives in UK organisations to identify the most important and problematic issues they face in managing information systems in order to compare the views in the two groups.

Hicks, J. O. (1993) *Management Information Systems: A User Perspective*, West, Minneapolis.

This describes the business cycle and has detailed and thorough discussion of the different levels of decision making in organisations. It discusses the different information needs of users and also the characteristics of information. A discussion of strategies for prioritising projects can also be found.

Porter, M. (1985) *Competitive Advantage*, Free Press, London.

Provides a detailed discussion of issues relevant to competitive advantage along with a definition of strategy.

Reynolds, G. W. (1992) *Information Systems for Managers*, 2nd edition, West, Minnesota.

This contains case studies and examples to support the material discussed in this chapter. The aims, objectives, goals and strategy of businesses are examined and the text provides further useful reading on the prioritising of projects.

Questions

1. What is a system?
2. Explain what an information system is.
3. Give examples of the kind of information that might be required by a video shop?
4. What are the different types of information systems?
5. Discuss the benefits that organisations can derive from information.
6. What is competitive advantage?
7. Describe the possible effects of information systems failure.
8. What are the main categorisations of computer-based information systems?
9. Compare the different types of planning that are required for information systems development.
10. What categories might projects in the project portfolio belong to?
11. What are the three main issues that have to be addressed at the top level of strategy development?
12. In what way can business plans and goals be established?
13. Why must current systems be evaluated as part of the process of developing an information systems strategy?
14. What is involved in identifying opportunities for information systems?
15. Distinguish between information systems and information technology.
16. What are the architecture elements of an information technology strategy?

Areas to debate

1. The main information systems issues affecting organisations as identified by Price Waterhouse (1993) are as follows:

- *Cost containment:* The last decade has been marked by ever-increasing IT expenditure, and this becomes a major target for cutbacks during a recession. However, organisations have found it difficult to reduce expenditure due to the nature of these costs and a great deal of investment has already been made.

- *Integrating information systems with corporate strategy:* In large organisations, information systems have often been characterised by a 'culture gap', in other words, a lack of understanding and co-operation between those in charge of implementing information systems and those they are aimed at benefiting. In the past, systems have often fallen short of their expectations due to a lack of integration and consultation.

- *Meeting deadlines:* Organisations have faced problems in achieving their targets for information systems in the time expected. This has often led to a backlog of information systems needing attention.
- *Open system v proprietary strategies:* The advent of open systems, which aim to be inter-connectable, has meant a move away from traditional proprietary systems and from the traditional computer manufacturers. Open systems from one vendor ought to be connectable with those of other vendors. The effect of this is that organisations are not tied to one particular vendor in order to meet their current hardware and software needs nor for their future expansion. Proprietary strategies involve organisations buying systems from them that do not interconnect and organisations hooked into this have to migrate along paths largely determined by the vendor.

Which issues do you think will still be important today and what new issues might be important? You can obtain help by getting the latest IT review from Price-Waterhouse at:

Milton Gate
1 Moor Lane
London EC2Y 9PB.

2. It is frequently argued that the information systems issues differ greatly between large and small firms. What do you think are the differences (if any)?

Some starting points to the debate might be:

- In large organisations, information systems are well established in the organisation, and are usually managed by separate departments or staff dedicated to the information systems function.
- Small organisations are also constrained by the availability of capital for information systems investments. Rather than containing high costs already, they are concerned with getting value for money without incurring excessive cost.
- It is of fundamental importance in a small organisation with limited capital that any investment in information systems will help the organisation achieve its objectives in an efficient way as possible. It must be integrated with the overall strategy.
- Time also constitutes a significant constraint. For example, with limited staff availability, any time devoted to learning new and complex systems is time lost on other activities, which could jeopardise the future of small organisations.

- While small organisations are unlikely to have large-scale systems or mainframes to manage, the need to keep abreast of developments is also an issue for them. It is important both for the future growth of the organisation and to ensure that information systems benefits are fully exploited, that small organisations maintain an external awareness of changes in the market and of new products which could help their business. It is particularly difficult to keep abreast of developments where there is no one person or group of people specifically in charge of the information systems function. Often, in the case of small companies, responsibility for information systems lies with those who decide to take a particular interest in it, but whose role involves various other activities as well.

- In small organisations, there is a lack of specifically trained managers to make informed decisions. Issues of co-ordination and consultation are less relevant, as this is easier and less formalised in small organisations. Any organisation in its early stages of growth is going to face relative poverty of people, time and capital resources.

CASE STUDY

Toni Asifiori is the owner of a chain of *Asifiori* hairdressing salons. They are rather exclusive salons usually in city centres around the country. What do you think are the information needs of Asifiori, his salon managers and other salon staff?

Asifiori hairdressing salons are considering computerising many aspects of their business.

1. Describe the kind of information that might be of use to such an organisation.
2. Identify the information systems that such an organisation might wish to develop and show how these might be classified.
3. What competitive advantage might be gained?
4. What are the possible effects for this organisation if its information systems projects fail?

Chapter 2

THE ORGANISATION

2.1 Structure of the organisation

In this chapter we look at types of organisations and their need for particular information systems. Organisations will vary in their structure and we discuss the various forms of organisational structure. We look at the processes in typical organisations. Data is processed in different ways in order to meet the information needs of different levels of users in the organisation. A model for representing the different levels of management is presented and the underlying difference in information needs at these different levels is discussed. Computer-based information systems can be used to meet these information needs effectively.

We have established that we need to develop computer-based information systems. We need to develop appropriate information systems to support the activities of the organisation, such as those to support the day-to-day operations, meet its longer-term goals and objectives, and support strategic management. The specific projects that will be developed will be those in the project portfolio. An organisation needs information about its own internal operations, activities and plans but it also requires information that provides an insight into the industry and markets in which the firm competes.

An organisation is a person or a group of people united for some purpose. Individuals or groups of individuals have specific responsibilities to carry out in meeting the purpose of the organisation. Some examples of the specific functions for which responsibility exists are accounting, marketing and production. Information systems operate within organisations and are crucial to their functioning.

An organisational information system collects, transmits, processes and stores data, in order to retrieve and distribute information amongst various users in the organisation. Hicks (1993) identifies four basic organisational forms. These are the functional, product, bureaucratic and matrix forms. Each of these is now described.

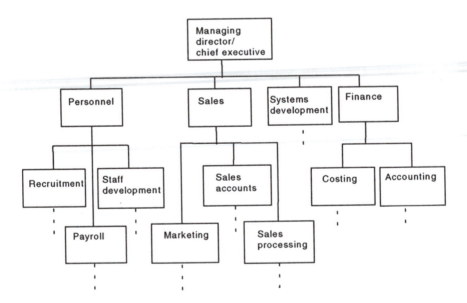

Fig. 2.1: Functional organisational form

- *Functional:* in this form of organisation, structure is aligned with basic managerial functions. As shown in Figure 2.1, these include accounting, personnel and sales. It enables clear assignment of responsibilities and also increases the potential for supporting employees carrying out similar work. A possible disadvantage is that it may narrow people's perspectives, confining them to their function only. Information systems for this form of organisation are usually hierarchical in nature, reflecting the hierarchical model of the organisation. It is often difficult to produce information which is aggregated across functions. In addition, information systems might be built that support only individual functions. It can be difficult to produce systems that span several functions. For example, implementing computer-integrated manufacturing would be difficult because it requires a system spanning the activities of several functional areas including marketing, manufacturing and accounting. Most organisational structures are hierarchical, though attempts are being made to change this.

- *Product:* in this form of organisation, activities are grouped together by outputs or products. As shown in Figure 2.2, each product division is organised internally by functions, such as marketing, design and manufacturing. An advantage of this approach is that it allows individuals to develop expertise of specific product types rather than spread their abilities over many different product types. Disadvantages include the consequent duplication of activities and personnel which are common across product divisions. Further, there is the danger of not reporting according to a managerial function, such as engineering, though reporting across product lines will be straightforward.

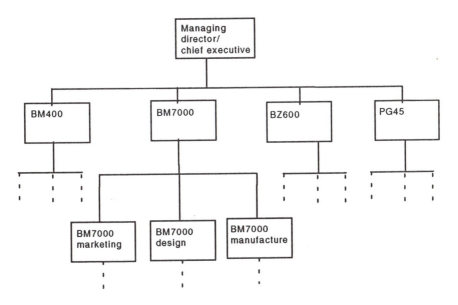

Fig. 2.2: Product organisational form

- *Bureaucratic:* in this form of organisation, it is assumed that individual employees cannot be entrusted to perform their task satisfactorily without specific rules and procedures. The characteristics of bureaucratic organisations are:
  - a specific hierarchy of authority is defined and division of labour based on functional specialisation exists;
  - a set of rules governs the actions and responsibilities of specific individuals in specific roles;
  - procedural specifications provide a sequence of steps that an employee must follow in carrying out tasks and dealing with difficulties;
  - employees as well as outsiders are treated in an impersonal manner;
  - technical competence is used as the main measure in the recruitment, retention and promotion of employees.

  Organisations of this form are usually mechanistic and impersonal. Such a form tends to be traditionally associated with government agencies, such as inland revenue and social security departments.

- *Matrix:* in this form of organisation, the dual nature of systems - authority and information reporting - is recognised. In this form the

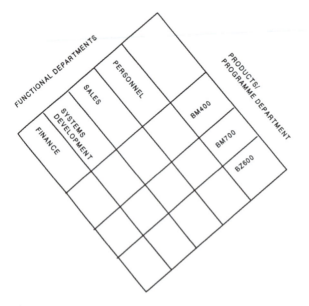

Fig. 2.3: Matrix organisational form

organisation is divided into functional departments. Simultaneously, each major product line or programme is assigned to a different product/programme department which is usually headed by a senior executive in the organisation (see Figure 2.3). The matrix form of organisational structure is a hybrid of the functional and product forms with individuals in the organisation reporting to both functional executives and to programme executives. This organisational form allows firms to respond quickly to new products. The members assigned to individual programmes bring a broad and rich level of expertise to the specific programme. A disadvantage of this approach can be the ambiguous nature of authority that results and problems of split loyalties for some individuals.

Organisational structures vary and it is important that systems analysts understand this aspect of the organisation in order to establish good communications as well as design information systems which are appropriate.

2.2 Processes in typical organisations

In this section we look at the general nature of processes that take place in organisations. Some specific processes which typically take place in organisations, such as payroll and stock control, are discussed. We look at how these result in the generation of data which is required for the production of information.

Regardless of the organisational structure, all organisations are concerned with dealing with a series of organisational **events** to do with their business. Every event of significance to the organisation will result in the generation and transmission of some data. The activity of the organisation consists of a series of transactions, which can be described as a business cycle. The data generated as the result of an event provides the permanent record of the event. As Figure 2.4 shows, the business cycle can be seen simply as a three-part activity: sales, purchasing and production. A customer orders and pays for products or services which the organisation sells. The organisation is able to do this as a result of some sort of production activity which involves obtaining raw materials from its suppliers and results in the product that the organisation is supplying to the customer.

There are many events that occur during this business cycle. Each of these will result in the generation and transmission of data which will be required for the production of information at some later stage. Examples of typical events are:

- *Placing of an order:* this will result in data about the customer who placed the order and the products required
- *Delivery of some goods:* this will result in data about what goods were delivered and to whom.

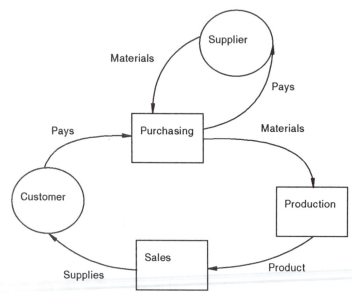

Fig. 2.4: Typical business cycle

Events not included in the diagram but pertinent to the operation of the business include hiring an employee, ordering machinery for manufacturing and paying in cheques to the bank. Clifton and Sutcliffe (1994) suggest that many organisations will have some or all of the following processes:

- *Payroll:* identifies employees, their personal details and rates of pay, and computes employee earnings, tax payments and pension payments.

- *Sales control and accounting:* ensures that orders from customers are received, recorded and dealt with in an organised and efficient manner. Sales control procedures will be used to ensure that customer orders are actually fulfilled. Sales accounting procedures are concerned with the financial side of customers' orders.

- *Purchase control and accounting:* ensures that all equipment, materials, tools and components are available where and when the organisation requires them and that they have been purchased at appropriate cost to the company. These procedures will be concerned, for example, with:

- obtaining quotations of prices, delivery dates and quantities
- placing orders with suppliers, monitoring delivery and following up any non-delivery of orders
- checking the goods are actually received
- checking supplier invoices and making payments
- aggregating information about supplier prices.

- *Management accounting:* ensures the activities of the organisation are carried out at acceptable cost and any discrepancies in costs are accounted for. These procedures are concerned with setting predetermined estimated costs and regularly comparing actual with these standard costs.

- *Stock control:* tries to minimise the money tied up in stock while ensuring there is enough stock to be able to meet demand. It involves the maintenance of records relating to stock levels, stock issued, outstanding orders, reorder levels and so on.

- *Production control:* decides what to make and how to make it. It ensures that planned production is achieved by monitoring and controlling the process, equipment and people involved in production. Information required for production control includes:
  - material requirements for each period of time
  - quantities of components and sub-assemblies to be made in each period
  - equipment needed for each stage of the production
  - amount of each type of labour category needed during each planned production period.

In this section we have considered the general nature of processes that take place in organisations and how these result in data being generated. In the next section we look at information from a number of perspectives, such as why the need for it arises, the different information needs and how data becomes information.

2.3 Characteristics of information

In this section we consider why the need for information arises, what these information requirements are and how these information needs are linked to the user role and activities in the organisation. We look at the different information needs of different users at different levels of the organisation. We distinguish between data and information and we discuss the characteristics of information.

We need information for reducing uncertainty in order to help us in our decision making. Information differs from data. The latter are the raw figures concerning day-to-day activities. Data do not enable decisions of any consequence to be made. It is information which enables this. Data arise from facts concerning the organisation. For example, the video shop has a certain number of employees and the working hours of each employee every week will need to be computed. The information that results from this data might relate to the running costs of the shop for particular times of the week. This information might be used to change the times when staff work.

Data is processed to produce information. Information facilitates decision making and planning. Information can represent actual values, for example, quantity sold, average service time and variation in the level of product costs. In our example, the number of loans of a given video, is an example of such quantitative information. Alternatively, it can relate to quality factors, for example, variations in the quality of video tapes purchased from different suppliers. This is referred to as qualitative information.

Data is the representation of facts, concepts or instructions in a formalised manner suitable for communication, interpretation or processing by human beings or by automated means. The same data can be represented in different ways. In order to interpret the data we need to know the rules or conventions for understanding it. Information is the meaning that an individual assigns to data, by applying a particular set of conventions to it.

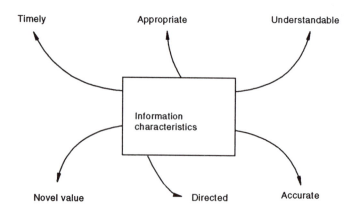

Fig. 2.5: Characteristics of information

Information has a cost associated with it. This is the cost of collecting, processing and storing the data which is used to produce the information.

Information also has a value. This value is subjective, depending on the context and intended use. What is perceived as information depends on the characteristics of the target personnel and their particular situation. What one person sees as data may be seen as information by someone else.

Information should reduce uncertainty, help in more informed decision making and be communicated effectively. As natural language is ambiguous, this can cause difficulties. Thought must be given to the possible interpretations (and potential misrepresentations) of the information by the recipient. As Figure 2.5 suggests, there are a number of characteristics that potentially useful information should have:

- *Information must be timely with respect to its intended use.* Information is of its highest value if it is provided at a time when it is most useful for the purpose intended. There is a cost involved in creating information: an increase in the speed of producing information normally increases its cost. If information arrives too late or is out of date when it reaches its target then it is of little or no use, indeed, it might even be of 'negative' benefit if incorrect decisions are made because it is out of date. For example, information about the video titles that are requested but not stocked or video titles that are stocked in insufficient quantities, needs to be available before, for example, the title has been on television after which the demand for the video is likely to decrease substantially.

- *Information must be appropriate for the type of task being undertaken and the personnel involved.* The task might relate to planning, decision making or control. Particular information will be for specific users due to their role in the organisation and the tasks that they are involved in as a result of these roles. For example, in the video shop, information about the availability of a specific video is useful to an employee dealing with the loan of videos. Information about usage of the shop will be specifically for the manager to enable the planning of staffing for different days and different times of the day. Information produced will be used for different purposes and its value will be influenced by its purpose. In our example, information about customers, what titles they rent, how much money they spend, which videos they wish to rent or pricing information about competitors all have different uses.

- *Information must be in a form that is understandable to the target recipients.* The style and format of the information must be suitable for the technical knowledge, numeracy and literacy levels of the recipients, otherwise it is of little use to them.

- *The degree of accuracy of the information must be appropriate for its usage.* There is little point in striving for a level of accuracy that is not required, as this incurs time and cost. For example, the video shop manager and the accountant are both interested in the value of video rentals. The shop manager needs to know that the value of the rentals over a particular period of time is about £60000 while the accountant needs to know the exact value of the rentals, which might be £60359.

- *Information calling for action must be directed to the person who can initiate the appropriate action.* The information provided should include sufficient facts and figures to enable effective and immediate action to be taken. For example, a report on goods out of stock for the stock controller should contain information about how to reorder the goods. The expected outcomes as a result of particular information being provided should also be anticipated. The information might be used to reduce staffing levels, change the prices of rentals or change suppliers of videos.

- *The value of some information depends on its unusualness.* Many information reports should emphasise the exceptions, so that the person who requires the information is aware of difficulties that need addressing rather than things which are going smoothly. The information that will be really useful to the manager of the video shop is about the people that still have not returned videos loaned despite several reminders. The manager is less interested in those that have returned their videos on time.

We can also think about information in terms of whether it is formal or informal. Formal information is generated by the formal organisation structure. The information is produced by standard procedures, that is, by known rules and is presented in a standard, predefined way. The data used to produce formal information appears on formal documents and is usually quantitative, that is, it represents actual values, for example, number of videos sold, average waiting time before being served and variations in the prices of video suppliers. Formal information has a well defined representation and the means by which it can be produced from the original data is similarly well defined. This means that it is easy to produce by computer-based systems.

Integrated with the formal organisation there exists an informal organisation which gives rise to informal information. This might be subjective and passed around verbally as rumour or opinions. Informal information can arise due to the following:

- *Patterns of social relationships and behaviour:* people meeting at lunch or tea breaks or socialising together out of business hours may well exchange information relevant to the business.
- *Work carried out outside the framework of existing predefined procedures:* There may be agreed but informal mechanisms about how work is organised and tackled by individual groups of users.
- *Differences in opinions:* The various groupings might have differing objectives and values which are likely to give rise to conflict. This is commonly referred to as 'organisational politics'.
- *Influences due to membership of organisations external to the organisation:* The most obvious of these are trade unions, but membership of political parties or other committees can give rise to informal information.

The informal structure is intrinsic to the organisation and is impossible to remove. It is often viewed as a negative force, but it can be beneficial and make the operations of the formal structure run smoother. It can deal with some of the omissions and inefficiencies of the formal structure. Informal information tends to be qualitative in nature. For example, the manager of the video shop might be said to have trouble retaining staff due to a brusque style of management. This is a subjective view but potentially a useful, if informal, piece of information. Though informal information is not produced as a result of predefined and known procedures, it is still an extremely important aspect of decision making. However, the nature of informal information means that it does not lend itself to collection, manipulation and transmission by computer-based systems.

We can further classify formal and informal information in terms of whether it is internal or external. Some information which is classified as external is actually internally generated, its classification in this way arises from the fact that it is for external consumption. Published accounts or a press release provide examples of these. Figure 2.6 shows that these two different classifications can be paired as follows:

- Formal external
- Formal internal
- Informal external
- Informal internal.

Information is also commonly classified as private or public. Public information is known to exist by most if not all people in the organisation but it can only be accessed by those in the organisation who have authority to access it. Private information is that kept by individuals which may either supplement or duplicate public information.

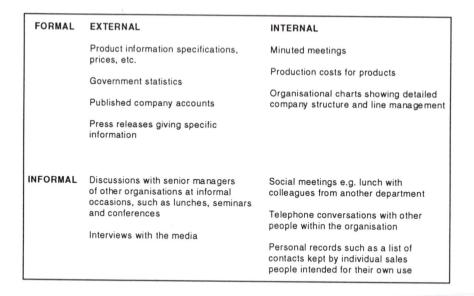

FORMAL	EXTERNAL	INTERNAL
	Product information specifications, prices, etc.	Minuted meetings
	Government statistics	Production costs for products
	Published company accounts	Organisational charts showing detailed company structure and line management
	Press releases giving specific information	
INFORMAL	Discussions with senior managers of other organisations at informal occasions, such as lunches, seminars and conferences	Social meetings e.g. lunch with colleagues from another department
	Interviews with the media	Telephone conversations with other people within the organisation
		Personal records such as a list of contacts kept by individual sales people intended for their own use

Fig. 2.6: Formal/informal and internal/external information

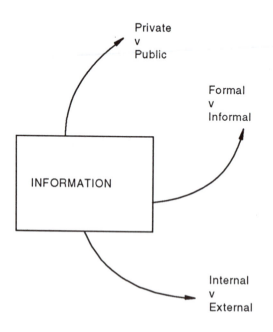

Private
v
Public

Formal
v
Informal

INFORMATION

Internal
v
External

Fig. 2.7: Dimensions of information

It can be seen that information has many dimensions that need to be considered. In the development of information systems, certain dimensions have significance for the specification of levels of security and other factors.

Within the organisation as a whole, the information needed will vary from individual to individual depending on the job or the role that they are fulfilling within the organisation. One way for us to think about the information requirements within an organisation would be to consider what the requirements are in relation to the level within the organisation. In the next section we look at these different levels within the organisation and the different information needs at each level.

2.4 Information requirements

In this section we look at how we might produce a simple model of the management of organisations. We then discuss the different levels in the model. We consider the different decisions that are made at these levels and the kind of information that is needed to enable those decisions to be made.

Since the managing of organisations is very complex, there are many different ways of modelling organisations suggested in the literature. The traditional view models organisations as having three layers of management. This is a simple view, but proves very useful. These three levels of management are:

- Strategic
- Tactical
- Operational.

The strategic level of the model is the top level of management and corresponds to the board of directors or their equivalent. They are responsible for overall organisational strategy and direction. The next level of the three-level view is middle management, typically heads of departments. They are responsible for ensuring that the policies for achieving the strategic objectives of the organisation are carried out. They will carry out suitable actions when information monitored indicates digression from the established norms. The third layer of the three-level view corresponds to the operational level of organisations. People at this level are responsible for the everyday activities of the organisation and typically include foremen and chief clerks who are in charge of daily operations, such as production, distribution and ordering.

The business information related to these different levels can also be classified into three main categories corresponding to the information requirements of these three levels:

- *Information for strategic management.* Senior managers are concerned with long-term planning and the setting of organisational objectives. They will require information that will help in addressing the following types of questions, for example:
  - Where do we want to be in five years time?
  - What markets do we want to be in?
  - Where shall we locate the new factory?
  - Which products shall we stop selling and when?

  The information required at this level is highly selective and usually in graphical form. Information required at this level is more likely to originate outside the firm. It will have value for a much longer period (years rather than months) and will require a higher degree of experience and judgement in its application. Patterns in expenditure from market surveys and trade publications are typical examples of this kind of information. The decisions made at this level tend to be unstructured. For example, deciding how much money to spend on research and development is unstructured because the factors on which this decision is to be based are not known precisely, nor are they quantifiable.

- *Management information for monitoring and control.* Managers at this level are concerned with monitoring and control of the activities of the organisation. They are responsible for the allocation of resources within departmental budgets. They are required to make decisions on the forecasting and the scheduling of work. They will require information that will help in addressing the following types of questions, for example:
  - Which products are we selling the most of?
  - Are the sales teams reaching their targets?
  - What are our projected sales for the next quarter?
  - In which areas do we need to recruit more staff?

  This level of management utilises information originating from both inside and outside the organisation. The degree of experience and judgement that needs to be applied to the information is less than that at the strategic level. Middle management requires condensed and summarised information in the form of reports, graphs and tables. This is largely derived from information collected at the operational level. Information at this level is used in shorter-term planning - months, rather than years - and is usually concerned with the departmental level. The following provide examples:

- *Analyses:* these are groupings of information to provide a summary of results within the various groupings. For example, sales analyses might be grouped according to product lines or to a period of time.
- *Forecasts:* these are predicted information based on previous figures projected into the future. The most obvious of these is sales forecasting information.
- *Regular reports:* these are generated at a particular time of the week or month and are linked to a particular cycle of activities.

The decisions made at this level tend to be semi-structured. Deciding how many products to schedule in the production line next week provides an example. This is partly unstructured because all the factors which affect this decision, such as staff availability, customer demand and work-in-progress, may be difficult to quantify.

- *Operational data for enabling and recording routine business activity.* It is at this level that computers have had a considerable impact. At the operational level, the day-to-day routines and activities of the organisation are carried out. Information is required for making the decisions necessary to ensure the effective and efficient use of existing resources to meet the objectives of the organisation. They will require information that will help in addressing the following types of questions, for example:
  - What is the stock level for a given product?
  - How much stock of a given part should be ordered ?
  - Can this customer be given credit?
  - When will the customer's order be fulfilled?

  Operational information is very detailed, highly specific and is generated internally. A typical process at the operational level is order processing, involving invoices and order forms. At the operational level we are concerned with the decisions made in the day-to-day operations of the business. It is used for weekly, daily or hourly decisions concerning the immediate situation and affecting the operation of a particular department. Thus it is considered very short-term in nature. Operational information could be about:
  - *Stock levels:* information about specific items and the quantity in stock
  - *Customer orders:* information about outstanding and overdue customer orders
  - *Overdue purchase orders:* information about invoices that have not been paid and which require further action.

The decisions made at this level are structured, since they are based on a relatively firm understanding of the underlying factors. Determining the level of inventory for certain products, for example, is structured, since all the factors are quantifiable.

Figure 2.8 shows how the information needs at the three levels vary in terms of the information type and its use. At the strategic level there is interest in patterns and trends over long periods of time. Decision making at this level is complex. At the middle management level we are interested in information that summarises the organisational activities, the information is to be used for monitoring, controlling and prediction purposes. At the operational level the need is for detailed information which is very short range and available in real time.

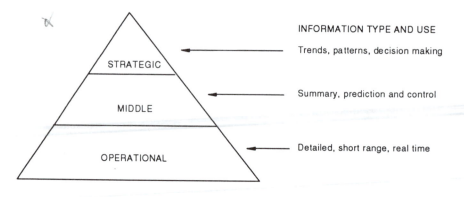

Fig. 2.8: Information type in use at the three levels of management

Figure 2.9 shows how the information at the different levels of management is used for different purposes and it gives examples of information systems that might provide appropriate information for use at each of these levels.

Figure 2.10 gives a summary of different information requirements of each of the levels in the three-level management architecture. Each level of the organisational hierarchy requires information with different characteristics in terms of the time scales, level of detail, source, degree of certainty and frequency. The continuum ranges from information at the operational level which is characterised by being for immediate use, very highly detailed, almost entirely internally generated, with a high degree of certainty and very frequently generated, to that at the strategic level of management where information is required for long-term planning, it needs to be highly aggregated and summarised, is from mainly external sources and tends to be uncertain and infrequent.

Information requirements vary at each level of management. Different kinds of decision making take place at each level and this requires different types of information.

	STRATEGIC MANAGEMENT	MIDDLE MANAGEMENT	OPERATIONAL MANAGEMENT
PURPOSE OF INFORMATION	Modelling and simulation for decision support	Monitoring and control	Transaction processing
EXAMPLES OF SYSTEMS	Financial models	Production planning	Stock control
	Profit margin change simulations	Sales forecasting	Payroll
		Market research	Accounting

Fig. 2.9: Purpose of information and examples of systems

	OPERATIONAL MANAGEMENT	MIDDLE MANAGEMENT	STRATEGIC MANAGEMENT
TIME SCALES	Immediate	$\longrightarrow$	Long term
LEVEL OF DETAIL	Highly detailed	$\longrightarrow$	Aggregated/ summarised
SOURCE	Internal	$\longrightarrow$	Mainly external
DEGREE OF UNCERTAINTY	Certain	$\longrightarrow$	Uncertain
FREQUENCY	Frequent	$\longrightarrow$	Infrequent

Fig. 2.10: Characteristics of information required (adapted from Curtis, 1995)

2.5 Data and information

We have looked at the different levels of management and identified their differing information needs. In addition, we have discussed how data and information might be distinguished. It should be apparent that what one person views as data, another might view as information. It very much depends upon the role of the users within the organisation and the purposes for which the information is required.

We now look at some examples of data that might be generated within an organisation and what information might be produced by appropriate processing of that data. We look at three examples. The first relates to a marketing information system, the second to a production control system and the third to a personnel information system.

In a marketing information system the following data might exist:

- *Competitors' accounts:* giving detailed data about their published accounts.
- *Product data:* giving details about specific products and their specifications.
- *Market intelligence:* data from market surveys about products and their actual or potential markets.
- *Accounting data:* giving details about the sales and profits of the organisation.
- *Contacts data:* giving details of potential customers at whom our marketing efforts could be targeted.

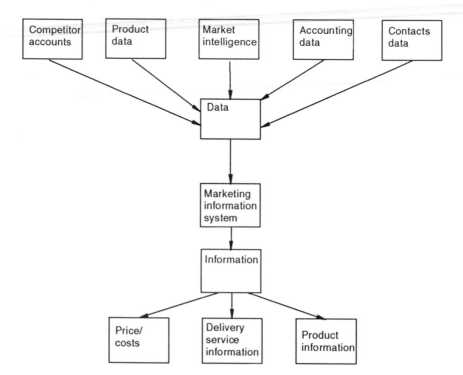

Fig. 2.11: Data and information in a marketing information system

As Figure 2.11 suggests, this data could be processed to produce information that might be useful for a number of different purposes, such as planning and scheduling of activities. The following could be derived from such data:

- *Information about product prices and costs,* for example, to establish how our prices compare with those of our competitors. Another example could be to identify what it is that forms the largest aspect of our costs and, once we have identified the contributory factors, how these costs might be reduced.
- *Information about delivery of our products or the services that we provide,* for example, we could discover what the time scales are for delivery and how this compares with the expectations of our customers with respect to service. This information could then be used to modify delivery and service if deemed necessary.
- *Information about specific products,* for example, which products might benefit from special promotions. Information about marketing effectiveness, in terms of market share and sales growth, could be produced from such data. This information could also be used to determine marketing efficiency, in terms of advertising and sales force performance.
- *Information about organisations where we might target specific promotions and campaigns,* for example, if customers have previously bought our products and services or expressed an interest in them, they will form a good potential customer base for new products.

If we consider a manufacturing organisation, what might be the data generated by a production control system? The data will concern the products that we are manufacturing, the raw materials that are required and the processes that must be gone through in order to produce our products. Data could therefore be derived from:

- *Work orders:* indicating what to make, when these are required and relevant manufacturing instructions.
- *Raw materials:* indicating receipt of raw materials, issues of particular quantities of raw materials for use in the production process of particular products, amounts of defective material and current stock levels.
- *Work-in-progress:* indicating completion of operations, locations of bins and the number of components involved.
- *Machine usage:* indicating time spent on a job, reasons for any breakdown and idle time when the machine is not in use.

- *Labour:* indicating time spent on a job, reasons for any non-productive time and clocking times.

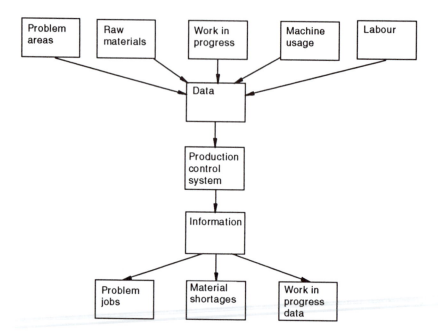

Fig. 2.12: Data and information in a production control system

As Figure 2.12 suggests, information about various aspects of the production process, its use of materials, the labour involved and details of difficulties experienced or problems anticipated could be derived from this data. The following could be derived:

- *Information about problem areas can be provided.* Picking lists can also be produced and information about stocks can be provided. Such information can enable decisions to be made, such as whether overtime is required to keep scheduled production on track.
- *Information about material shortages, material costs and material stocks.* Decisions regarding the need to chase up suppliers for non-delivery of materials, change arrangements with our suppliers or change production methods might be made.
- *Information about the progress of jobs, the work still outstanding and specific information about jobs running into trouble.* This information will assist in the task of rescheduling the jobs.
- *Information about processing costs and machine efficiency.* This will enable decisions regarding whether to change production methods to be made.

- *Information about wages and labour shortages.* Decisions could be made regarding whether to add a shift or to add more people to an existing shift.

Most, if not all, organisations will need to keep data about their employees. They need to know who their employees are, where they live, and know their tax and other details to be able to pay them for their work. In a personnel information system, data could be as follows:

- *Personal data about the employee:* will include the name, date of birth, address, qualifications, previous job history, current job historical information, current assignments and training record for each employee.
- *Employee data about periods away from work:* will include holiday entitlement, previous year's holiday entitlement carried over, holidays already taken, holidays scheduled, periods of sickness and length of absences.
- *Job description data:* will include detailed information about different organisational job roles, qualifications and skills required and wage and salary structures.

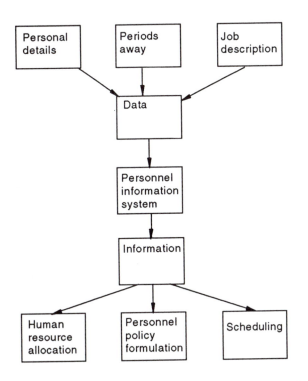

Fig. 2.13: Data and information in a personnel information system

As Figure 2.13 suggests, information could be derived from this data about the various profiles of the workforce, their qualification and skills, the days lost by the organisation due to absences, the patterns of absences from work and when best to schedule the shutdown of operations. More specifically, the following could be derived from such data:

- *Information to facilitate human resource allocation within the organisation.* This may be provided through details about the age and skill profiles of the workforce. Information to determine redundancy and retirement provision could also be produced from such data, as can information concerning staff turnover. It could provide assistance in formulating the future recruitment policy of the organisation.
- *Information to facilitate control of labour input about frequency, nature and length of absences from work.* This can be used to help formulate personnel policy, for example, regarding how many absences employees are allowed before they are cautioned or counselled about them.
- *Information to enable appropriate scheduling of shutdown of factory or production operations.* Related information for scheduling jobs and projects may also be produced.

As we have seen, data can be generated within organisations. This is processed in appropriate ways to produce the required information. In this section we have seen some specific examples of information generated from the raw data.

2.6 Organisation of information systems

In this section we consider the ways in which information systems can be organised. We also identify the components of an information system as people, hardware, software and data. We discuss the use of computer-based information systems by organisations and suggest some applications for which computers might be used by organisations.

As information is an important organisational resource, it is essential that it is efficiently utilised. It is therefore necessary to plan and allocate resources to manage information carefully. There are different approaches to organising information system resources and these will vary from organisation to organisation. For example, some organisations centralise the resources under a single organisational unit, while others delegate authority to functional units. This might take the form of an information systems section within functions, such as personnel, marketing and accounting. Another aspect is the physical location of relevant resources.

Some organisations concentrate their computing equipment and associated staff in the main office, while others may well distribute computing equipment and associated staff at different geographical locations.

Traditionally, computer-based information systems have tended to be designed around the functions of an organisation. These information systems have been developed to support functional activities, such as finance, production and accounting. There is now much more awareness of the need to build integrated organisational information systems capable of providing managerial and strategic as well as operational support.

Information systems development and operational support can be provided through the formation of **information centres**. An information centre is a unit of the organisation which provides hardware, software and personnel to support the computer users in an organisation. In the past, it would normally have been part of an information services department. However, it can also be found in individual user departments. The information centre helps users by supporting the use of:

- *Hardware:* personal computers, printers, scanners, digital cameras and so on;
- *Software:* word-processing packages, spreadsheet packages, databases and so on;
- *Personnel:* systems analysts, programmers and operators, whose aim is to help users make efficient and effective use of their hardware and software resources.

Different arrangements occur due to the fact that organisations tailor information systems resources according to their particular needs. The implication of this is that there is no single generalisation to model the organisation of information systems appropriately. However, we still need to discuss the main roles involved in IS development and support, and the organisation of IS development.

Over the years there have been changing trends with respect to whether information services are **centralised** or **decentralised**. In the early years of computing and data processing, decentralisation was the only option. Since computers were of limited capacity and power, they were only able to handle the workload of a single department. As mainframe computer technology developed along with advances in networking and telecommunications, the trend was towards large centralised computing facilities composed of hardware, software, databases, and information systems personnel. The next stage was the development of powerful minicomputers and personal computers which resulted in organisations moving towards decentralisation or **downsizing** of resources. This distribution of information systems resulted in the shift of information systems specialists to departments, and the creation of information centres has resulted from this.

Subsequent trends have included organisations centralising, although some have gone for hybrid measures, with both centralised and decentralised aspects to their structure. Some companies have moved their information systems function into separate companies or subsidiaries which provide relevant services to both the parent company and to other organisations. **Outsourcing** is another trend whereby a company hands over its IS operation (or part of it) to an outside agency known as an **IT facilities management** company, while continuing to focus itself on its core business activities. It is apparent that businesses are continually trying new and different approaches to providing, controlling and managing information systems resources. It is also apparent that certain core functions, such as telecommunications infrastructure, specifying standards and information systems strategic planning are likely to remain centralised information systems functions.

An important concept in information systems organisation is that of information resource management (IRM). In this approach there are five explicit areas that must be managed (see Figure 2.14). These are:

Fig. 2.14: The five areas under information resource management

- *Strategy:* This is concerned with managing information technology so that it contributes to both the organisation's strategic goals and competitive advantage, as well as its operational and management decision support activities. The IRM approach recognises that the emphasis on information systems must be aligned with organisational strategy to enhance business competitiveness. In line with this approach, many organisations have created a senior management position referred to as the **chief information officer** (CIO). The CIO's role is to oversee the organisation's use of IT. The emphasis in this role is on long-term information planning and strategy rather than on day-to-day information service activities.

- *Resources:* This is concerned with managing all the components of the information system, that is, people, software, hardware and data, in the same way as other organisational assets. These are valuable organisational resources that are to be managed in a way that benefits the whole organisation. It advocates the use of the information resource as a base for enabling strategic planning and innovation in products and services.

- *Functional:* Historically, the information systems function has tended to be treated as a special case due to its technically complex nature. In the IRM approach, it is treated in the same way as the other business functions and the same management approach and techniques are expected to be used as any other business unit. Managing information services involves:
  - Information systems development, that is, managing and controlling all the information systems development life cycle activities
  - Operations, such as data entry, equipment, production systems control and job processing monitoring
  - Technical services and support, such as managing and advising on equipment purchasing, maintenance, telecommunications, systems programming and data administration.

- *Technological:* This aspect emphasises the importance of managing all organisational technologies for handling data as integrated organisational resources. The IRM approach bridges the various technologies, such as telecommunications and computer-based information systems, and they are all under the overall responsibility of the CIO. All the technologies are co-ordinated and directed in line with the strategic objectives of the organisation.

- *Distribution:* This aspect recognises that computing technology is dispersed throughout the organisation. The implication of this is that information resources have to be managed at a number of levels throughout the organisation and not only by the CIO. The IRM approach ensures that this distribution of information management is recognised and that organisations see the need to establish and enforce appropriate policies for purchasing hardware and software, for information systems development by ensuring that relevant standards are adhered to, and that the security and integrity of corporate and departmental data is ensured.

As we have seen, information systems can be organised in different ways according to business needs. Information resource management helps to ensure that the five basic areas of strategy, resources, function, technology and distribution are managed in the process.

2.7 Components of information systems

The information systems of the organisation will consist of a number of components. As shown in Figure 2.15, people, hardware, software and data are the four basic components of information systems. In this section we discuss these components.

INFORMATION SYSTEM

Hardware - computers - peripherals	Software - systems software - applications software

Data
- About organisational
  activities
  e.g. employees,
  products, services,
  transactions
	People
	- end users
	- information systems
	  specialists

Fig. 2.15: Components of an information system

People
People are necessary for the operation of all information systems. They can be categorised into two main groups:

- *End users:* sometimes referred to as users or clients. They might be accountants, engineers, administrators, clerks, customers or managers. They are the people who use an information system or the information it produces. They may also be a source of the data which is input into the information system.

- *Information systems specialists:* who are the people who develop and operate information systems. They include systems analysts, programmers and operators. Other titles of information systems specialists include software engineers, information engineers, systems engineers and systems designers. The main activities carried out by various IS specialists include analysing requirements of users, designing information systems based on the information requirements of the users, developing programs based on the specifications produced, and operating computer systems.

Hardware

This includes all the physical devices and materials used in information processing (see Figure 2.16). It includes machines, such as computers, and all data media on which data is recorded, such as disks. Examples of hardware in information systems are:

HARDWARE	
Computers	Peripherals
Supercomputers Mainframe Personal Mini Laptop Notebook Hand-held	Graphics tablets Scanners Printers Mice Touch screens Pens Voice recognition devices

Fig. 2.16: Examples of hardware

- *Computer systems:* for example, mainframes, supercomputers, minicomputers and personal computer (PC) systems (see Figure 2.17). Mainframes are very large, fast systems which can support several hundred on-line terminals connected to them. Typically, they are used by very large organisations for processing massive volumes of transactions.

    Supercomputers are even larger and faster mainframes that are used primarily for scientific applications where very complex mathematical calculations need to be carried out very rapidly. They tend to be used by large scientific and research organisations. Minicomputers tend to be medium-sized computers with more processing power than PCs, but less than that of mainframes. They are capable of supporting a number of users at the same time, but obviously significantly less than those supported by mainframes.

COMPUTER TYPE	TYPICAL APPLICATION TYPES	TYPICAL ORGANISATIONAL TYPE
SUPERCOMPUTER	Complex, scientific and numerical applications	Government research agencies Military organisations Large time-sharing networks
MAINFRAME	Large volume and complex data processing applications	Major national banks National stock exchange
MINICOMPUTER	Business and scientific applications. Engineering analysis and manufacturing systems	Departmental office computers for large organisations Main computer for smaller organisations
PERSONAL COMPUTER	Word processing and other personal productivity tools. Graphics, communications and applications development. CAD.	All types of organisation Personal home use
HANDHELD COMPUTER	Applications for mobile workforce to enable data entry and local access to data e.g. paramedics service, personnel, gas, telephone, etc.	All types of organisation where off-site personnel have to collect and receive data

Fig. 2.17: Application and organisational types for various hardware

Minicomputers tend to be used by small and medium businesses as their main machine and by large organisations at the departmental level. PCs are the smallest and least expensive computers and are used by a single person at a time (hence personal computer). They can be in various forms, such as desktop, laptop, notebook and hand-held. They will be used by all kinds of organisations, both large and small, since their use is by individuals for improved personal productivity.

- *Computer peripherals:* for example, devices such as keyboards, optical scanners, bar-code readers, touch screens, light pens, joysticks, trackerballs, graphics tablets, speech recognition devices and electronic mice. These are all used for the input of data and commands (instructions to the computer in order to get it to do something). Magnetic or optical devices are used for data storage. Printers, voice synthesisers and video screens are used for the output of information.

Software

Software includes all information processing instructions (see Figure 2.18). It is obvious that computer programs are included in this category. However the procedures, that is the sets of information processing instructions needed by people, are also sometimes included. A program is a set of instructions which is executable by a computer. The executed instructions cause the computer to perform a particular task. Examples of software in information systems are:

SOFTWARE		
Systems	Applications	
Operating Networking	PACKAGES Word processing Spreadsheet Database	BESPOKE Accounting Payroll Sales Manufacturing

Fig. 2.18: Examples of software

- *Systems software:* this is a set of general programs which manages and controls all of the operations of a computer system so that its use is optimised. An operating system is systems software which provides the interface to the computer hardware and is the buffer between users and the hardware. It is the means through which the hardware is operated to perform the required tasks. Operating systems are very large and complex software for which the term systems software denotes that they are an integral part of the computer system. An operating system is constantly active while the system is on.

   The modern trend is for operating systems to support WIMP (Windows, icons, menus and pointing device, typically a mouse) graphical user interfaces which allow easy user interaction with the computer. Communication is multimedia-based and also interactive and across networks.

   The next generation of user interfaces have been described as 'post-WIMP' (Van Dam, 1997). These do not use menus, forms or toolbars but rely on, for example, gesture and speech recognition for specifying the operation and the operand. They are based on a three dimensional (3D) spatial metaphor rather than the two dimensional desktop metaphor for organising information. Commercially available examples are pen-based, hand-held personal digital assistants (PDA) such as the Apple Newton, arcade games and driving simulators with steering wheels, golf simulators where the player hits a real golf ball with a real golf club and the computer simulates the trajectory and displays it. Van Dam describes the future hardware consisting of wearable computers, PDAs and wall-sized displays where the user sees computer-generated information superimposed on real-world objects via optical or video merging to provide, for example, annotation or X-ray vision. Voice recognition will be natural language based. The software and hardware will be able to handle large volumes of continuous information from many input channels simultaneously. Figure 2.19 shows the four ages of user interfaces.

Batch mode, punched card input line printer output	Time-sharing mainframe and minis Alphanumeric displays Interaction via commands	Raster graphics based Networked workstations Point and Click WIMP GUIs	Post WIMP user interfaces; 3D spatial metaphor including sound video, etc
1950 1960 1970		1980 1990	
1st age 1950s-60s	2nd age 1960s-early 1980s	3rd age 1980s-	4th age 1990s-

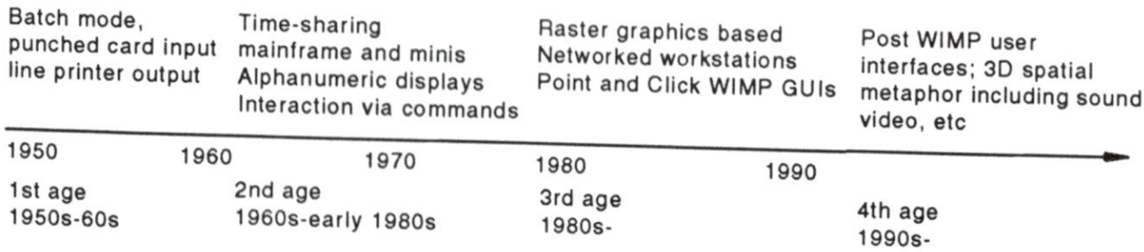

Fig. 2.19: The four ages of user interfaces

- *Applications software:* this is software that performs a specific set of tasks related to business functions. A common classification of applications software is into two main categories. One group, commonly referred to as software packages, is general purpose applications software. Word processing software is a typical example. Globally, there are an enormous number of word processing systems being used for work which is similar and since a word processing program is long and complex and required to do exactly the same kinds of tasks, then there is little point in each organisation developing its own word processing software. Software vendors sell relatively cheap packages for word processing which can be purchased by anyone who wants to do this type of work using a computer. The advantages to users are that, as well as being much cheaper, packages will have fewer errors than individually developed systems, as each version takes into account the experiences of a large number of users of earlier versions. Because of this, it is much cheaper to purchase applications software 'off the shelf'. The currently emerging trend in this area is that of voice input directly into a microphone. The appropriate software converts this into text format for manipulation by word processing software.

Electronic spreadsheets are another example of generalised software packages, which are relatively inexpensive but invaluable in terms of their typical use. The spreadsheet software package will enable relatively easy and rapid construction of a spreadsheet, which is a table consisting of rows and columns containing numbers on which calculations can be performed. A cell in the spreadsheet is the intersection of a row and a column and will be used to hold data. The data in a cell can hold a number, an item of text or a formula. If a formula is held in a cell, it is used to calculate the number in the cell from numbers in other cells. Spreadsheets are a powerful tool for those manipulating tables of numbers since the data held in cells can be recalculated whenever a change to any part of the spreadsheet is made.

In modern package software it is common to find spreadsheet packages to be integrated with other software such as word processing, database and electronic mail. The advantage of such integrated software is that users can easily move data around between the different packages and that data can more easily be automatically updated in one package when it is updated in another.

- *Specific-purpose or bespoke software:* this is software specifically developed for a particular purpose within a specific organisation as opposed to general purpose software. It is sometimes referred to as 'tailor-made' software. Examples of such software include payroll processing software developed for a specific organisation or an organisation's sales analysis software: indeed most of the application types discussed in this text are likely to be of this kind. Such software is used only for the application and organisation for which it was designed.

Data

This is the remaining component of an information system. Data is the basis for the informational aspects of the information system and hence is a key element of any IS. This component of information systems has already been discussed in some detail in Section 2.5.

2.8 Using information systems

We have discussed how information systems might be organised and also described the four components of an information system: people, hardware, software and data. We now consider where information systems might be used in the organisation and what specific systems might have been developed or purchased for use.

Most modern organisations depend on computers for virtually all aspects of their business, at least to some extent. For example, financial institutions, such as banks, insurance companies and investment companies, depend on computer networks and telecommunications for much of their basic activities. Computers are used to record all financial transactions. Prices of stocks and shares and exchange rates are quoted using electronic systems. Large quantities of such information can be handled speedily and accurately by using computers. Organisations are likely to have computer-based systems for accounting, order processing, invoice processing, stock-control, payroll processing and forecasting, amongst others.

Electronic point-of-sale systems (EPOS) are used by most large retail companies to record sales as and when they are made. By linking the terminals directly to computers, they manage the timely ordering and distribution of stock, as well as keeping accounts and providing detailed up-to-date information for further analysis. The use of computers helps reduce the volume of paperwork, reduce repeated entry of the same data, enable records to be more up-to-date, and increase cost-effectiveness. Much of the organisational correspondence will be computer-generated, either produced on word processors or using electronic forms, and is increasingly being exchanged via electronic means.

Organisations require information systems for their business activities with external clients, such as customer information. They are also used for managing and controlling resources in the business. We now consider some example applications that might be used by organisations. This is not intended as a comprehensive list covering all possible information systems. Some of the example systems have previously been mentioned. They may now be presented in the context of another way of categorising information systems.

- *Sales and marketing systems:* recording details to support marketing activities. Example systems include sales force management, mailing list management, sales forecasting, sales management, advertising, marketing and product management

- *Operations and production systems:* recording details of the stock situation for parts and products, allowing for ease of handling and distribution. Information in such systems could be used to identify problems with customer orders such as goods not sent but invoiced for, damaged goods and customer returns, for recording information about customer requests and the allocation of personnel and resources for dealing with these. Information in such systems could be used to understand the level and quality of service provided by the organisations and areas and ways in which it could be improved. Example systems include purchasing, goods-in, materials requirements planning, process control and computer-aided manufacturing,

- *Office automation systems:* which most organisations have introduced to allow their employees to benefit from the personal productivity tools that are included in such systems. Example systems include word processors, spreadsheets, databases and electronic mail.

- *Personnel and human resource systems:* for recording information about the employees of an organisation, such as their personal details, date of birth, salaries, qualifications, training courses and job histories.

Information in such systems could be used for identifying training requirements, or identifying the age profile of the organisation to influence recruitment procedures etc. Example systems include personnel records, training and development, human resource requirements forecasting, employee skills records and statutory reporting.

- *Ledger, accounts, financial, purchasing and planning systems:* for the financial and accounting functions, for recording information concerned with selling the services and products of an organisation, as well as information about its procurement activities. Information in such systems might be used to overview the financial situation of the organisation and how it could improve its purchasing activities. Payroll systems are required to ensure that the workforce is paid for its work. Example systems include cash and credit management, capital budgeting, financial forecasting, order processing, accounts payable, accounts receivable, budgeting, general ledger, inventory control and payroll.

2.9 Summary

Information systems can be organised in a number of different ways in organisations and we have considered some of the possibilities. We have also identified the four components of an information system as data, people, software and hardware and looked at examples of these. Examples of different type of information systems typically found in organisations have also been given.

We need to develop information systems that are appropriate for the business activities of the organisation in terms of short, medium and long range objectives. Specifically, we will develop projects that have been included in the project portfolio. Organisational structure has a bearing on the types of information systems developed. We have looked at typical business processes and how these result in the generation and transmission of data. From this data, information is produced to aid decision making within the organisation. The various characteristics of information have been discussed. We have presented some examples of data, and looked at information that might usefully be generated from such data. Four major components of information systems were identified, namely, hardware, software, people and data. Finally we looked at the ways that organisations use information systems for different parts of the business.

The next chapter looks at the process of developing information systems.

Further reading

Ackoff, R. (1967) Management misinformation systems, *Management Science*, **14**, 4, pp. 147-56.

This is a seminal paper which was among the first to recognise the failure of computer-based management information systems to get the right information to the right person at the right time.

Clifton, H. D. & Sutcliffe, A. G. (1994) *Business Information Systems*, 5th edition, Prentice-Hall, Chichester.

This contains a very thorough and detailed explanation of organisational processes, data and information, and the characteristics of information. It also discusses the different levels of management and the differing information needs at those levels.

Curtis, G. (1995) *Business Information Systems: Analysis, Design and Practice*, 2nd edition, Addison-Wesley, Wokingham.

This also contains a detailed discussion on data and information and the different information requirements of users in different levels of the management structure. It also contains a discussion of formal and informal information.

Gorry, G. A. & Scott Morton, M. (1971) A Framework for management information systems, *Sloan Management Review*, **13**, 1, pp. 55-70.

This provides a classification of decision making situations

Van Dam, A. (1997) CACM: the next 50 years, *Communications of the ACM Special Edition*, Hopes, visions and plans of future computer-based technology, **40**, 2, pp. 63-69.

Questions

1. What computer-based information systems might be developed to support the organisation's activities?
2. What are the different ways in which organisations can be structured?
3. Describe the business cycle.
4. Give examples of events that occur during the business cycle.
5. List a typical organisational process.
6. Distinguish between data and information.
7. State the characteristics of information.
8. Distinguish between formal and informal information.
9. How does informal information arise?
10. Distinguish between internal and external information.
11. List the components of a simple three-level model of the management of organisations.

12. Discuss the different information requirements at these levels.
13. Give examples of the kind of decisions made at each of these levels.
14. Think of questions that managers at each level in an educational organisation might ask. Can a computer information system provide information to address these questions?.
15. For an organisation of your choice, suggest data that might exist and also suggest information that might be produced from that data.
16. What are the different approaches to organising information systems?
17. For an organisation that you might come across in your day-to-day activities, list examples of computer-based systems for its employees and clients.

Areas to debate

1. You are planning to open a chain of pizza restaurants. What would be the information needs of such an organisation? Remember to consider information requirements at the different levels of management.
2. Search appropriate literature to find a variety of definitions for the term information. Discuss these different definitions and their particular perspective.
3. Identify an organisation with which you come into contact on a day-to-day basis. For this organisation identify three or four main levels of management and discuss the types of decisions being made at each of these levels and their differing information needs. Discuss appropriate information systems for meeting these information needs. What hardware, software and types of users are involved?
4. Identify several different types of organisation, for example, retail, manufacturing and health-care, and discuss with examples the different dimensions of the information. Such dimensions might include formal v informal, public v private and internal v external.
5. Joe Smith is a builders' merchant. He is experiencing problems due to a build-up of customer queues in the showroom. These queues are due to: (a) the length of time it takes to process a customer order which involves checking prices, product specification, filling out order forms and calculating order value; (b) when customers go out to the yard they often find that the items are not in stock and so they have to return to the showroom to select an alternative and have their paperwork altered. There is considerable friction between showroom and yard staff due to this. Showroom staff think that yard staff are uncommunicative whilst yard staff feel that showroom staff do not understand what is going on in the yard. Joe Smith thinks that these problems need addressing.

Furthermore he is contemplating relocation to newer premises. What are the information needs of this organisation? What information systems might be appropriate?

6. Identify different sized businesses. How might the information systems vary between each type of organisation?

CASE STUDY

The types of information required for Asifiori hairdressing salons includes _____ and information systems that might provide this include _____. Some of this information, for example, _____, is potentially able to give the chain advantage over its competitors. This is because of the following reasons: _____. The risk of failure is _____ and this may, in consequence, cause _____.

1. Fill in the gaps by providing suitable examples.
2. What processes will exist in a business such as the Asifiori Salons?
3. For the Asifiori organisation, identify the different levels of management that might exist in such a company. What kinds of information might be required at each of these levels and what characteristics would need to be emphasised for each of these levels.

Chapter 3

THE INFORMATION SYSTEMS DEVELOPMENT LIFE CYCLE

3.1   Requirements of a methodology

Having established a strategic information systems plan, which includes priorities for developing its information systems, the organisation now needs a suitable framework within which individual information systems can be developed. This is the central theme of this book. The development of an individual information system involves a number of phases which are often collectively referred to as the information systems development life cycle.

We now look at the reasons and problems which led to the formulation of the information systems development life cycle and discuss some important general principles which have been suggested for its use.

Early computer applications were developed without an explicit methodology and many aspects of these early information systems were problematic:

- In applications development there was a far greater emphasis on programming than on understanding requirements

- Developers were technically trained but usually poor at communicating with non-technical people, such as end users
- The needs of users were often not properly established and the systems that were developed tended to be inappropriate
- Estimating completion dates was difficult since the scope and phases of the tasks were not well established
- Small changes to one part of a system might cause undesirable effects in other parts of the system
- Staff left or moved to other posts in the organisation frequently, and this often meant that the people who maintained the systems were not the people who had written them
- Applications did not interact since they tended to be developed independently, leading to redundant data as well as introducing the risk of inconsistencies in that data
- Systems satisfied the needs of individual departments, but not the needs of the organisation as a whole. Since an organisation is more than a collection of departments, it has needs and characteristics as a whole entity in its own right which are not simply an aggregation of those of its departments.

Because of these difficulties, there was a move towards an appreciation of analysis and design and of the need for integrated information systems. The information systems development life cycle was introduced as means of producing better information systems in a more controlled and systematic way.

The information systems development life cycle can be considered to be a model of the stages in the life of an information system (and of any product). It is a process by which systems analysts, software engineers, programmers and end users build information systems. It can be considered to be a project management tool used to plan, execute and control systems development projects.

Some general principles that have been suggested for systems development by Whitten *et al.* (1994) are given below:

- *The user should be involved.* User involvement is essential for successful information systems development. Unfortunately, there is tendency for an 'us-and-them' attitude to exist between professional systems developers, such as systems analysts and programmers, and users. Misunderstandings between these groups continue to be a significant problem in information systems development. User involvement and education can help to minimise these problems. This aspect of IS development is looked at in greater detail at the end of this chapter.

- *A problem-solving approach should be used.* The information systems development life cycle is a problem-solving approach. The term 'problem' refers to opportunities and instructions from management as well as actual problems. Problems exist in a **problem situation**, that is any organisation. This might be a department, a factory or a whole business. A problem-solving approach involves establishing the problem clearly, along with identifying its environment and possible causes and effects. An understanding of the problem should lead to a definition of the requirements of any suitable solution. Alternative solutions meeting those requirements are identified and the 'best' among these is selected. The appropriate solution is designed and implemented. The implemented solution is observed and evaluated and refined accordingly. Further, it should be suitable within the context of the problem situation as a whole.

- *Phases and activities should be determined.* The size of the overall problem can be reduced by breaking it down into a number of phases so that detail is introduced into the information systems development life cycle as an on-going process. Early phases are concerned with the organisation and its activities, and later phases with the technology that will support the organisation and its activities. It may appear that all phases and the activities are carried out top-to-bottom and in sequence, but this is rarely the case. At any time analysts may be performing activities in more than one phase simultaneously. They may also backtrack to previous phases and activities to respond to new requirements or problems that have been identified since carrying out that phase.

- *Appropriate standards for consistent development and documentation should be specified.* These should be established for each phase of the life cycle and should describe the activities to be carried out, responsibilities, documentation requirements and quality checks. Doing this will enhance communication and ensure consistency between a potentially changing base of users and information systems professionals.

- *Circumstances requiring the cancellation or revision of scope should not be ignored.* One advantage of a phased approach is that several opportunities are provided to re-evaluate feasibility. There is often a temptation to continue with a project because of the investment already made in it. What is important is that the continued feasibility of the project should be assessed. Implementing an unfeasible project is likely to have more serious consequences (and costs) than cancelling it at an earlier stage. Checkpoints can be built into a phased approach where consideration is given to cancelling a project if it is no longer feasible, recalculation of costs and budgets if project scope is to be increased, and reducing the scope of the project if the project budget cannot be increased to cover all original project objectives.

- *Systems should be designed for growth and change.* It is important to recognise that organisations are constantly changing and therefore their needs in terms of information systems will also be changing. The trap of developing systems to meet the system requirements of today should be avoided, since such systems are difficult to change in response to new requirements and the resulting 'patched-up' system will cause problems in the long term.

In this section we have introduced information systems development methodologies as an appropriate framework for planning, executing and controlling information systems projects. We have suggested general principles which enhance the effectiveness of the development process. In the next section we look in more detail at the information systems development life cycle.

3.2   Stages of the life cycle

The idea of a life cycle is not unique to information systems. An analogous concept applies to the development of a new product. An essential element of the life cycle is that the development and operation of any system or product must evolve through the same consistent and logical process without omitting any phase. An analogy that can be made is that the development of an information system resembles the construction of a building. In most cases, buildings are not identical, but their construction phases are identical. As shown in Figure 3.1, the major phases of an information systems development life cycle are:

- Feasibility study
- System investigation
- Systems analysis
- Systems design
- Implementation
- Review and maintenance.

Each of these stages are discussed in detail as separate chapters in this book. A brief summary of these stages is now given.

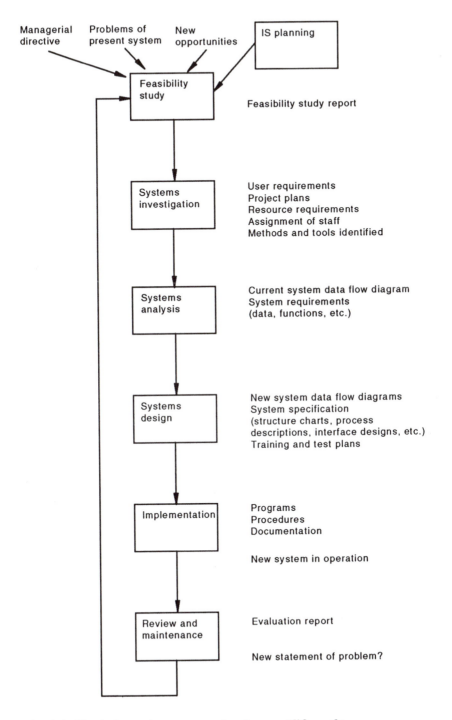

Fig. 3.1: The information systems development life cycle

- *Feasibility study:* During this stage, a systems analyst, or team of systems analysts, identifies the initial framework for the application. An investigation must be carried into whether it is feasible to carry out the project given the available organisational resources. Alternative costed solutions should be considered. The result of the feasibility study is a feasibility report which is presented to relevant personnel in the organisation who will make one of a number of decisions regarding the project. This might vary from keeping the present system or opting for the recommended or an alternative option.

- *Systems investigation:* Once the project has been given the go-ahead then its subsequent stages must be planned in more detail. Such detail will include data types, volumes, problem areas and so on. Analysts may use techniques such as data flow diagrams to represent the present system design. During this stage it is necessary to determine the data items associated with the system and to identify the sources and destination of data. The boundary of the system will need to be defined. Techniques for achieving this might include examining existing documents, interviewing, using questionnaires, observing present methods of work and sampling. The systems analysts need to know:
  - *Data to be processed.* They need to consider what data is created, received, manipulated and transmitted and the relationships between the different items of data.
  - *Processes that are performed on the data.* They need to consider what transformations of the data need to be carried out so that the information requirements of the organisation can be met.
  - *Files that are used.* They need to consider how the data is grouped and organised.
  - *Technical equipment that is used.* They need to consider what equipment is used to capture and output data.
  - *User views.* Systems analysts also need to investigate and understand the views of the various users. They need to consider what aspects of data different users or user groups wish to see and how these differ between them.
  - *Personnel and departments involved.* Systems analysts also need to investigate the interaction between different personnel or groups of personnel or departments.

- *Systems analysis:* Analysis of the current system is carried out in detail to determine the requirements of the new system. This is expressed as a logical model of the data and processes in the system. This phase should result in a detailed description of the system required by the clients. The clients need to agree that this is an accurate description of the system they require.

- *Systems design:* The purpose of this phase is to produce a design of the system to be developed to meet the requirements identified. This includes consideration of different hardware and software alternatives. These might include centralised or distributed systems and file or database systems. The logical design is translated into a design consisting of hardware, software, file and database specifications, program specifications and procedures. Technical design of the system requirements must be produced. This involves the preparation of:
  - File (including database) structures and organisation
  - Report layouts and contents
  - Screen designs, again in terms of layout of individual screens and the sequencing of screens and contents
  - Program specifications, giving detailed information from which appropriate code is to be developed
  - Specifications of devices that are to be used for the input and output of data
  - Plans about how the system is to be tested and the data with which it is to be tested along with the expected results
  - Detailed criteria for and against which the final system will be evaluated for acceptability.

- *Implementation:* During this stage the information system is built. This stage involves coding the programs, designing the operating procedures and producing the accompanying documentation. Testing the system is also undertaken to see if it works and meets user requirements. In addition, the installation of the tested physical system and conversion from the old system to the new system is carried out. Training of staff involved in the use and operation of the new system also takes place. Equipment is installed and the changeover to the new system is made.

- *Review and maintenance:* This phase consists of activities triggered by the identification of problems when using the operational system. At some point in time, the system will become too expensive to maintain, or it will cease to provide adequate business support. At that time the life cycle starts again.

Other texts may have slightly different phases or names for the phases. An example of another description of the life cycle is:

- Definition
- Construction

- Implementation
- Operation.

The important feature of these various approaches is that they do not vary greatly in terms of the actual activities or the order in which they are carried out. They may be called by different names or grouped into different stages, but the overall approach and its constituent activities are broadly similar. We will examine each of the phases that we have identified as part of our information systems development life cycle in more detail later in the book, indeed, each phase forms a chapter in the book:

- Chapter 4: The feasibility study
- Chapter 5: Systems investigation
- Chapter 6: Systems analysis
- Chapter 7: Systems design
- Chapter 8: Implementation
- Chapter 9: Review and maintenance.

3.3   Methodologies for IS development

The early applications of computers were implemented without the aid of any explicit IS development methodology. In these early days, the emphasis of computer applications was towards programming. This meant that systems developers were technically trained but were not necessarily good communicators. This often meant that the needs of the users in the application area were not well established, with the consequence that the IS design was frequently inappropriate for the application. Few programmers would follow any formal methodology. Frequently, they would use rule-of-thumb and rely on experience. Estimating the date on which the system would be operational was difficult and applications were frequently behind schedule. Programmers might spend a very large proportion of their time on correcting and enhancing the applications which were operational. Typically, a user would come to the programmers asking for a new report or a modification of one that was already supplied. Often these changes had undesirable effects on other parts of the system, which also had to be corrected. This vicious circle would continue, causing frustration to both programmers and users. As computers were used more and more and management was demanding more appropriate systems for their expensive outlay, the situation could not continue. There were three main changes:

- The first was a growing appreciation of the part of the development of the system that concerns **analysis and design** and therefore the **role of the systems analyst** as well as that of the programmer.
- The second was a realisation that as organisations were growing in size and complexity it was desirable to move away from one-off solutions towards a more **integrated** approach.
- The third was an appreciation of the desirability of an accepted **methodology** for the development of information systems.

It was to answer these problems that methodologies were devised and adopted by many organisations.

A **methodology** is a collection of procedures, techniques, tools and documentation aids which will help systems developers in their efforts to produce a new information system. It will consist of phases, themselves consisting of sub-phases, which will guide the systems developers in their choice of the techniques that might be appropriate at each stage of the project and also help them plan, manage, control and evaluate information systems projects. A methodology represents a way to develop information systems systematically.

Methodologies may differ in the techniques recommended or the contents of each phase, but sometimes their differences are more fundamental. Some methodologies emphasise the humanistic aspects of developing an IS, others aim to be scientific in their approach and others attempt to automate as much of the work of developing the project as possible.

Tools and techniques feature in each methodology. Particular techniques and tools may feature in a number of methodologies. A **technique** is a way of doing a particular activity in the systems development process and any particular methodology may recommend techniques to carry out many of these activities.

Each technique may involve using one or more **tools** which represent some of the artefacts that might be used. In the context of information systems methodologies, tools are normally computer-based. Some of these have been designed specifically to support activities in a particular methodology. Others are more general purpose and are used in a number of methodologies.

An information systems methodology in attempting to make effective use of IT will also attempt to make effective use of the techniques and tools available. But information systems are about balancing the technical aspects with behavioural (people-oriented) aspects. There are many views as to where this balance lies and how the balance is achieved in any methodology. At one extreme are the methodologies aiming at full automation of information systems development as well as the information systems itself. At the other extreme are attempts at full user participation in information systems development.

Over the last 15 years, systems developers have begun to rely on structured methodologies. Many organisations have developed their own 'in-house' methodology, selecting appropriate tools and techniques from commercial methodologies. The tools are used at specified points in the methodology to produce a series of **models** which form the basis of program and data design. Not all structured methodologies address each phase of the information systems development life cycle, although most address the analysis and design phases.

A structured approach divides the project into smaller, well defined activities. It specifies the sequence and connection between the activities. It provides a clear statement of requirements. It also aims to improve project management and control leading to better quality systems.

In this text we propose a generic approach to information systems development. Most, but not all, commercial information systems development methodologies, such as SSADM, Merise and Information Engineering, are based on this. Towards the end of the text we look at one particular commercial methodology, Structured Systems Analysis and Design Method (SSADM), but as we shall see, it is not too different from the generic information systems development life cycle described in Chapters 4-9.

3.4 Tools for project planning and control

An information systems development project requires that a number of tasks are carried out. Broadly, these tasks can be divided into the following areas:

- *Planning:* This enables the judgement of the progress of a project and consists of producing an overall project plan involving:
  - Specifying milestones/events which signify the end of a particular stage in a project
  - Costing activities
  - Identifying how objectives are to be met
  - Sub-dividing larger activities into smaller, manageable chunks
  - Allocating appropriate staff to carry out tasks.

  Estimation plays an important part in project planning. The project manager must estimate the risk involved in a project before deciding whether to continue with it. One important risk factor is the likelihood of a project exceeding its estimated budget or timescale.

- *Organising:* This involves establishing the skills and personnel required to carry out the project. Individual responsibilities and lines of communication should be clearly specified. This includes communications between project staff and between designated project staff and customer/client staff.
- *Staffing:* This involves selecting, promoting and training appropriate personnel to fill the positions previously identified. It is important to recognise the potential of existing members of staff and encourage those with potential into more senior positions. Doing this will ensure continuity of staff with the appropriate skills and knowledge.
- *Monitoring:* This is the means of measuring the progress of a project. As stated earlier, planning will have identified how major objectives are to be met; monitoring will check that these objectives are being met.
- *Controlling:* This involves ensuring that a project is on target to meet its objectives. This might mean the reallocation of resources, or rescheduling of activities. It is a day-to-day activity, that is short term when compared to planning, and involves solving problems and finding solutions to difficulties.

As discussed in the previous section, the information systems development activity will require effective planning and control. This will help to ensure that projects are completed on time, within budget and are of the required functionality and quality. As this has traditionally been a particularly problematic aspect of information systems development, tools and techniques have been developed. For example, software tools are available which help to document the plans and progress of activities for the project. Project management requires detailed analysis of:

- Tasks involved in the project
- Relationships between the tasks
- Allocation of resources to the tasks.

Software tools can help in drawing up appropriate representations, such as charts or networks. Outputs from such software are useful for management reviews of the projects as they progress. Useful techniques for these type of tasks are:

- *Gantt chart:* This is a visual aid to planning, offering a mechanism for showing linked activities, their relationships and the time taken to complete them. They are also called bar charts. As shown in Figure 3.2, a Gantt chart uses bars or lines to show the amount of time needed by an activity. The length of the line is proportional to the length of time that activity takes to complete. The position of the line indicates the earliest point in time from which the activity can start. The end of the line shows the earliest time the activity can end. In Figure 3.2, the light blocks show the estimated time for completing activities and the shaded blocks show the actual times. A vertical line denotes the present position.

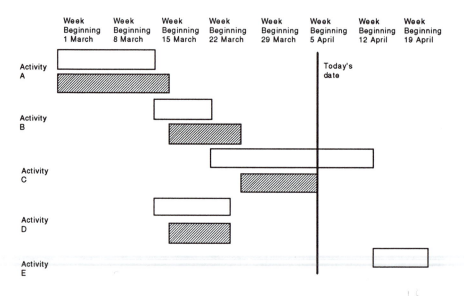

Fig. 3.2: Gantt chart

- *Critical path analysis*: With this technique, the project is reduced into its component sub-tasks or activities. Events are identified which mark points in time where some activity starts or stops. In a given project, the analyst will produce a list of all activities which constitute the project with an estimate of how long each activity will take to complete. The analyst must also identify the other activities which must be completed before the activity can start. As shown in Figure 3.3, a critical path analysis network is drawn showing linked activities, their relationships, and the time taken to complete them. Analysis is carried out to identify those activities which constitute the critical path for the project. Activities making up the critical path are those in which any delay will cause a delay in the whole project. Delays in activities not on the critical path will not affect the overall project completion time unless they are excessive.

We have so far described software tools which can help in the planning and control of an information systems project. In fact there are a number of software tools available to help in the development of information systems. We now briefly discuss PRINCE which is a method for project management. PRINCE stands for Projects in Controlled Environments. It is a project management method which was first developed by the Central Computer and Telecommunications Agency (CCTA) in 1989 as a UK government standard for the management of IT projects. It is now used in both the public and private sector and both for IT and non-IT projects. Indeed, the latest version of the method, PRINCE 2 (1996a) has been designed by the CCTA to incorporate the requirements of existing users and to enhance the method so that it can be used for managing all kinds of projects.

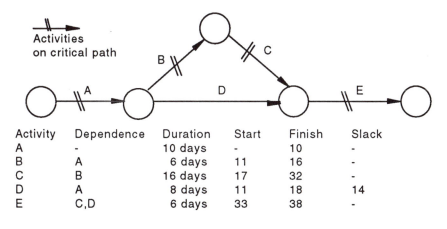

Activity	Dependence	Duration	Start	Finish	Slack
A	-	10 days	-	10	-
B	A	6 days	11	16	-
C	B	16 days	17	32	-
D	A	8 days	11	18	14
E	C,D	6 days	33	38	-

Fig. 3.3: Project control - the network and critical path

PRINCE 2 (1996b) is a process-based approach for project management that is intended to be tailorable and scaleable for the management of different types of projects. Processes are defined with their key inputs and outputs as well as their specific objectives and the activities to be carried out. The approach divides the project into a number of manageable stages in order to provide efficient control of organisational resources. Under the PRINCE 2 method a project is driven by its business case which is the organisation's justification for the project. This business case is reviewed during the project to ensure that the business objectives, which may have changed during the life of the project, are still being met. It aims to provide the means for involvement of management and stakeholders at appropriate times during the project. It also establishes communication channels between the project team, project management and the rest of the organisation.

3.5 Role of the user

In the final section of this chapter, and before looking at the stages of the IS development life cycle in more detail, we return to the role of the user in IS development and it is essential to emphasise this for successful information systems. We also look at end-user computing.

Figure 3.4 places the roles of the personnel, introduced in Section 2.7, in the context of the information systems development life cycle. Users are the employees of the organisation who perform the functions and activities necessary for the business to operate. They are the people who know about the business, what activities need carrying out, how these activities should be carried out and what the difficulties are in carrying these out. From the point of view of the systems analyst, it is the users who will be able to provide information about the organisation that is necessary for the analysts to carry out their information systems development activities. Unless there are major problems, the users will use the information system when it is implemented.

From the point of view of the organisation, it is essential that users accept the information systems developed for them, since these systems are an important factor in achieving organisational objectives. The industry is rife with reports of systems which are either never completed or are not used when they are, even though they may be technically adequate, because of a lack of user acceptance of these systems. They may express their lack of acceptance of the system by not using it and by returning to the manual procedures or the previous systems to perform the same tasks.

There are a number of factors which can lead to an improvement in acceptance by users of the systems developed for them:

- Participation of the users in the development of the system means that they are more likely to use the system when it is implemented
- Demonstration that the system is needed and that it will be of some benefit to users
- Consideration made to users' job satisfaction in the design and development of information systems.

When users, who are not information professionals develop software themselves, it is known as 'end-user computing'. One of the most significant developments over recent years has been the increased direct involvement of business end users in the design and implementation of software systems using fourth generation languages, spreadsheet packages and so on. Some of these are specifically designed for end-user computing. In end-user computing, the eventual users of an information system will normally play a major role in all of the following:

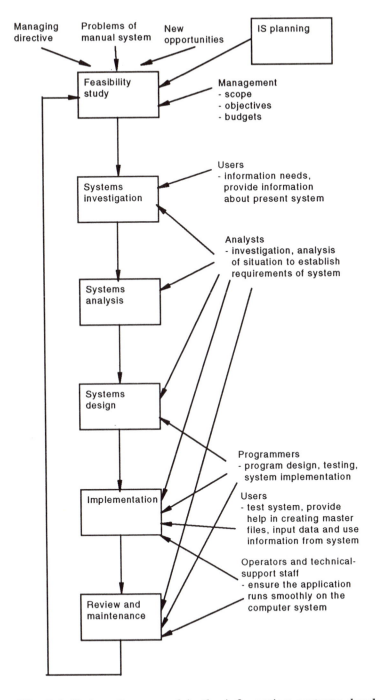

Fig. 3.4: Roles of personnel in the information systems development life cycle

- Establishing the need for the system
- Specifying the type of hardware and software systems to meet that need
- Providing the appropriate resources for hardware and software
- Developing the system
- Defining and managing appropriate security and backup procedures for the system.

We look at the reasons for the growth in end-user computing. The features of end-user computing and the factors which increase participation are suggested. The potential risks of end-user computing are also described.

The introduction of networked personal workstations in recent years has reduced the cost of computing in terms of hardware and software. It has also precipitated the emphasis away from centralised IT departments to the business personnel intending to use or benefit from the system. There appears to be an increasing demand for individuals to control their information and the design and operation of computer systems to provide it.

End users may be non-programming, IT-naive users, which is often the general perception. However many are more 'computer literate'. Many users who support functions carried out by computer may not be IT specialists, but have used computers for some time and may begin to develop applications for other end users and themselves. Others become computer enthusiasts and develop expertise. Thus there are many degrees of involvement in the user community. This differing 'sophistication' of end users has been the subject of considerable research. Attempts have been made to design methods of measuring the sophistication of users involved in end-user computing.

As illustrated in Figure 3.5, there are three fundamental aspects to the level of end-user computing sophistication (Rockart and Flannery, 1983, Nelson and Cheney, 1987 and Huff et al., 1992). These are:

- *Breadth of end-user computing capability:* that is, the end users' knowledge and skill of computing as applied in the business area.
- *Depth of end-user computing capability:* that is, the mastery of computers and information technology in terms of features and functions.
- *Finesse:* that is, the ability to apply end-user computing creatively and produce IT-based solutions to business problems.

Research studies have shown that end users who develop applications tend not to depend on information systems professionals for support and that the large majority of applications are of the 'query and reporting' or 'simple analysis' type. Typical examples are spreadsheet applications. Only a very small percentage are shown to be of a 'complex' type, which might involve complex data analysis and simulation. Most of the applications are developed and used by a number of users within the developer's own department.

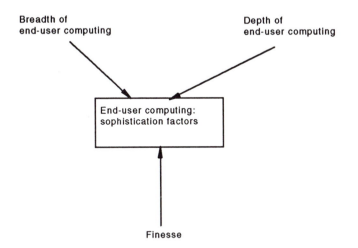

Fig. 3.5: Sophistication factors for end-user computing

As seen in Figure 3.6, the growth of end-user computing has progressed through a number of stages The intensity of participation in end-user computing is related to a combination of three groups of factors shown in Figure 3.7 (Ein-Dor and Segev, 1991).

- *Organisational factors:* such as the build-up of a backlog of computer applications awaiting development. This meant that users were becoming increasingly frustrated with their information systems development function. The widespread proliferation of affordable and powerful personal computers with software specifically designed for end users has provided the potential for autonomy.
- *Management leadership:* the above developments and the improvement in computer literacy has led to management looking outside their information systems department for their business systems.
- *Individual factors:* such as personal motivation, the rank and role of the individual in the organisation, and the opportunity he has for getting involved in end-user computing.

The potential benefits of end-user computing that Khan (1992) has identified are seen in Figure 3.8.

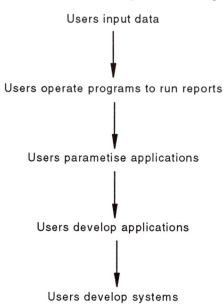

Users input data

Users operate programs to run reports

Users parametise applications

Users develop applications

Users develop systems

Fig. 3.6: The multi-stage growth of end-user computing (after Shah and Lawrence, 1996)

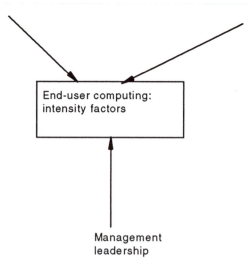

Organisational

Individual

End-user computing: intensity factors

Management leadership

Fig. 3.7: Integrity factors for end-user computing

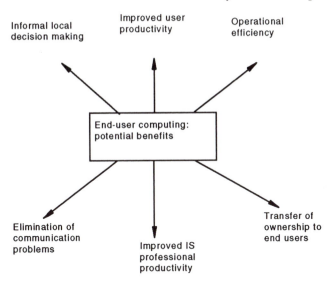

Fig. 3.8: Potential benefits of end-user computing

- *Improved user productivity:* because end users are now able to satisfy their own requirements in many cases. This means that waiting times for applications development are reduced and the applications backlog is also reduced.
- *Operational efficiency:* because of the shorter time between the need for the system being identified to the time that a system becomes used in the organisation's day-to-day business activities.
- *Informed local decision-making capabilities:* because of the opportunity to exercise control over the design, adoption and operation of their information producing applications.
- *Eliminating the problems associated with ineffective communications between analysts and end users:* because end users are able to directly translate their requirements into solutions without needing to go to an analyst.
- *Ownership transfers to the end users:* because this gives the opportunity for innovation and control over their own information provision, encourages autonomy and also responsibility in users.
- *Enhanced productivity of information systems professionals:* because they are able to concentrate on developing information systems that are not suitable for end-user computing. They will also be able to offer advice and guidance to end users in their new role of facilitators. They

provide this in particular with regard to the technological aspects of the systems development process and this will enable end users to make appropriate decisions for the application.

There are also some potential risks associated with end-user computing. Among the risks identified by Alavi and Weiss (1985) and Amoroso and Cheney (1987) are:

- *The potential for poor requirements analysis, documentation, and training resulting from the elimination of the IS specialist role.* Research has also shown that end users involved in end-user computing projects tend not to follow some of the practices traditionally followed in conventional systems development projects, for example, thorough data validation, documentation and security.
- *The potential for producing 'islands of information':* with individual end users or groups of end users producing their own information which does not interact with those produced by others and therefore is not easily shareable. Where end-user computing activity is carried out, mechanisms need to be in place to enable the sharing of information.
- *The potential for end users being 'distracted' from their primary business responsibilities.* Users might spend more of their time to do with information systems development activities rather than the activities they were originally employed to carry out.
- *The potential for end-user computing to be poorly managed:* there is a strong need for more control and guidance in an environment encouraging end-user development.

Although, as we will see in Chapter 10, there are appropriate software tools available, we would suggest that end users would gain much from information systems experts whose job was to assist them in the task of systems development. Whilst end users should accept responsibility for application development, it should be information systems professionals who play the role of advisor, trainer, guide, facilitator and technical expert.

Further, the monitoring and control of end-user computing activities should be managed by business 'line' managers carrying out the role of information systems managers. We regard this to be part of their general management duties and responsibilities. However, this contradicts those who suggest that centralised information systems departments should retain this control.

Whichever emphasis is given, IS development needs to be a balance of end user and computer professional contributions, but not the sole province of the 'experts'.

3.6 Summary

The information systems development life cycle is proposed as a systematic approach and context within which to consider the development of individual information systems that have been identified as necessary within the broader framework of the information systems plan. The individual phases of the information systems development life cycle have been identified.

Information systems development methodologies were introduced as a means of more effectively managing and controlling the development of systems for organisational activity. We have also stressed the role of the end user in information systems development projects.

The next six chapters are each devoted to one of the six stages of the information systems development life cycle. The next chapter looks at the world of opportunities available to us in terms of the potential solutions that might be proposed when we are undertaking systems development projects. Before we go down any particular opportunistic route, we need to assess its feasibility and that of other possible solutions.

Further reading

Alavi, M. & Weiss, I. R. (1985) Managing the risks associated with end-user computing, *Journal of Management Information Systems* **2**, 3, pp. 5-20.
  Examines risks associated with end-user computing.
Amoroso, D. L. & Cheney, P. H. (1987) A report on the state of end-user computing in large North American insurance firms, *Journal of Information Management*, **8**, 2, 1987, pp. 39-48.
  Looks at the range and numbers of end users participating in end-user computing.
Amoroso, D. L. & Cheney, P. H. (1992) Quality end-user developed applications: some essential ingredients, *Data Base*, **23**, Winter 1992, pp. 1-11.
  Discusses some of the potential benefits of end-user computing. Also identifies some of the potential risks.
Avison, D. E. & Fitzgerald, G. (1995) *Information Systems Development: Methodologies Techniques and Tools*, 2nd edition, McGraw-Hill, Maidenhead.
  This discusses methodologies in more depth.
Ein-Dor, P. & Segev, E. (1991) Intensity of end-user computing, *Data Base*, **22**, 1/2, pp. 30-37.

Identifies the groups of factors related to intensity of participation in end-user computing.

Fitzgerald, B. (1996) Formalised systems development methodologies: a critical perspective, *Information Systems Journal*, **6**, 1, pp. 3-23.
This paper discusses some arguments and pressures which support the use of methodologies for systems development. It also identifies a number of arguments and pressures which question the value of methodologies and reports the results of a field study which investigated the role of methodologies in practice.

Huff, S. L., Munro, M. C. & Marcolin, B. (1992) Modelling and measuring end user sophistication, *Proceedings of ACM SIGCPR Conference*, April 1992, Cincinnati, Ohio.
Establishes the three fundamental aspects of end-user computing sophistication.

Iivari, J. & Hirschheim, R. (1996) Analysing information systems development: a comparison and analysis of eight IS development approaches, *Information Systems Journal*, **21**, 7, pp. 551-575.
This paper analyses two sets of assumptions in eight ISD approaches: the organisational role of information systems and the view of information requirements. The organisational role distinguishes three alternatives: technical, sociotechnical and social.

Khan E. H. (1992) The effects of information centres on the growth of end-user computing, *Information and Management*, **23**, 5, pp. 279-289.
Discusses some of the potential benefits of end-user computing.

Nelson, R. R. & Cheney, P. H. (1987) Training end users: an exploratory study, *MIS Quarterly*, **11**, 4, pp. 547-559.
Again looks at end-user computing sophistication.

PRINCE 2 (1996a) *PRINCE Version 2 Reference Manual*, Stationery Office, London.
The definitive guide for PRINCE 2.

PRINCE 2 (1996b) http://www.open.gov.uk:80/ccta/prince
The CCTA's web pages for PRINCE.

Rockhart, J. F. & Flannery, L. S. (1983), The management of end-user computing, *Communications of the ACM*, **26**, 10, pp. 776-784.
Some of the early work on end-user computing sophistication.

Shah, H. U. & Lawrence, D. (1996) A Study of end-user computing and the provision of tool support to advance end user empowerment, *Journal of End-User Computing*, **8**, 1, pp. 13-21.
This details research that explores the extent and nature of end-user computing.

Whitten, J. L., Bentley, L. D. & Barlow, V. M. (1994) *Systems Analysis and Design Methods*, Irwin, Boston, Ma.
A very readable and comprehensive coverage of systems analysis and design.

Questions

1. Identify the stages in the development of an information system.
2. What aspects of information systems development were problematic in early information systems development?
3. Identify some general principles for information systems development.
4. What aspects of the information systems project must be planned for?
5. Consider the most appropriate phase of the information systems development life cycle for the following activities: (a) the accountant complaining about the number of erroneous data entries into the purchasing system; (b) the systems analyst observing that the salesman takes details of orders and agrees discounts with customers; (c) The systems analyst obtaining approximate costs of a network-based solution; (d) producing the code for processing the sales team's commission.
6. What is end-user computing? List the three fundamental aspects of end-user computing sophistication. List the three groups of factors for end-user computing.
7. Identify the potential benefits and risks of end-user computing.

Areas to debate

1. A senior member of management in an organisation has a reputation for complaining about the time taken to develop information systems. He is particularly critical about the time taken in the early stages of a project where 'nothing is being delivered'. Discuss the arguments that might be put forward to such a person, identifying the possible consequences of reducing the time spent on these early stages of the life cycle.
2. 'End users are the ones that truly understand the business, not technical staff, therefore it makes sense for all the information systems of the organisation to be developed by end users.' Discuss this statement, giving consideration to the types of system, potential problems and the role of the technical staff.

3. Many organisations develop information systems without due consideration being given to project planning and control aspects. Debate the reasons for this. Consider the contents of a report to senior management defining the important implications and nature of such an activity.

4. What is end-user computing and what are its associated opportunities and risks? Investigate the literature to discover the extent of end-user computing activity in the context of information systems development.

5. Discuss the importance of project planning and control in information systems development. Identify some project planning methods and tools.

CASE STUDY

Toni Asifiori wishes to develop information systems for his hairdressing salons. He is wondering whether he can develop these systems himself, use his staff or hire experts from consultancy firms. In view of the information systems that you have already identified for Asifiori, what recommendations would you make to him for developing the information systems?

Chapter 4

THE FEASIBILITY STUDY:
A WORLD OF OPPORTUNITIES

4.1   Feasibility study stage

In this chapter we look at the feasibility study stage in the life cycle of an information systems project. During this stage different information systems alternatives are proposed and evaluated. Priorities are established. In order to enable this to be done, information is gathered and analysed, and costs and benefits of the alternatives are considered. Decisions will then need to be made as to which aspects of the proposed solution might be computerised. The analyst carrying out the feasibility study must make recommendations as to whether it is reasonable to develop a new information system. A decision might be made to design and develop the system as proposed, but normally the application area will be investigated further. Figure 4.1 shows the feasibility study phase in the context of the information systems development life cycle.

There are always many ways in which a particular problem situation can be dealt with. It is at this stage that the feasibility of the various opportunities is assessed. This needs to be done in a systematic way. The feasibility study is a crucial stage in the information systems development life cycle. It determines whether the project actually goes ahead or not. It is

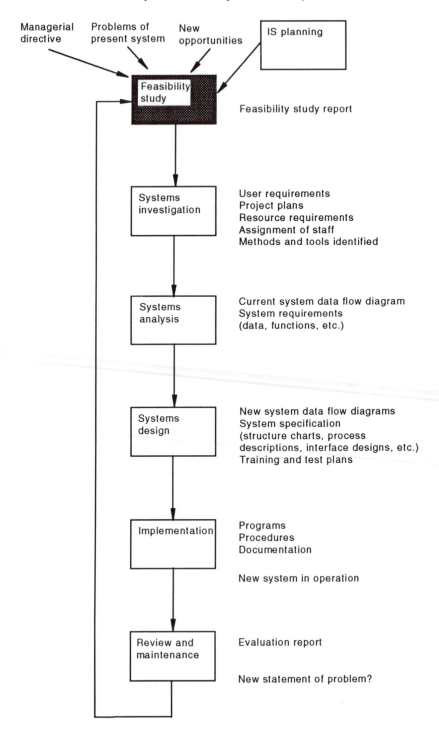

Fig. 4.1: The information systems development life cycle

the last stage before a considerable amount of resources are invested in a project, and therefore needs to be handled very carefully. The feasibility study is a preliminary study to investigate the information needs of prospective users and to determine the resource requirements, costs, benefits and feasibility of the project. At the end of the study a report is produced for the client. As Figure 4.2 shows, the information about problems and existing practice are supplied by the users as well as details of any new requirements. The objectives and scope of the study as well as its constraints are identified by management. Information about costs will include those provided by potential suppliers. The feasibility report that will be produced as a result of the study will be for the benefit of management in order to decide how to proceed.

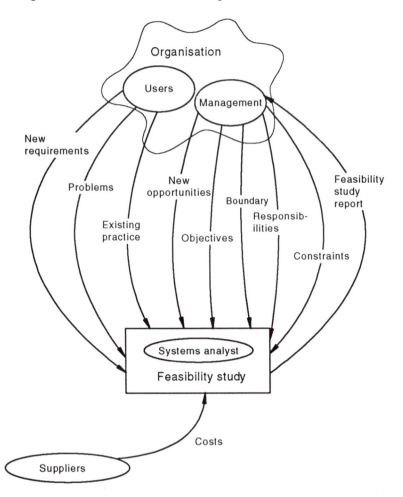

Fig. 4.2: The feasibility study stage - inputs and outputs

In this section we discuss the concerns that lead to a feasibility study stage, the issues involved, and the tasks which are carried out. The need for a feasibility study is likely to come about when a problem arises in an application area or a need for change is recognised. For example, one problem might be that the company is losing customers because sales orders are being processed late. An example of an opportunity might occur if a consultant suggests that 'it might be worth introducing a computer-based stock control system in the warehouse'. An important aspect of initiating the study is that the true nature of the problem needs to be revealed. This may well be different from the stated problem.

A feasibility study is essentially a scaled-down version of the whole systems investigation, analysis and design process. However, the study has a narrower focus, and is undertaken in a much reduced time. The findings of the feasibility study should assist the user in making a decision about whether the project is to carry on 'as is', be amended, postponed or cancelled. The study will help the user make an informed decision, particularly when the project is large in size, complex or expensive. The study is not a substitute for the detailed and thorough analysis that will still be required if the project is not very simple.

Before carrying out the feasibility study, project objectives and terms of reference must be identified. A number of fundamental questions need to be addressed. The client, that is, the person who initiated the project, needs to be identified along with the objectives. The analyst also needs to ascertain the client's role in the organisation. Gaining an understanding of objectives will lead to them being addressed in the proposal. The explicitly-stated objectives of the client will be recorded in the **terms of reference** of the feasibility study. It is essential to agree these with the client before the start of the study as these define the scope of the investigation that is to be undertaken.

The terms of reference consist of the following:

- *Project objectives:* a clear and precise statement about the expectations of the client who has initiated the project.
- *System boundary:* this will identify the area of the organisation that is to be the scope of the feasibility study.
- *Responsibility:* it will be necessary to identify who has responsibility for supervising the project. It needs to be made clear who has the authority to give permission for changes that might be necessary during the study. An example may occur where the scope of the project needs to be extended.
- *Constraints:* it is important to identify factors, such as budget, resources and time scales, which may have implications on the study or the project in some way.

- *Report:* this is the mechanism by which the findings will be relayed to the client.

In carrying out the feasibility study, we establish the broad requirements of the client. An important aspect of these requirements are the priorities that the client assigns to them. However, this is more difficult than it appears at first sight, as there is likely to be a considerable range of opinions on what are the requirements and their priorities. It is the analyst's job to narrow the range of these disparate views to form some consensus. In doing this the analyst must arrive at requirements and priorities that are in the best interests of the organisation as a whole rather than those of specific individuals or groups. The analyst also needs to be aware that user requirements and priorities are likely to change over time.

Yeates *et al.* (1994) identifies the following tasks to be carried out during the feasibility study stage of the information systems development life cycle:

- *Study the current situation:* The analyst tries to obtain a more thorough understanding of the problems or opportunities that triggered the project in the first place. This phase may well identify new problems and new opportunities. It is also important that the analyst tries to determine whether the problems really exist and, if confirmed, to consider how serious these problems are. It is often the case that the initial problems are symptoms of more serious or subtle problems. While carrying out the feasibility study, the causes and effects of the problems need to be identified.
- *Analyse requirements:* It is important to identify what the capabilities of the new system should be. We need to establish what data it will require and what information it will produce. These are all decisions about what the system will do, not how it will do them. The analyst will need to approach the clients and users to find out what is needed from the new system.
- *Consider alternative solutions:* This phase should produce a number of alternative solutions which meet the identified requirements. Each of the alternatives will consider:
  - *Technology:* the hardware and software needed for the proposed solution to meet the requirements.
  - *Schedule:* the plan to complete the project within the required time constraints, given the on-going activities and existing projects, planned projects and available resources of the organisation.
  - *Organisation:* the implications for the organisation in terms of human, organisational and political aspects.

- *Economic analysis:* the initial and continuing costs of the proposed solution.

A report on the findings of the feasibility study, including recommendations, should be produced, containing the following information:

- *Background:* This will include the terms of reference and the reasons for the study. It will give an outline of the background to the project and the way it relates to the stated objectives of the organisation.
- *Current situation:* This should give an overview of the current situation as well as the problems identified.
- *Proposed system:* This should detail the requirements of the new system and the various options concerning implementation. Details of the technical, organisational and economic implications of these proposals should also be given.
- *Recommendations:* This should summarise the findings of the previous parts of the report and include recommendations about the next stage which could be:
  - *Progress with complete and detailed analysis.* In this case, the report should include a project plan for the subsequent phases of the project.
  - *Amend the terms of reference or the scope of the study before proceeding any further.* In this case the report should include recommendations on how to proceed.
  - *Abandon the project due to its lack of feasibility.*

Once the feasibility study report has been delivered and any recommendation by the analyst to proceed is agreed by the client, then the detailed systems analysis phase can begin.

4.2   Information gathering

During the feasibility stage, the analyst is gathering information to gain a good overview of the situation. As stated earlier, the feasibility study is a miniature version of the systems investigation, analysis and design stages of the information systems development life cycle itself, except that the level of detail is in overview form only. The techniques for fact finding used at this stage are those that will be used in the systems investigation stage of the life cycle, that is, interviewing, observing, sampling and so on. Analysts must gather the information without being constrained by their own preconceived ideas, and they should avoid:

- *Presenting their own solutions:* to information problems when interviewing the users.
- *Imposing constraints:* to implementing users' suggested features, for example, by suggesting that they would cost too much.
- *Undermining the users' confidence:* by telling them that superiors have either rejected their suggestion or are considering a completely different approach.

The analyst should keep all options open while gathering information, since potentially innovative ideas might be stunted by the analyst airing any preconceived bias. At this stage the analyst might find the technique of rich picture diagramming useful in helping the process of understanding the problem situation as well as documenting the findings. A rich picture is a means to represent the information given following on from the interviewing process. A rich picture is a pictorial caricature of an organisation, and is an invaluable tool for helping to explain what the organisation is about. It should be self-explanatory and easy to understand. Figure 4.3 shows a rich picture for the video shop.

One may start to construct a rich picture by looking for elements of structure in the problem area. This includes things like departmental boundaries, activity types, physical or geographical layout and product types. Having looked for elements of structure, the next stage is to look for elements of process, that is, 'what is going on'. These include the fast-changing aspects of the situation such as, the information flow, the flow of goods and so on. The relationship between structure and process represents the climate of the situation. Very often an organisational problem can be tracked down to a mismatch between an established structure and new processes formed in response to new events and pressures.

The rich picture should include all the important hard facts of the organisational situation, and the examples given have been of this nature. However, this does not represent all the important information. There are many soft or subjective aspects of the situation which should also be represented, and the process of creating the rich picture serves to tease out the concerns of the people in that situation. This softer information includes the sorts of things that the people in the problem area are worried about, the social roles which the people within the situation think are important, and the sort of behaviour which is expected of people in these roles.

Typically, a rich picture is constructed first by putting the name of the organisation that is the concern of the analyst into a large 'bubble', perhaps at the centre of the page. Other symbols are sketched to represent the people and things that inter-relate inside and outside that organisation. Arrows show these relationships. Other important aspects can be incorporated, such as crossed-swords to indicate conflict and 'think' bubbles to indicate worries of the major characters. Techniques such as these can be used to clarify and bring into focus the overall picture of the problem situation.

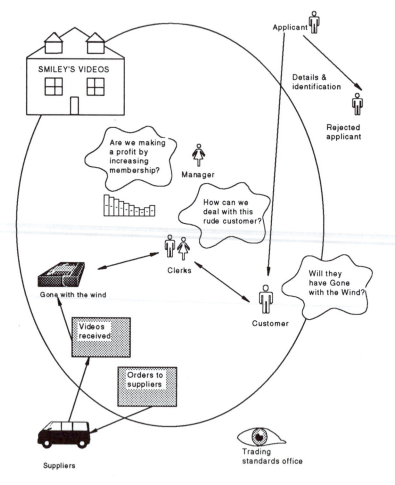

Fig. 4.3: Rich picture of a video shop

4.3   Costs and benefits

To help us decide on the feasibility of a project we have to assess its costs and benefits. Feasibility has four main dimensions. A successful project will be:

- Technologically reliable
- Reasonable to schedule
- Economically worthwhile
- Organisationally acceptable.

Many projects are unsuccessful because each of these dimensions were not considered fully. In particular, there is a tendency to overemphasise the technological aspects to the detriment of the organisational aspects. We will consider each of these dimensions in turn.

Technologically reliable

In attempting to overcome an information problem, we need to look at currently available hardware and software technology as a step towards recommending a possible solution. In the three-level management architecture that we have presented in Chapter 2, it is unlikely that any problems are encountered in identifying appropriate technology for operational information systems. At this level of system, appropriate hardware and software are well catered for and proven. However, if more sophisticated applications are required, for example, to provide support at the strategic level, such as decision support systems or systems requiring advanced technology, such as voice recognition, then it is necessary to investigate the technology further.

Reasonable to schedule

There are two aspects to scheduling. Having established that appropriate technology is available for the project, we need to consider whether we have or can obtain expertise in that technology and, given the technical expertise, whether the project deadlines are feasible. It must also be established whether the suggested deadlines are mandatory or desirable. Mandatory deadlines may be necessary because of a change in legislation which is to apply from a fixed date. With deadlines that are desirable rather than mandatory, the analyst may propose different schedule possibilities.

Economically worthwhile

Having established the feasibility of the project from the point of view of technology and scheduling, it is necessary to consider whether it is economically feasible. Economic feasibility is usually considered using some sort of cost-benefit analysis. This means that costs and benefits have to be estimated and then compared in a way that determines economic feasibility. This process can be complex and there are many techniques.

The cost and time scales need to be appropriate for the organisation and the potential returns need to justify the initial outlay. This involves assessing whether the benefits merit the costs. In estimating costs, consideration has to be given to development, capital and operational expenditure. If the costs exceed management expectations or they do not justify the costs, then the project will normally be abandoned.

Costs can be categorised in two ways: those one-off costs incurred in developing the system and those incurred in operating the system once operational. These can only be estimated once specific solutions have been proposed. The development costs can be attributed to specific phases of the project and can be assigned to standard cost categories, such as:

- *Staff costs:* the salaries of systems analysts, programmers, operators, clerical and administrative staff
- *Computer costs:* the cost of any new computer equipment and software, and any charges for computer time that may be incurred
- *Training:* the costs of training information systems personnel to use particular packages, programming languages and so on. The costs for training end users must also be included.

Operating costs are sometimes overlooked. Any envisaged benefits of the system must recover both the costs of developing and operating the system. The operating costs will be of two types:

- *Fixed:* these are leasing or rental costs, and costs for software licences which will occur at fixed intervals in the life of the system. They also include the costs of computer operators and support staff.
- *Variable:* these are costs which occur in proportion to some usage factor. For example, costs which relate to the amount of computer usage, supplies, such as stationery, and overhead costs will also be included under this heading.

Potential benefits are those that are likely to increase profits or decrease costs. As far as possible, benefits should be quantified in monetary terms. Benefits can be classified as:

- *Tangible:* these can easily be quantified, such as a reduction in processing errors, decreased response times, reduced expenses and the like. These might be measured as monthly or annual savings or as profit.
- *Intangible:* these benefits are difficult or impossible to quantify, such as better service provision, better decision making or improved staff morale.

If a benefit cannot be quantified, it might be difficult for the decision-maker to accept the validity of the associated cost-benefit analysis. Decisions will therefore be based on incomplete data. Although there are those who argue that intangible benefits do not exist and that all benefits are quantifiable (it is just that some are harder to quantify than others), we believe that some benefits cannot be quantified in this way. In these cases the decision maker needs to assess whether an improvement in the level of staff morale, for instance, is worth the associated costs. The decision maker makes a value judgement.

Three techniques for assessing economic feasibility are return on investment, payback analysis and net present value.

- *Return on investment (ROI):* this compares the lifetime profitability of alternative solutions. The ROI is a percentage rate that measures the relationship between the amount a business gets back from an investment and the amount invested. It can be calculated as follows:

$$\text{ROI} = \frac{\text{(Estimated lifetime benefits - Estimated lifetime costs)}}{\text{Estimated lifetime costs}}$$

The figure produced represents the lifetime ROI and could be divided by the estimated lifetime of the system to yield an average annual ROI.
- *Payback analysis:* this determines how much time will lapse before accrued benefits overtake accrued and continuing costs. This is referred to as the payback period.
- *Net present value:* this determines the profitability in terms of today's value of the money involved (it assumes that one unit of currency today is worth more than that same unit in one year's time). Costs are represented by negative cash flows while benefits are represented by positive cash flows.

We need techniques to assist us in our comparison of alternative solutions. One way in which this might be done is to use a matrix-based documentation technique. Such a technique can be very useful as a documentation aid for the comparison, and it is also useful when presenting this information to others. Using a feasibility analysis matrix (Figure 4.4) we can carry out a feasibility analysis of possible solutions. The rows of the matrix correspond to the candidate solutions. There are columns in the table corresponding to different feasibility criteria of operational, technical, schedule and economic feasibility and a final column indicating the overall ranking of a particular solution. The cells contain feasibility assessment notes for each candidate and a rank or score for each criterion. When all alternative solutions have been ranked or given a score, the last row is used to record the overall ranking or score.

FEASIBILITY CRITERIA PROPOSAL DESCRIPTION	TECHNOLOGICAL	SCHEDULE	ECONOMIC (a) Cost to develop (b) payback period (c) Net present value	ORGANISATIONAL
Proposal 1 Packaged solution for lending and purchasing systems	Few well-established robust and low cost packages. Risk of major changes to business processes	Approximately 4 months	(a) £3000 (b) 6 months (c) £8200 For detailed calculations see Appendix 1	Concern amongst staff about significant changes to their role and tasks
Overall Ranking =	Score = 70	Score = 90	Score =	Score =
Proposal 2 Tailor-made development of lending and purchasing systems	Required technology and skills to build the system are readily available	Approximately 12 months	(a) £6000 (b) 1.5 years (c) £9000 For detailed calculations see Appendix 2	Managers are concerned about the length of time to develop a system which is urgently required and also lack of opportunity to evaluate software as in proposal 1
Overall Ranking =	Score =	Score =	Score =	Score =
Proposal 3 -------------- -------------	Proposal 3 -------------- -------------	Proposal 3 -------------- -------------	Proposal 3 -------------- -------------	Proposal 3 -------------- -------------

Fig. 4.4: Feasibility analysis matrix (part completed)

Organisationally acceptable

This addresses the question of whether the envisaged impact on the organisation is appropriate. In considering the organisational feasibility of a project, we should be able to anticipate the difficulties that might be faced and this should enable us to prepare measures for dealing with these difficulties. The organisational dimension must be considered, since information systems will impact on the organisational environment. The feasibility study must consider how the environment (for example, user departments, customers and managers) will react to the proposed system. An assessment needs to be carried out as to whether the intended users are capable of operating the system and gaining full benefit from it. The risk that users perceive the system to be a challenge to their status or job security needs also to be assessed. Changes to the work and conditions of employees, and the impact of these, will also need to be considered. A further organisational dimension is a consideration as to whether the proposed system is compatible with existing systems.

In this section we have considered the need for assessing costs and benefits to ascertain the feasibility of a project. We have identified technological reliability, ease of scheduling, economic and organisational acceptability as being the four dimensions of feasibility.

4.4   Different types of proposal

The systems analysts may suggest alternatives to a new computer information system. It is possible in some situations, having examined the current system, that non-computerised solutions will be among those proposed. It should not always be assumed that all problems will be solved by the use of technology. There may be other ways in which a given problem can be addressed and these should be explored further, and possibly included amongst the alternatives recommended.

The systems analysts may also suggest keeping the present system. While it may appear that there is overwhelming pressure to go ahead with the project, doing nothing must be an option that is considered. At this decision point all costs that have been incurred so far in carrying out the feasibility study should be considered irrecoverable and the feasibility of going ahead should be assessed without taking these into account. This concept of ignoring past costs sometimes causes considerable problems in the development of information systems. There is a tendency to continue some projects well beyond their actual feasibility because of the investment already made in them.

A decision to go ahead with a project might mean one of three things:

- *Go ahead with the project:* on the basis of one of the alternatives identified and costed in the feasibility study.
- *Increase the scope:* beyond that originally identified and dealt with in the feasibility study and this will necessitate a re-evaluation of costs and schedule for the project
- *Reduce the scope:* if the project budget and schedule are fixed but have been found to be insufficient to cover all the project objectives identified.

This decision will have to be made by the instigators of the information systems project. Clearly the recommendations of the analysts will be an important factor in this decision.

4.5 Summary

Figure 4.5 gives an overview of the feasibility stage of the information systems development life cycle. We have seen that a feasibility study is initiated as a result of a problem or a need for change being recognised. The study should investigate the problem or opportunity in further detail. The feasibility stage is a scaled-down version of the whole systems analysis process and is used to help make a decision about whether a project should be pursued further and, if so, the way in which it should progress.

We have described the activities that must be carried out during the feasibility stage, namely a study of the current situation, an analysis of requirements, consideration of alternative solutions and the production of a report presenting the feasibility study findings.

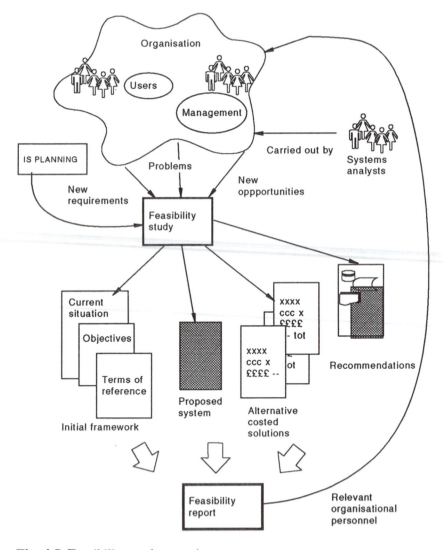

Fig. 4.5: Feasibility study overview

Priorities must be established and appropriate information gathered by interviewing personnel in the organisation. Methods for comparing costs and benefits were discussed briefly. On the basis of the feasibility study, a decision must be made whether to go ahead with a new information system, which may be computerised. If so, the life cycle proceeds to systems investigation, the subject of the next chapter.

Further reading

Ahituv, N., Neumann, S. & Riley, N. H. (1994) *Principles of Information Systems for Management*, 4th edition, B&E Tech, New York.
Hicks, J. O. (1993) *Management Information Systems: A User Perspective*, West, Minneapolis.
O'Brien, J. A. (1991) *Introduction to Information Systems*, Irwin, Boston, Ma.
Yeates, D., Shields, M. & Helmy, D. (1994) *Systems Analysis and Design*, Pitman, London.
All the above texts discuss the feasibility study stage of the development of the information systems project.

Ballantine, J. A., Stray, S. J. & Galliers, R. D. (1996) Information Systems/technology evaluation practice: evidence from UK organisations, *Journal of Information Technology*, 11, pp. 129-141.
Van Wegen, B. and De Hoog, R. (1996) Measuring the economic value of information systems, *Journal of Information Technology*, 11, pp. 247-260.
These are two good sources on IT investment evaluation.

Questions

1. What is a feasibility study?
2. Discuss the various situations that might lead to a feasibility study.
3. Explain what the terms of reference are for a feasibility study.
4. Discuss the tasks that are carried out during this phase of the information systems development life cycle.
5. List the information that should be included in the feasibility study report.
6. What are the possible recommendations that the analyst can make to the managers and users who have initiated the information system?
7. Explain how developing a rich picture of the problem situation might be useful to the analyst.
8. What are four different dimensions that must be considered in assessing the feasibility of a project.
9. List the techniques that might be used to assess economic feasibility.

Areas to debate

1. Assume that you have been asked by management to develop a system for a sales director of an organisation. At the outset, before you know what the director wants from the system, you are told that the system is to be operational in six months and that you have a budget of $100,000 for its development. How do you proceed?
2. Investigate and debate the potential risks of an information systems development project.
3. Draw a rich picture for an organisation with which you are familiar, for example, your college, university, library or bank. Compare your solutions with those of your colleagues. How are the differences caused?
4. You are the director of human resources at a large telecommunications company requiring a new human resources system. Debate the possible objectives and terms of reference of such a system. How would you like to relate with the developers of such a system?

CASE STUDY

Toni Asifiori is considering computerising all aspects of his organisation concerned with purchasing and managing stocks of hairdressing products. These include the stock bought for salon use as well as stock which he sells on to his customers. Ideally he would like the system to cater for stock control at all of the salons in the chain.

You are required to establish the feasibility of this computerisation. Develop a skeletal feasibility study report. Where you are unable to provide the information, identify the questions you would need to ask to be able to resolve those issues.

Sketch a rich picture for Asifiori salons.

Chapter 5

SYSTEMS INVESTIGATION: FINDING OUT MORE

5.1   Planning the systems investigation

In this chapter we consider the systems investigation stage of the information systems development life cycle. This is the stage where we find out more about the project situation. In this chapter we discuss the types of skills that the systems analyst should possess to be effective in this role.

In trying to find out more about the problem, we require appropriate fact finding techniques. Suitable techniques include interviewing key personnel, observing appropriate organisational activities, examining document usage and gathering information using questionnaires.

Figure 5.1 shows the systems investigation phase in the context of the information systems development life cycle.

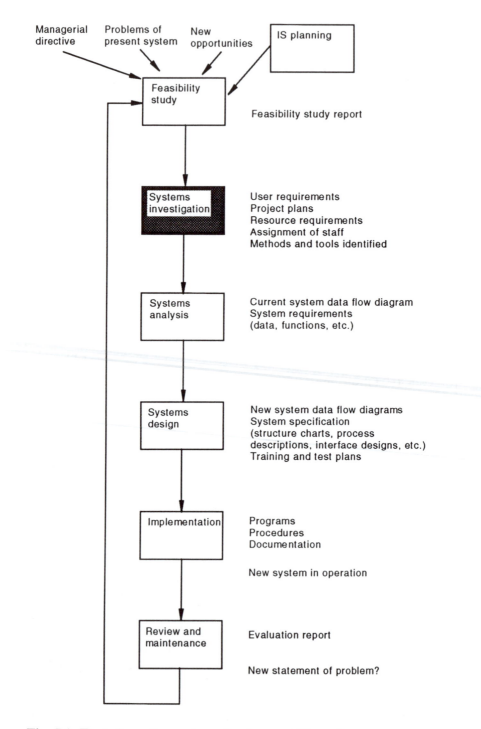

Fig. 5.1: The information systems development life cycle

A basis for controlling all the activities of the development process for a particular project is usually a detailed and comprehensive project plan. The plan provides details about what the end results of the project should be, how the project will be carried out, when it will be carried out and what resources will be required to carry it out. The project plan provides the mechanism for monitoring project progress as well as providing a mechanism for control.

An initial plan will be produced as a result of the feasibility study activity. This is made more detailed and precise during the systems investigation stage. The plan may well need to be modified during subsequent phases of the life cycle. The project plan needs to include the following elements:

- Details of the project's objectives, background, problems and solutions.
- Definition of the phases and activities of the development, including dates and duration, as well as the expected outputs of each activity. To aid understanding, various charts can be used to document these activities.
- Details of the organisation where the project will be carried out including the functions and responsibilities of each of the groups in that area.
- Assignment details about individuals by name if known or by skill category, and the activities that they are to perform and when. Again, an appropriate charting technique can be used to document these.
- Details of the resources, such as technical staff, equipment, computer time and administrative support, that will be required to complete this project. The resources plan should show when these resources will be required as the project develops. This should also be expressed as a budget plan which is the translation of the required resources into monetary terms.
- Details of the methods and tools to be used for reporting the progress of the project and the timing, scope, objectives, participants and personnel involved in the review.
- Details of the training requirements for everyone involved in the project or affected by it in terms of their role in the organisation.
- Details of any documents to be produced during the project. It should outline the contents of the document, the creators of the document, deadlines for the production of the document, the approval procedure and the personnel who should receive them.
- Details of the tools, procedures and responsibilities for all testing involved in the project, including individual module testing, program testing, system testing and acceptance testing.

- Details of how the system, once operational, will be managed. It specifies the responsibilities of the users and the developers when the new system is installed.
- Details of how changes to the system are to be managed, since the development of information systems is an evolving process, procedures for controlling, co-ordinating and documenting change need to be defined. This is done in the change control plan.

A project plan which includes these elements will be comprehensive in its coverage of all the important aspects.

5.2   Role of the systems analyst

To develop appropriate organisational information systems, the analyst must establish the facts concerning the information that is generated and used by the organisation. In essence, in the early phases of information systems development, we are attempting to identify and collate the following facts about the organisation or the organisational area that is of concern in the particular information systems project:

- When is the information required?
- What information is required and by whom?
- For what purpose is the information required?
- What are the activities that give rise to the data that is used to produce the information?

The work of the systems analyst is very specialised and requires certain skills, quality and approaches from the analyst. The work is investigative and analytical, and requires appropriate basic but essential skills if it is to be done properly, in depth and without alienating the users. Investigative skills are required to know what questions must be asked and what information must be unearthed. Analytical skills are required to identify what constitutes relevant and appropriate information. It needs to be broken down into its fundamental components and reorganised into a logical framework applicable to the given situation. The analyst must be observant in order to be able to identify potential inconsistencies and omissions in the information. Expertise is required in order to resolve such difficulties. Having gathered the information and reorganised it, the analyst must be able to draw appropriate conclusions and justify them based on the findings of the investigation and analysis.

Systems analysts also require excellent communication skills for talking to users in order to establish their needs, for giving oral presentations to users and management at various stages of the project, for producing written documentation concerning the analysis and design aspects of the information systems development process and for being able to communicate the requirements of the users to the people responsible for the technical development of the system. Much of the systems investigation activity is based around people, and looks at human activity in the situation that is the focus of the information systems project. This requires very good social skills in order to relate to people at all levels of the organisational hierarchy, from senior personnel, such as directors and executives, to the most junior staff involved in the day-to-day activities of the organisation. Their activities will require them to communicate effectively with other information systems professionals who might work at a greater level of technical detail.

The analyst will need to be able to deal with conflict, since different people in the organisation will have different views and priorities. The analysts must take a broad organisation-wide view in resolving such conflicts. They will need to gain an understanding of the business as a whole and of the various organisational interfaces in particular. In many situations, the analyst will find that there is a very limited view taken by people in different departments. They may have little understanding of the activities of departments other than their own. They may view those activities to be generally obstructive to them, even the cause of all their difficulties and problems.

The analysis activity requires attention to detail, a disciplined approach and persistence. Planning skills are also essential, as the analysts will be responsible for planning their own work and will be carrying out this work with little or no supervision or guidance from others. The analyst will also be responsible for planning the project. This will involve planning the 'people' aspects of the system, that is, changes to the work environment, in terms of individual jobs, as well as the computer aspects of the system.

5.3   Fact finding techniques

There are a number of ways by which systems analysts carry out their role:

- *Talking to people in the organisation about their jobs and the activities that they are involved in.* This will be to establish, amongst other things, the different activities that take place, the different roles of the personnel involved, the data that the activities give rise to, the information that this data produces and the data or information used in their activities.

- *Studying documentation for existing systems within the organisation.* This will include both manual and computerised systems, as both are sources of information. The documentation might consist of forms that are completed and the description of procedures that are carried out in different parts of the organisation. For example, this will include the documents that need to be completed when a person joins the organisation as a new employee.

- *Reviewing the causes and effects of problems.* It will be necessary to do this since what appears to be a problem may well be a symptom or effect of a different and more deep-seated problem. It is important that the analyst investigates to establish the true situation in terms of the causes of difficulties and the effects that those difficulties produce.

- *Taking account of anticipated changes.* It is important that the activities of the analysts are carried out in a context which recognises that the organisation (or the part of the organisation that is the subject of the information systems project) is an evolving and changing thing. It is important that the analyst does not completely fix on the way the organisation is at the present time, but also tries to establish the changes or nature of potential changes that might be on the horizon. It is important that analysis and the complete information systems development is done in the correct context.

- *Collating and documenting the information obtained.* The activities of the analyst will result in a wealth of information. It is of major importance that this information is collated, documented and organised in ways which contribute to the subsequent activities of the information systems developers. It is wasteful and potentially a more major problem if data that is needed is collected but not used appropriately, simply because it was not documented and organised so as to be subsequently accessible.

Systems analysis should result in a description of how given processes work. It is not about how they are implemented. Feedback throughout this activity is essential because of the complexities and uncertainties of real-world situations and processes. It is unlikely that the first description will entirely reflect how a process functions.

For the purposes of information systems development, we need to establish relevant facts regarding the given situation. To do this successfully, appropriate fact-finding techniques need to be employed. There are a range of different techniques that can be used to assist us. Different ones will be appropriate to different situations. The techniques that might be considered for use during the analysis activities are:

- Interviewing key personnel
- Examining document usage
- Developing questionnaires and analysing responses
- Observing appropriate organisational activities.

In a given information systems development project, it is likely that a combination of these techniques needs to be used. They each involve different methods and activities, and each has its advantages and disadvantages. We will look at each of these fact finding techniques in more detail.

5.4   Interviewing and note taking

Interviews normally involve the analyst in one-to-one discussions with particular users. They present a significant opportunity for detailed investigation of specific aspects of the situation under investigation. The interviewees (the users) will be the most knowledgeable about the business (or business area). They are likely to have a detailed and in-depth understanding. The interview is used by the interviewer as the mechanism for getting the user to communicate the most important and vital aspects of this knowledge of the business.

However, the process of trying to transfer knowledge is fraught with difficulty. There are problems that might arise when using interviews to establish information. In the interview the analyst is to a large extent relying on the user being able to communicate what the analyst needs to know. The problem with this is that users are not always articulate enough to communicate this knowledge to the analyst. The user may well make assumptions about the analyst's knowledge of the problem situation, thinking it to be greater than it actually is. There are things that will be obvious to the user that are not obvious to the analyst. The analyst has to ask the right questions and these must be understood as intended by the user. If not, then the analyst gets a response to a different question and confusion results.

The analyst must carry out interviewing in an organised and systematic way. It is important to think about who to interview and the sequence of interviews, so that the analyst is assisted in developing a top-down understanding of the organisation, that starts off with a global overview (probably as the result of interviewing the chief executive or other senior personnel), followed by interviews which successively provide more and more detail, until information has been obtained to an appropriate level of detail for the information systems project under development and the current stage of the information systems development life cycle. The following is one possible approach:

- *Preparing for the interview:* The purpose of the interview is to obtain the information required. This will need to be obtained from various people working at different levels of the organisation, in different roles, all contributing to the activities of the organisation. Prior to arranging the interviews, the analyst needs to think about whom to interview as well as to decide what questions need to be asked in order to obtain the information required. The analyst must go to the interviews with a number of questions already well formed. Other questions will be added during the interview. These will arise as a result of specific responses received from the interviewee. These further questions will enable the analyst to go deeper into a particular issue, as well as enabling the analyst to check understanding. It is also necessary to think about where the interview will take place. It may be appropriate to interview users near or around their place of work or to interview them elsewhere. The exact location can be established in discussions with the user. It is best to be guided by the interviewee's choice, as it is important that all interviewees are comfortable about the location, for example, in terms of privacy. Once the interviews have been arranged with them, it is useful to send a memo to confirm the arrangements. It is also a good idea to telephone on the day of the interview to re-confirm the interview arrangements.

- *Carrying out the interview:* During the interview the analyst will ask the prepared questions and amplify and clarify points raised in the responses through follow-up questions. It is important that in situations where the interviewee is not personally known to the analyst, that the analyst ensures that the right person is present through introductions. The information produced as a result of the interview may be recorded in different ways. In most situations the analyst will make the appropriate notes. The analyst might also make use of appropriate secretarial support to record the questions and responses. A further possibility is for the analyst to use a tape recorder. This is sometimes problematic because some users may feel uneasy and unable to talk freely. The analyst should therefore not use a tape recorder without prior agreement from the user. Even if the interview is being recorded, thorough notes should be taken, but again, only after gaining permission. The analyst can reassure users by suggesting, for example, that information provided will not be attributable to individuals. It goes without saying that the analyst should be polite and courteous with the user at all times.

- *Asking the questions at interview:* The analyst should make an attempt to put the interviewee at ease and not launch straight into a tirade of questions about the job and activities. For example, the interview can be started off with general comments and a statement about the objectives of the interview and what to expect during the interview. Questions which might be used to begin with are commonly referred to as open questions. An interviewer might sensibly ask the following opening questions in an interview:
  - Could you tell me about the essence of the business? Is it concerned exclusively with the rental of video tapes, or does it sell other things, such as tape accessories or confectionery?
  - Could you tell me about the organisational structure of the business? What is the role of each member of staff including yourself?
  - Could you describe the sort of problems that you have? An example might be given, such as 'are there areas in which you lack information?'.
  - What improvements do you think could be made to make your job easier?
  - Where do you see this business going in the future?

  It is unlikely that the responses to opening questions will contain everything that the analyst wants to know. Sometimes the analyst may well have difficulty understanding what the user is trying to explain. In this case, the interview will continue by following up the open questions by checklist questions such as:
  - So the core of the business is loaning videos?
  - The sales manager has four junior sales staff working for him?
  - The company wants to expand into other areas?

  In general, systems analysts should seek to confirm their understanding of what has been explained by the users through relaying the understanding of what the users have expressed back and get them to either confirm or correct that understanding.

  The interview should be drawn to an end when the information that was required by the analyst has been elicited. The interview should be closed by asking questions that will be useful in checking whether the user has any additional information that might be useful to the analyst, establishing who else needs to be interviewed and ensuring the availability of the user should further amplification or clarification be necessary. The final type of questions should be closing ones, such as:
  - Is there anything else which you would like to tell me about?
  - Who else would you recommend I talk to and why?

The interviewee should then be thanked and permission sought to come back if necessary.

- *Ending the interview:* It is possible that the time allotted for the interview has been insufficient due to the complexity of the business area and constituent activities that have been discussed. The analyst cannot complete the tasks until sufficient information has been obtained. If this situation arises and the interview is running over the scheduled time, then if the analyst is able to continue and does not have any other scheduled meetings for that time, the analyst should see if the interviewee is willing to continue the interview. If the user is not able to continue, then a mutually convenient time should be arranged to continue the interview.

- *Confirming the main points of the interview:* The interview should be concluded by the analyst summarising the main points discussed during the interview and thanking the interviewee. It is important to send the interviewee a letter to confirm the main points agreed from the interview. This gives the interviewee an opportunity to give more information about something that was discussed, raise other matters and confirm that the information has been correctly understood.

An important aspect of interviewing is recording the information obtained. If this is done by taking notes, then it should be systematic and thorough. Failure to take full notes will result in wasted time and effort, both on the part of the analysts and users. Taking notes is therefore a skill that is essential for the information systems professional. There are a number of areas within the context of information systems development in which good note-taking is important, for example, when at:

- Client interviews
- Project management meetings
- Product demonstrations
- Courses and lectures.

Note-taking is required to recall the information obtained and our ability to do this is improved if we write the notes down ourselves. The objective of note-taking is to record the key points of the meeting. It should then be possible to recall the detail of the meeting from a review of the key points noted.

We will examine three forms of note-taking:

- *Outline Format:* This is the 'traditional' format of indented lists. An example is shown as Figure 5.2. An agenda for a meeting may be prepared in this structured format and notes taken during the meeting may follow the same structure.

The following difficulties may arise when this form of note-taking is used:

- It may be difficult to maintain logical order when discussion backtracks to a previous point or digresses from the point
- It may be difficult to avoid recording unnecessary detail by copying visual material presented or by quoting participants verbatim
- It may be difficult to review notes easily
- It may be difficult to obtain an overview of the points discussed and the conclusions drawn from the meeting because of the rigid list structure
- It may be difficult to make connections between the ideas presented because they are obscured by the form of notes.

```
Making notes in the IS development process

1 ...............................................
   1.1 ........................................
2 ...............................................
   2.1 ........................................
   2.2.........................................
3 ...............................................
```

Fig. 5.2: Outline format

- *Mind mapping:* In the 1970s Tony Buzan developed the mind mapping technique which is based on the workings of the human mind (Buzan, 1993). The technique adopts a holistic approach to note-taking and memory recall. Mind maps are simple to create. The main idea is first written in the centre of a piece of paper. Branches are then added from the main idea labelled with keywords. Creativity is the key for developing successful mind maps. The use of colour, illustrations and symbols assist in improving the recall of the material and detail discussed. An example of a mind map is illustrated in Figure 5.3.

  The simplistic power of mind maps has many applications beyond note-taking. Mind maps can be used, for example, in brainstorming sessions, project planning, structuring material to assist in report writing and for the preparation of presentations. Mind maps are very flexible and one of their strengths is the ability to assist in the identification of relationships between concepts in the material.

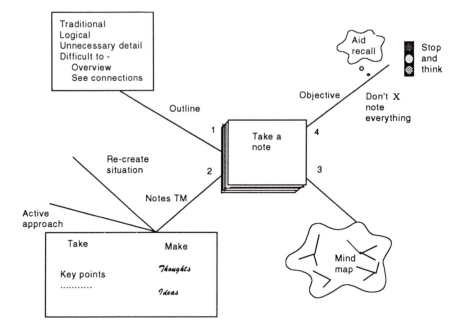

Fig. 5.3: Mind map

- *Notes:TM:* (Notes: Taking and Making) is a technique which records the note-taker's thoughts and conclusions, in addition to the key concepts which are discussed. This technique promotes an active approach to note-taking and has been called 'constructive day-dreaming'. The technique suggests that a piece of paper is divided into two sections by drawing a vertical line about one third of the way in from the right hand side of the page. The left hand side of the page is used to 'take' note of key points. The right hand side of the paper is used to 'make' notes of thoughts, impressions, questions, ideas and points to follow up later. The use of symbols and illustrations in the right hand column in addition to the thoughts recorded, later help to re-create the situation. The cognitive re-creation of the situation aids recall of the points discussed during the meeting. An example of this form of note-taking is shown in Figure 5.4. This technique is particularly useful in meetings and interviews where the manner in which the words were spoken are as important, if not more important, than the actual words themselves. Expressions of uncertainty, anxiousness, apprehension and concern, for example, are important indicators which need to be addressed for the successful implementation of information systems.

Poor, incomplete and incomprehensible notes are worthless. In contrast, good notes aid recall of the details presented, and assist in the identification of relationships between ideas. After a twenty-four hour period, as much as 80% of detail is 'lost' from memory. Systems development projects can take years to complete. Comprehensive notes are therefore important during all stages of systems development. Commitment to developing note-taking skills therefore enhances the systems development process by:

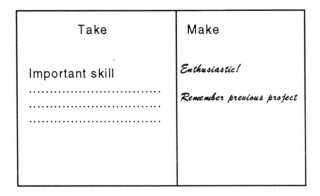

Fig. 5.4: Notes: TM

- Reducing the percentage of detailed material 'lost' during the development.
- Reducing the time spent searching through poor notes of a previous meeting, to find that some material may not even have been recorded.

Note-taking is therefore an essential skill for the information systems professional.

5.5   Examining document usage

Another important source of information for the analyst is the existing literature and documentation that might exist which relates to the situation under investigation. It is important that the analyst establishes what exists and examines relevant material in detail.

It is through generating information that the organisation is able to plan and control its activities. Companies have a large body of literature and documentation. It is possible for the analyst to become overwhelmed by the quantity of this and care must be taken to avoid this. Literature that might potentially be of interest includes:

- Documentation of any previous investigations and their findings
- Company literature describing its organisation and activities
- Sales literature and product information
- Job descriptions describing the duties and responsibilities of staff
- Procedure manuals describing how activities are carried out
- Management reports providing information on the range of management information that is used, and this might also be a useful starting point for discussions about future requirements
- Forms and documents that contain much of the information that flows within the company.

Much information can be gleaned from examining forms and documents, indeed, any form, card, list or file. Many documents which are commonly used in organisations today are computer-generated. From the point of view of systems investigation, these are no different from other, non-computer documents.

Sources for documentation may be internal or external to the organisation. After generation, documents are passed around before being sent off, filed or destroyed. In examining a particular piece of written material, the following points about it need to be considered:

- Where does it originate and how many copies are produced?
- What is its purpose?
- What entries are made on it and what work does this involve?
- Where does it go after it is generated and during its life?
- Who uses it, what data is extracted from it and for what purpose?
- When, if at all, is it filed, for what purpose and for how long?

This type of investigation will involve cross-checking between departments, and any inconsistencies will need to be resolved by further investigation.

Documents typically consist of two essential parts: headings and entries. Headings will identify the document and major aspects, such as the project, version and who generated the document. The entries will list the detail. There are also subtle differences in terms of externally-generated and internally-generated documents:

- *Internal documents:* are pre-headed but otherwise blank, and entries will be added during their life in the organisation as they are processed.
- *External documents:* arrive with entries already inserted, and further ones may be added internally.

Steps should be taken to ensure that the documents being examined are current and up-to-date and that they are correctly headed. Users should be asked to validate their contents. If entries involve the use of special symbols or different colours, the analyst must establish the reasons for these as they may well be significant information in their use.

One way to record the detailed information about a particular document is by completing a document specification form which describes the data to be found on any document. Figure 5.5 provides an example form. The entries of this particular document consist of a list of items and information about them.

DOCUMENT SPECIFICATION FORM

Name of Doc   *Video title form*   Originator   *Shop manager*

Doc Ref *73*   Date completed *25/10/97* No of copies *2*   Orig. *JBL*

Form distribution   *1 Head Office (white copy)*
                     2 Manager (yellow copy) for filing

Remarks   *Admin. clerk to tick off videos as received*

Entry ref.	Item description	Max items	Structure	Entered by	Remarks
A	Date originated	1	date	manager	day/month/year
B	Video title	1	40 chars	manager	taken from catalogue
C	Video director	1	15 chars	manager	
D	Description	1	80 chars	admin	synopsis
E	Run time	2	6 num	admin	
F	Production year	1	4 chars	admin	
G	Release year	1	4 chars	admin	
H	Certification	1	3 chars	admin	
I	Film category	2	3 chars	admin	
J	Rental category	1	1 char	admin	
K	Format code	2	6 chars	admin	

Fig. 5.5: Document specification form

Another useful technique for recording details of entities to be found on various forms is through the use of a data usage chart. A given entry on a document may appear on several different documents as a result of having been copied from one document to another. Entries are also derived by calculation from other entries, as a result of some organisational activity, or from some external source. A data usage chart, an example of which is provided in Figure 5.6, can be used to record details of data entries and their usage, and to avoid unnecessary duplication. The data usage chart can also be used for cross-referencing to the data flow diagrams.

Document/display Name	Ref	Video title	Catalog number	Date out	Member number	Pay code	Date due	Fine to pay	Date in	Member name	Remarks
Scrap report	S1	T2	T3								
Tape hire	T1	T2	T2	I	M1	I	I	C	I	M1	Compute fine
Video order	V1	S1									
Customer details	M1	I	I		M1				I	M1	
Request details	R1				M1					M1	

Fig. 5.6: Data usage chart

5.6   Developing questionnaires and analysing responses

Questionnaires might be particularly useful where the users are remote from the analyst. Where the project concerns products in anticipated markets, then the users do not yet exist and are therefore not accessible to the analyst. In such situations, questionnaires can be used to gather relevant facts, identify attitudes and collate suggestions about the system. In comparison to interviews, questionnaires are limited as to the level of detail that can be collected. However, they are useful in obtaining information from a larger sample of users than is possible with interviewing. The specific situations which are amenable to the use of questionnaires as a method of fact finding are:

- Where the users are widely dispersed at different branches in different locations.
- Where the number of people whose views need to be heard is too large that interviewing is not a practical option.
- Where verification of information elicited by other means is necessary.
- Where the questions to be asked are simple and call for direct answers which can be selected from a list shown on the questionnaire.
- When a complete set of replies is not necessary to establish the facts. In general people tend to not give high priority to filling out questionnaires and therefore the number of responses will form only a proportion (perhaps a small proportion) of the total number sent for completion. Nevertheless it is important that the sample returned is large enough to provide a reasonable picture of the situation.

The design of a questionnaire is very important, as we need to encourage people to want to fill it in. Some guidelines for questionnaire design are:

- Keep the questionnaire as short as possible. If it is too long, people will not bother to fill it in.
- Keep in mind the level of intellect and likely interests of the people who are being targeted.
- Keep questions clear, concise, unambiguous and unbiased. Whenever possible, give multiple-choice answers from which the respondent is to select one. Questions requiring long answers should be avoided.
- Avoid excessive branching and skipping in the structure of the questionnaire.
- Group questions by topics and structure the questionnaire so that the questions and groups follow a logical order as far as possible.
- Give appropriate instructions for answering questions. It is important to consider the manner of response which will provide the right level of detail in the response. The response can be:
  - Selecting one from 'Yes/No' option
  - Selecting a number on a particular scale
  - Ticking, underlining or circling an appropriate response from a given reply set
  - Providing short descriptions.
- Avoid introducing bias into an answer because of the way the question is structured.

When the questionnaire has been designed and produced, it can be useful to carry out a trial run with a small number of representative targets, if time and resources permit. This will be useful in identifying any potentially problematic areas which can then be modified before the full survey. When the questionnaire is sent out, it is important that a covering letter is included with the questionnaire to:

- Explain briefly to the potential respondent the purpose of the questionnaire and why they have been selected to complete it.
- Indicate whether anyone else is going to see the completed questionnaire or whether the responses are to be anonymous. Also indicate who is going to be informed of its findings.
- Explain what the results are going to be used for, highlighting any advantages to the respondent that might motivate them to complete and return the questionnaire. A report that might be of use or a better

system catering for their needs might provide an incentive to the recipient to complete the questionnaire.

- State the deadline by which the questionnaire has to be returned.

The advantages of an analyst using questionnaires are that:

- A relatively high volume response is possible when compared with other investigative methods.
- Respondents may be permitted to be anonymous, and this might result in better information for the analyst because people are more likely to be honest rather than say what they think they ought to say.
- This approach is cheaper than mass interviewing, which is particularly time-consuming.

The disadvantages of using questionnaires are:

- They may limit the type of questions that can be asked to those which have a Yes/No response, rather than being able to ask questions that would provide more relevant information.
- Questions and answers may be open to misinterpretation, and there is no opportunity for clarification as there is with an interview.
- If the volume of returns is low, the sample may not be statistically significant. A less than 10% response rate is by no means unusual.

Questionnaires prove to be a useful method of fact finding, though as shown above they do have their limitations and very often the analyst uses a number of techniques.

5.7   Observing appropriate organisational activities

It might be appropriate for the analyst to gather information by observation of appropriate organisational activities. This is an important fact finding technique as it enables the analyst to gain first-hand information. Interviews are extremely useful, but they do not tell the analyst everything. A significant amount of organisational knowledge is tacit, and is never verbalised as the user mistakenly might assume that the analysts know what appear to them to be commonplace facts.

A way around this lack of expression of tacit knowledge is for the analyst to observe the user in the workplace, while trying to be as inconspicuous as possible. There is a risk that the presence of the analyst disturbs the situation, causing people to modify their behaviour. This requires the analyst to be diplomatic, and attempt to build up trust and rapport. Observation is a time-consuming activity, but it can provide a significant amount of information on working practices. The analyst needs to observe the flow of documents. This might be a good way of seeing exactly what goes on rather than be given a specific individual's interpretation of what goes on as an interview would do. The analyst may get the opportunity to observe:

- Exceptional conditions and how non-routine aspects are dealt with, such as interruptions to the normal work flow. These may be due to contact from callers and visitors (both internal and external to the organisation).
- Informal communications of information by others in the department and organisation or outside organisation. These might go undetected if not observed.
- The ways in which people work around the system.
- Normal routine activities involving defined formal communications.
- The balance of workload, and how it varies at different parts of the day and week and between the different members of staff.
- Operational problems, such as bad working conditions, equipment problems, absence of authority or leadership, and insufficient understanding of the procedures.

5.8   Summary

In this chapter we have looked at the systems investigation phase of the information systems development life cycle. It is carried out in order to find out more about the specific situation. Figure 5.8 provides an overview of this stage of the information systems development life cycle.

During this stage we need to plan various aspects of the project, including its phases, activities, how the project is to be organised, responsibilities, individuals assigned and resources. We also need to establish the methods to be used for reporting project progress.

To carry out our investigations we need to use appropriate techniques to establish the facts corresponding to the information required by using the information system. We need to know who requires the information, when they require it, the purpose and the activities for which the information is to be used.

The systems analyst requires certain skills to carry out this task. The main fact finding techniques of interviewing, examining document usage, questionnaires and observation were also discussed in detail.

In the next chapter we consider how the systems analyst analyses the information provided in the next phase of the life cycle.

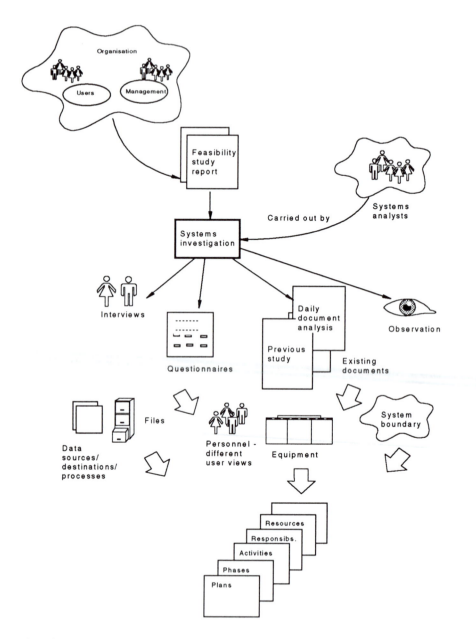

Fig 5.8: Overview of the systems investigation process

Further Reading

Buzan, T. (1993) *The Mind Map Book*, BBC, London.
   Mind mapping described in considerable detail.

Chatzoglou, P. D. & Macaulay, L. (1996) Requirements capture and IS methodologies, *Information Systems Journal*, **6**, pp. 209-225.
This paper presents the findings of a survey looking at current commercial practice associated with the requirements stage. The survey looks at the use of methodologies and project planning tools during requirements capture and analysis.

Dingley, S. & Shah, H. U. (1994) *Notetaking*, Internal report - Aston University (obtainable from Hanifa Shah at Staffordshire University)
Looks at the importance of note taking and effective ways of doing this.

Joshi, K. (1992) Interpersonal skills for co-operative user-analyst relationships: some research issues, *Data Base*, **23**, 1, Winter 1992, pp. 23-25.

Kappelman, L. A. & McLean, E. R. (1994) User engagement in the development, implementation, and use of information technologies, *Proceedings of 27th Hawaii International Conference on System Sciences*, **3**, pp. 512-521, Jan 1994.

Shah, H. U., Dingley, S. & Golder, P. A. (1994) Managing systems development - bridging the culture gap between users and developers, *Journal of Systems Management*, July 1994.
Looks at the barriers between users and analysts/designers.

Wood-Harper, A. T., Corder, S., Wood, J. R. G. & Watson, H. (1996) How we profess: the ethical systems analyst, *Communications of the ACM*, March 1996, **39**, 3, pp. 69-77.
Proposes a basis and rationale for conducting ethical analysis as part of the information systems development process enabling self-reflection by systems analysts on the ethical implications of their practice ensuring that ethical decisions are not made implicitly.

Questions

1. What aspects of the project must be planned for?
2. What facts about the information needed by the organisation are we trying to establish?
3. Discuss what qualities a systems analyst should have.
4. Explain how systems analysts carry out their role.
5. Why is feedback an important aspect of the analysis activity?
6. List the techniques that might be used during analysis.
7. Explain the importance and use of interviewing.
8. How should the analyst prepare for an interview?
9. How should the interview be carried out?
10. What are the kinds of question that should be asked at different stages of the interview?

11. Discuss examination of document usage as a fact finding technique.
12. What questions need to be asked about each document?
13. Discuss the use of questionnaires for analysis.
14. What are the advantages of using questionnaires?
15. Explain how observation might be used by the analyst in the fact-finding process.

Areas to debate

1. You are asked to carry out a systems investigation into the new human resources system for a large telecommunications company. Debate the different circumstances that prevail throughout relevant parts of the organisation. Consider appropriate fact finding methods for these and identify specific questions that should be asked and information that should be established.
2. Consider the role of the systems analyst in the above investigation. What are the required characteristics of the systems analyst and the potential difficulties of the role? What likely impact will the decisions of the systems analyst have on the various personnel in the organisation?
3. Discuss the literature on the 'ethical systems analyst'. Might there be any sources of conflict that the ethical systems analyst may have to resolve in the above example?

CASE STUDY

Toni Asifiori has agreed to the recommendations that the analyst made in the feasibility study report of the proposed system to manage and control stock purchasing which is for use at all the Asifiori Salons. You must now consider the systems investigation aspects of this project. What activities need to be carried out during this phase? Think about the type of planning that is required for such a project and also about the fact finding techniques that might be used. Produce a list of potential interviewees and the questions that you wish to ask them. Design a questionnaire for obtaining information from people in salons outside the area.

Chapter 6

SYSTEMS ANALYSIS: UNDERSTANDING THE MATERIAL

6.1 Systems analysis phase

In this chapter we consider the systems analysis phase of the information systems development life cycle. During this phase we are trying to get a detailed understanding of the material collected so far, so that we can identify the requirements of the system. We first look at what is done during the systems analysis phase. We then look in detail at structured systems analysis as a means of dealing with the complexity of an application domain. We discuss the problems of analysis and the techniques which have been developed to address some of these problems.

Figure 6.1 shows the systems analysis phase in the context of the information systems development life cycle.

We classify structured systems analysis and design techniques into three groups: data-oriented, process-oriented and time-dependent. We discuss in detail a number of techniques within each category. Data-oriented techniques include:

- Entity-relationship modelling
- Normalisation.

  Process-oriented techniques include:

- Data flow diagrams
- Functional models
- Decision trees
- Decision tables
- Structured English
- Tight English
- Data flow diagrams.

  Time-oriented techniques include:

- Entity life histories.

Systems analysis is the study of a problem situation, that is a situation where problems exist, before some action is taken, to gain an understanding of the situation and to specify the requirements of any action that might be required. In information systems development, the analysis is undertaken in some business area or application, and it leads to the specification of a new information system, perhaps involving computer systems, for that business domain. Following this systems analysis stage, the new system is designed and implemented. Systems analysis involves establishing a detailed understanding of all the important facets of the business area under investigation. Analysts working closely with users need to establish answers to the following questions:

- What is being done?
- Why is it being done?
- When is it being done?
- How is it being done?

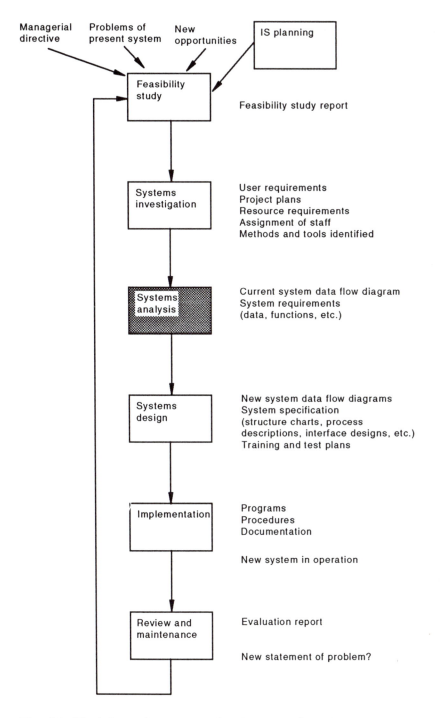

Fig. 6.1: The information systems development life cycle

- How frequently does it occur?
- How effectively is it being done?
- What problems exist?
- What are their effects?
- What are their underlying causes?

In answering these questions the analyst will gain a detailed and thorough understanding of the problem situation. In particular, the information needs will be identified and problems with the current system should also come to light. To establish this information, the analyst needs to talk to a variety of people to find out about the business processes. The analyst can also ascertain opinions about why things happen as they do and ideas for changing the processes. Of course, much of the basic information will have been obtained at the systems investigation phase.

Some approaches to information systems development advocate that this information about the existing system is expressed in a series of stages to eventually form the design of the new system:

- Express the present system in physical terms
- Express the present system in logical terms
- Express the new system in logical terms (using the logical information about the old system and the new requirements)
- Express the new system in physical terms.

The last two stages above will form part of the systems design phase (the subject of Chapter 7). Depending on the particular approach, the second stage may be considered part of either systems analysis or design. Some argue that it is unnecessary to model the current system as this can be very time-consuming and might lead to solutions which are too similar to the old system. Whether or not models are produced of the current system, effort will have to be expended in gaining an understanding of it. Studying the current system will enable the analysts to familiarise themselves with the activities and relevant terminology of the environment. It will also enable the analyst to set clear and identifiable boundaries for the investigation.

In Figure 6.2 we can see this concept represented as a 'V' diagram, in which the real-world needs result in a specification of requirements. These are then used in the systems analysis process to form a conceptual model of those requirements. This leads to a system design which will be used to develop an information system representing the real-world business solution.

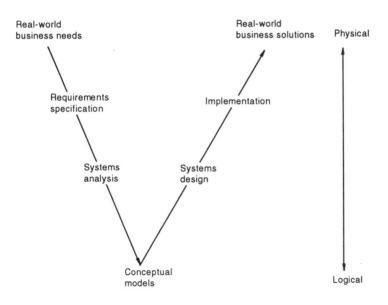

Fig. 6.2: The 'V' diagram

Figure 6.3 shows an example of organisational activity in which the 'work' involves using the data (items with quantities ordered by a particular customer) on one document (the sales order form) to produce the data (the cost to that customer of the items bought in those quantities) on another document (the invoice). This example illustrates that organisational activity can be modelled by looking at:

- data that is moved; and
- processes that are carried out.

Fig. 6.3: Multiple views - data and processes

Data and processes represent two complementary views about systems. This complementarity is the basis of modern structured methods. Modern information systems consist of databases and applications programs which represent tangible forms for this separation of data and the processing of the data. The data defines the nature of an organisation and is relatively stable. The processing is affected by organisational structure and its environment and by the technology employed. Hence it varies continually.

Staff will have different views about the data processing. For example, senior staff often do not know the detail of any processing, but see the activity as information flows. Views need to be elicited from different staff in an organisation. The two views (data and process) also act as a check on each other and enables the full structure to be identified.

During the systems investigation phase, natural-language descriptions of the information are used, but this is not sufficient to understand and describe large, complex systems. We need other techniques. Natural language is imprecise, ambiguous and informal. Structured methods aim to overcome this difficulty in two ways: first, by partitioning the system into components, and second, by constructing appropriate models of the system.

As Figure 6.4 shows, creating an information system involves starting off with a general statement in loose narrative language and refining this through a series of stages, eventually resulting in precise statements in a precise language which is machine executable.

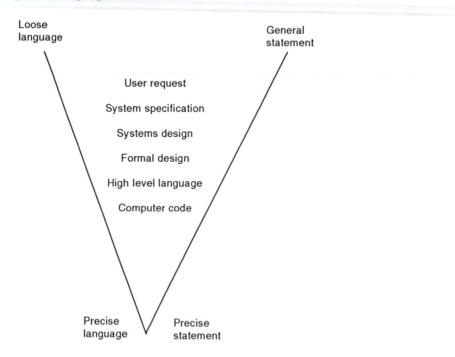

Fig. 6.4: Refinement from general to precise statements

6.2 Structured analysis

Due to the complexity of the products produced and the processes involved in information systems development, structured approaches have become widely used. In this section we discuss what the problems of analysis in general are, what structured systems analysis is and how structured systems analysis aims to overcome the problems previously identified.

Systems analysis is a complex activity, and there are a number of difficulties that might arise. DeMarco (1978) discusses these in detail. We summarise them below:

- *Communication problems between analyst and user:* These occur because the procedures that they are describing are inherently complex and therefore difficult to describe. A textual description of the procedures is not necessarily appropriate and this can be compounded by the lack of a common language (each seeing the other's language as jargon). Further difficulties are caused by the fact that there is no early system model that can be used as a discussion vehicle between analyst and user.
- *Lack of tools compared with programming:* There is a lack of tools to support analysis, especially when compared to the proliferation of tools for programming work. This has now been rectified to some extent with tools becoming available for analysis. We discuss these tools in Chapter 10.
- *Allocation of work:* Without modularisation of the problem, it is not possible to partition the work effectively. In this case, a backlog of analysis work will occur which may lead to the analysis work being done poorly in order to catch up.
- *Changing nature of requirements:* Organisations are dynamic entities and we cannot freeze the target document. On the other hand, as changes arise, the target document will be difficult to modify. Hence many large systems are never implemented.
- *Target document:* In order to counteract the previous point, care should be taken to avoid a target document which is tedious to read and write. The document should not be:
  - excessively redundant
  - excessively wordy
  - excessively physical.
- *Politics:* Organisational politics can make the task of analysis extremely difficult. It is not possible to eliminate this completely, though politics flourish in confusion and obscurity (often a result of a poor target document).

The target document is therefore crucial as it defines the final product. It represents the contract between analyst and client. There are a number of problems that can arise, concerned with the language of the document and its modifiability. The language should be easy to understand and the report should be easy to modify. It should be expressed in logical rather than physical terms. The document should contain a logical model of the system.

During systems analysis, we need techniques which are going to help us address the questions:

- What is the problem?
- What is the best solution for the problem we have identified?

Due to the complexity of the situation, we might be dealing with, there is no single technique that will help us. What we require are a number of techniques which we can use to form different models of the same situation. A **model** is a representation of real-world objects and events, and good models will be a fair representation of certain aspects of the 'real world'. Systems analysis in general is an art, not an exact science. There can be a number of ways to derive a reasonable model and there are a number of reasonable models (there are of course an infinite number of poor models). A model represents something, usually a simplification, which highlights aspects which are of particular interest to the user, and is built so that it can be used for a specific purpose, for example, for communication and testing. Many types of model are used in information systems work.

The essence of structured systems analysis and design is the decomposition of a system into processes, inputs, outputs and files. These are fundamental parts of any information system. However, structured approaches are not complete in themselves to assist in all aspects of information systems development. To give an example, analysts must rely on other techniques to collect facts, identify user requirements, identify candidate solutions and evaluate those candidates for feasibility. We have discussed some of these (for example, rich pictures) in the previous chapters on the feasibility study and the systems investigation stages. The modern information systems life cycle presented in this text, therefore, draws upon the techniques of structured systems analysis and design, where appropriate, while attempting to produce a framework for information systems development as a whole.

DeMarco (1978) identifies the goals of structured systems analysis and design as being to:

- Produce a maintainable product
- Produce a partitionable product
- Make use of graphical techniques to reduce ambiguity
- Distinguish the logical from the physical
  - **Logical** is the 'what' and is the concern of the user
  - **Physical** is the 'how' and is the concern of the analyst.

As we have already pointed out, complex problem situations cannot be described in appropriate richness by the use of a single technique. With this in mind, a number of techniques are available which help us to develop different perspectives of the situation. The techniques and tools of structured analysis and design are:

- Data flow diagramming
- Data modelling
- Data dictionary generation
- Process modelling techniques, such as:
  - structured English
  - decision tables
  - decision trees.

All of the above are described in detail in this chapter. Structured analysis should result in a structured specification which is composed of:

- Data flow diagrams
- Data models
- Data dictionary
- Process specifications making use of relevant techniques.

The techniques and tools listed above are not used only in the systems analysis phase. They are also used to specify the design of the new system, that is, structured design (the subject of the next chapter). The structured design documentation will include data flow diagrams, data dictionaries and process specifications of the new system. These will then be used to generate, amongst other things, appropriate programs in the systems design and implementation stages.

As we have seen, the three views of information systems - data-oriented, process-oriented and time-dependent - are not mutually exclusive, but are complementary views of the same system. Methodologies integrate techniques from each category to produce an integrated view of the system to be developed. We now look at these techniques, beginning with data-oriented techniques.

6.3 Entity-relationship modelling

Data-oriented techniques focus on the identification and analysis of the data requirements of the system. They consist of:

- Entity-relationship (E-R) modelling
- Relational modelling and normalisation.

We introduce conceptual modelling and discuss E-R modelling and relational modelling in detail, as these are well established and widely used conceptual modelling techniques. We demonstrate how a relational model can be produced from an E-R model. We also explain how we can produce an improved relational design by carrying out normalisation on our relational model in order to remove duplication and redundancy. Finally, we show how these techniques can be applied in a seven stage approach to conceptual modelling.

E-R modelling (Chen, 1976) is a technique of conceptual modelling which produces a high-level formal model of the organisation. This model is then used as a framework for current and future development of information systems. At this stage, we are not making reference to implementation details. This is important as it enables us to separate the needs of the organisation from how those needs are going to be implemented. This allows 'objective' decisions to be made about implementation later. We do not want a bias towards current implementation methods. The model is independent of processes and, in general, provides an unambiguous way of presenting ideas. E-R modelling proves useful in presenting ideas (especially between user and analyst). It is also an aid to understanding. We need to understand the concepts to draw the models. Further, E-R modelling allows the use of rigorous standards and conventions.

Information systems have become much more complex, and as they become more complex, we need to integrate data and minimise duplication. We also need to maintain integrity, which requires control over the data resource at an early stage in development using suitable documentation techniques.

As Figure 6.5 illustrates, conventional systems analysis procedures were applied to single applications that were the first to be computerised in the organisation. When applications being developed are an integrated part of a total system (to departmental systems, integrated operational systems and then management information systems), these analysis techniques prove inadequate. The situation which most obviously requires a different approach is the development of a database. In a database environment, many applications share the same data. The database is looked upon as a common asset. E-R modelling techniques were largely developed to cater for the implementation of database systems, although that does not mean that they cannot be applied to other situations. Data modelling may also be carried out as a step in conventional file applications.

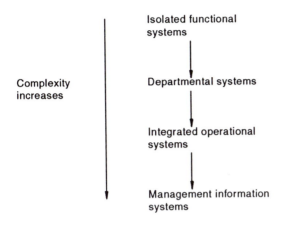

Isolated functional systems

Complexity increases

Departmental systems

Integrated operational systems

Management information systems

Fig. 6.5: The increasing complexity of information systems

E-R modelling can also be of interest to management as a way of understanding their organisation. The E-R model is just another view of the organisation, but it is a particular perception of reality and it can be used to help solve a number of problems. The model produced proves to be a very useful way of viewing the business.

The entity-relationship model is an abstract representation of the data within the organisation. It can be looked on as a discussion document and its coincidence with the real world is verified in discussions with the various users. However, the analyst should be aware that variances between the model and a particular user's view could be due to the narrow perception of that particular user. The model should be a global view. This model enables the computer specialist to design appropriate computer systems for the organisation, but it also provides management with a unique tool for perceiving the business process. The essence of rational scientific problem solving is to be able to perceive the complex, 'messy', real world in such a manner that the solution to any problem may be easier. As we shall see, it is easy to understand and to use.

The model has a number of components. An **entity** is a thing of interest to the organisation and something about which we want to ho' information. An entity instance might be some physical object, example, a person, or it might be a conceptual object, for example, about which we need to store information. An **entity type** is a collection of entity instances sharing similar properties. An entity is represented diagrammatically by a box with a name, as shown in Figure 6.6. The name is in the singular and shown in block capitals. The box may be of any size or shape sufficient to hold an unambiguous name and to make the drawing of the E-R diagram as convenient as possible.

ENTITY NAME

Fig. 6.6: Entity representation

Synonyms may occur where there are different words to name an entity which have identical meanings within this business context. One name is chosen as the primary name. Any synonyms may then be shown (in most conventions preceded by a '/'). One example might be EMPLOYEE/WORKER. Each entity must be uniquely identifiable, that is, each instance or occurrence of an entity must be separate and distinctly identifiable from all other instances of that type of entity.

Relationships associate or relate instances from one entity type with some of the instances of another entity type. Relationships occur because of:

• *Association:* for example, customer loans video
• *Structure:* for example, video-catalogue contains video-entries.

The above are binary relationships since they represent a link between two entities. Relationships can be more complex than this. For example, a relationship between three entities is a ternary relationship. Each relationship has a:

• *Name*
• *Degree or cardinality* (how many)
• *Membership class* (optional or mandatory).

These three features of a relationship are now explained further.

A relationship is represented by a line that joins entity boxes together. In a recursive relationship the line joins an entity box to itself. An important property of a relationship is its degree. There are three possible kinds of relationship **degree**, each corresponding to different pairs of business rules for the relationship:

- *One-to-one (1:1).* An example of this type of relationship could correspond to the business rule that a customer can only have one membership card. An example is shown in Figure 6.7.
- *One-to-many (1:m).* An example of this type of relationship could correspond to a business rule that a customer can borrow many videos. An example is shown in Figure 6.8.
- *Many-to-many (n:m).* An example of this type of relationship could correspond to a business rule that a given video can be supplied to us by many suppliers and that a given supplier can supply us with many videos. An example is shown in Figure 6.9.

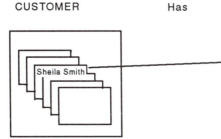

Fig. 6.7: A one-to-one relationship

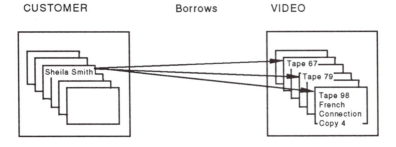

Fig. 6.8: A one-to-many relationship

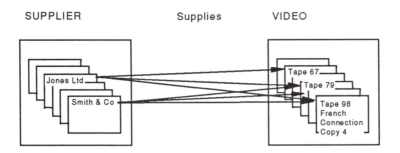

Fig. 6.9: A many-to-many relationship

The **membership class** of a relationship denotes whether it is optional or mandatory for every occurrence of the related entities to participate in an occurrence of the relationship. Where the relationship end is optional, a small circle is placed on the line at the appropriate end of the relationship. This is shown in Figure 6.10.

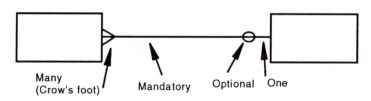

Many
(Crow's foot)   Mandatory   Optional   One

Fig. 6.10: Relationship representation

An example of a business rule that could result in an optional relationship is the rule that we wish to keep details of suppliers whether they already supply us with videos or whether they might potentially supply us with videos. This means that it is optional for occurrences of the SUPPLIER entity to be related to a VIDEO entity. This example is shown in Figure 6.11.

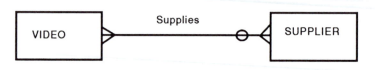

Fig. 6.11: An example of an optional relationship

A first approach to an E-R model for the video shop might result in the diagram given in Figure 6.12. The entity types are VIDEO, CUSTOMER, MEMBERSHIP and SUPPLIER. This reflects the fact that a CUSTOMER has a MEMBERSHIP and CUSTOMER borrows VIDEO which are supplied by SUPPLIER. The relationships shown in Figure 6.12 are examples of degrees of one-to-one, one-to-many and many-to-many.

The diagram also shows a few **attributes** of the entities. The particular attribute or group of attributes that uniquely identify an entity occurrence is known as the **key attribute** or attributes. The 'video-no' is the key attribute of the entity called VIDEO.

A mistake frequently made at this stage is to define the entities to reflect the processes of the business, such as stock control, credit control or sales order processing. This could be a valid model of the business but it is not an entity-relationship model. A database so created would be satisfactory for some specific applications, but would not be adequate for many applications and certainly not all. Where data analysis differs from conventional systems analysis is that it separates the data structures from the applications which use them. The objective of data analysis is to produce a flexible model which can be easily adapted as the requirements of the users change. Although the applications will need to be changed, this will not necessarily be true of the data. The model reflects data in the business, not processes. It is concerned with the data that exists, not how it is used.

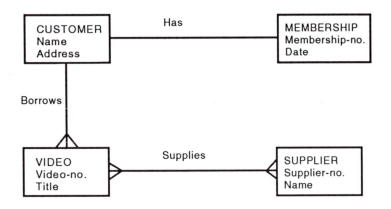

Fig. 6.12: A first approach to an E-R model for a video shop

As we have seen, the technique attempts to separate the data structure from the functions for which the data may be used. This separation is a useful distinction, although it is often difficult to make in practice. In any case, it is sometimes useful to bear in mind the functions of the data analysed. For example, CUSTOMER and an EMPLOYEE are both people, but it is their role, that is what they do, that distinguishes the entities. The distinction, formed because of a knowledge of functions, is a useful one to make. However, too much regard to functions will produce a model biased towards particular applications or users or the present ways of doing things.

An important preliminary step is therefore to define the area for analysis and break this up into distinct sub-areas. Again, the arrangement most suitable to the organisation should have been determined in the feasibility study stage.

Although it is relatively easy to illustrate the process of data modelling in theory, in real life there are problems in deciding how far one should go and what level of detail is appropriate. The level of detail must serve two purposes:

- It must be capable of explaining that part of the organisation that is being analysed
- It must be capable of being translated into the physical model.

It is important to realise that there is no logical or natural point at which the level of detail stops. This is a pragmatic decision.

Some informal guidelines for producing an E-R diagram are as follows:

- *Deciding what is an entity:* sometimes it is difficult to decide whether an item is an entity or an attribute. This obviously depends on the situation that is being modelled. An example of this could be entity occurrences of persons who are female, where they relate to:
  - patients in a hospital
  - students at university
  - readers in a library.

  In the first example, the fact that the person occurrence is female is important, so important that the patient entity may be split into two separate entities - male patients and female patients. In the student example, the fact that the person is female may not be of great significance and therefore there could be an attribute 'sex' of the person entity. In the reader example, the fact that the person is female may be of such insignificance that it is not even included as an attribute. In our video example, we may decide not to distinguish between the sex of our customers, though distinguishing them may show different renting patterns which might be useful.

- *More than one relationship between the same two entity sets:* there is no reason to prevent different relationships between entities in two sets. Thus we could have the relationships BUYS and LOANS between the two entity sets CUSTOMER and VIDEO. Each such relationship set contains relationships with different properties. A property of the LOANS relationship may be the length of the loan, whereas a property of the BUYS relationship may be the price of the video.

- *The organisation or part of the organisation being modelled should not be included in the E-R diagram:* this is a common source of difficulty. It is important to remember that ·the organisation being modelled should not itself appear in the E-R diagram (see Figure 6.13). Adding the business itself as an entity can cause confusion because it is now being given the same importance as its own components. Further, there is only one entity in the entity set VIDEO-SHOP and there would have to be a relationship between VIDEO-SHOP and every other entity set. The correct model for this is shown in Figure 6.14.

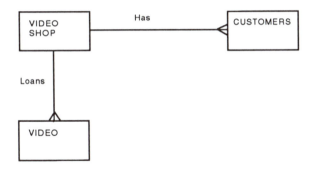

Fig. 6.13: Incorrect model since it includes organisation being modelled

Fig. 6.14: Correct model does not include organisation being modelled

- *An attribute acts as a relationship:* we may replace it by the relationship. For example, the relationship between PREMISES and EMPLOYEE shown in Figure 6.15.

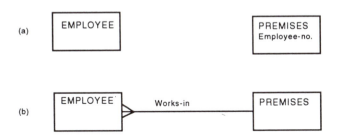

Fig. 6.15 (a) Incorrect representation of a relationship (b) Correct representation of a relationship

- *Entities with only one attribute:* These should be removed. The attribute SPOUSE-NAME in Figure 6.16 could become an attribute of EMPLOYEE.

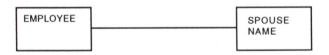

Fig. 6.16: Entity with single attribute only can be removed

- *Redundant or derivable information:* these should also be removed. We are trying to model only the essential features. For example, if we have decided to hold as attributes of a product, the quantity in stock and the unit price, then the attribute giving the total value for that stock item need not be included as it can be derived from the other two.

In developing a conceptual model of the organisation we need to go through number of phases, these are discussed next.

6.4 Phases in conceptual modelling

- Define the area for analysis (this will have been decided at the feasibility study stage)
- Define the entities and the relationships between them
- Establish the key attribute(s) for each entity
- Complete each entity with all the attributes
- Map to relational representation
- Normalise
- Ensure all events and operations are supported by the model.

After the area of analysis is agreed, the entities can be defined. The obvious and major entities will be identified first. The analyst will attempt to name the fundamental things of interest to the organisation. As the analyst is gathering these entities, the relationships between the entities can also be determined and named. As we have seen, their degree (or cardinality) can be one-to-one, one-to-many, or many-to-many. It may be possible to identify those which are optional or mandatory. The analyst will begin to assemble the entity-relationship diagram. The diagram will be like a doodle in the beginning, but it will soon be useful as a communication tool. There are software tools available which can help draw up these diagrams and make alterations easily.

The key attribute of each entity will also be determined. The key attributes will uniquely identify any entity occurrence. There may be alternative keys, in which case the most natural or concise is normally chosen. The analyst has now obtained the model in outline and is in a position to fill in the detail. This means establishing all the attributes for each entity. Each attribute will say something about the entity. The analyst has to ensure that any synonyms and homonyms are detected. For example, a product could be called a part, product or finished product depending on the department. These are all synonyms for 'product'. On the other hand, the term product may mean different things (homonyms), depending on the department. It could mean a final saleable item in the marketing department or a sub-assembly in the production department. These differences must be reconciled and recorded in the data dictionary and possibly on the E-R diagram. The process of identifying attributes may itself reveal entities that have not been identified. Any data element in the organisation must be defined as an entity, an attribute or a relationship and recorded in the data dictionary. Entities and relationships will also be recorded in the entity-relationship diagram.

As we shall see, the next stages are to map the E-R model to its relational representation. At this stage normalisation is carried out. The final stage of entity analysis will be to look at all the events within the area and the operations that need to be performed following an event, and ensure that the model supports these events and operations. Events are frequently referred to as transactions. For this part of the methodology, the analyst will identify the events associated with the organisation and examine the operations necessary on the trail of each of the events.

Entity-relationship modelling has documentation aids like other techniques of systems analysis. It is possible to obtain forms on which to specify all the elements of the data analysis process. The separate documents will enable the specification of entities, attributes, relationships, events and operations. These forms can be pre-drawn in some software tools and their contents automatically added to the data dictionary. E-R modelling is a communication tool as well as a technique for finding out information.

The entity-relationship diagrams, which are particularly useful in the initial analysis and as an overview of the data model, prove a good basis for communication with managers. They are much more understandable to non-computer people than the documents used in more traditional data processing, although they are also a good communications aid between computer people. They provide a pictorial description of the business in outline, showing what the business is about, not what it does. Managers and users can give 'user feedback' to the analysts and this will also help to tune the model and ensure its accuracy. A user may point out that an attribute is missing from an entity, or that a relationship between entities is one-to-many and not one-to-one as implied by the entity-relationship diagram. The manager may not use this terminology, but the analyst will be able to interpret the comments made.

6.5   Relational modelling and normalisation

Although an E-R diagram describes many of the important features of a conceptual model, using most notations it does not show the attributes associated with the entity and relationship types (we have listed one or two attributes in the entity boxes, for illustrative purposes). This additional information can be represented conveniently in the form of a set of fully normalised table types in the relational model - for relations are tables. In principle one could define a table type for each and every entity and relationship type, but the number of table types so generated would often be unnecessarily large.

As a first step in deciding which tables are required in practice, it will be helpful to develop criteria for deciding how different kinds of relationship can be best represented. Bear in mind that the initial objective is to define a simple high-level, implementation-independent model which can be used as a basis for further refinement.

The columns of the tabular relation represent attributes. Each attribute has a distinct name and is always referred to by that name, never by its position. Attribute names have no underlying order.

Each attribute has an associated **domain** which consists of all the allowable values of the attribute. Attribute values in a relation must be single, non-decomposable data items. Each row (often called a **tuple**) of a tabular relation is distinct: no two tuples may have identical values for all their attributes. Further, the ordering of tuples is immaterial. The **cardinality** of a relation is the number of tuples which it contains at any instant in time.

A key of a relation is a subset of the attributes of the relation which have the following properties

1. *Unique identification*: the value of the key attribute(s) uniquely identifies each tuple in the relation.
2. *Non-redundancy*: No attribute in the key can be discarded without destroying property 1.

Since each tuple in a relation is distinct, a key will always exist. That is, a key consisting of all the attributes of the relation will always have property 1. It then remains to find a subset with property 2. A relation may have more than one candidate key. That is it may have more than one set of attributes which satisfy 1 and 2 above. In this case we must choose one as the **primary key**. An attribute which participates in the primary key is called a prime attribute. The value of a prime attribute in any tuple may not be null (undefined). In specifying relation types the unique identifier (primary key) is underlined.

A phase in conceptual modelling is to map the E-R model produced to a relational representation. The following is a set of guidelines for mapping an E-R diagram into a relational model. They are not hard and fast rules and the database designer must use them in conjunction with common sense and a good understanding of the application. Used wisely, they should lead to a good first-cut design of the relational model.

- *Entity types:* become relations and their attributes become the attributes of the relation as shown in Figure 6.17.

Fig. 6.17: Mapping an entity to a relational representation

- *Representing relationships - 1:m:* This is done in two steps. First a relation is created for each of the entities on the E-R diagram as shown in Figure 6.18.

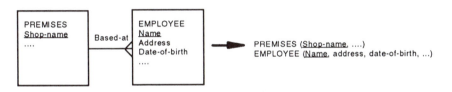

Fig. 6.18: Mapping two entities in a one-to-many relationship - first step

The above relational schema does not describe totally the E-R diagram. The entities are represented by their respective relations but there is no representation of the relationship between PREMISES and EMPLOYEE. One way to do this is as shown below in Figure 6.19. This is the second step. The primary key for the entity PREMISES is posted into the EMPLOYEE relation, to represent the relationship between EMPLOYEE and PREMISES. The attribute shopname in EMPLOYEE is called a 'posted identifier' or more commonly a **foreign key**.

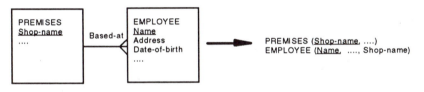

Fig. 6.19: Mapping entities in a one-to-many relationship - second step

- *Representing relationships - 1:1:* This can be done in one of two ways. Either the primary key of the first entity (CUSTOMER) is posted into the relation representing the second entity (MEMBERSHIP) or *vice versa*. This is shown in Figure 6.20.

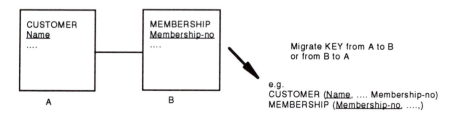

Fig. 6.20: Mapping two entities in a one-to-one relationship

- *Representing relationships - n:m:* In this case we would create a relation for each entity and one to represent the relationship between the two entities as shown in Figure 6.21.

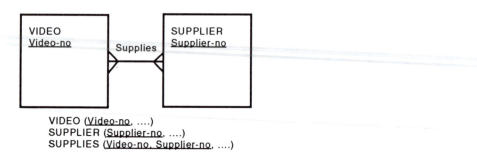

Fig. 6.21: Mapping two entities in a many-to-many relationship

If the above n:m relationship had been decomposed into two 1:m relationships as shown in Figure 6.22, the relational schema produced would still be the same.

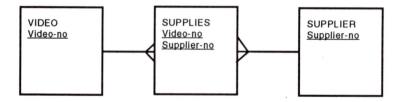

Fig. 6.22: Another representation of the m:n relationship

A relational model designed according to the guidelines of the previous section may still contain ambiguities or inconsistencies which must be resolved. This process of refinement is known as **normalisation**. Normalisation is the application of a number of rules to the relational model which will simplify the relations. These rules prove to be a useful guideline because we are dealing with large sets of data and the relations formed by the normalisation process will make the data easier to understand and manipulate.

There are three nested levels of normalisation, and the third and final stage is known as **third normal form (TNF)**. As well as simplifying the relations, normalisation also reduces anomalies which may otherwise occur when manipulating the relations. Normalised data is stable and a good foundation for any future growth. It is a mechanical process, indeed the technique has been automated, but the difficult part of it lies in understanding the meaning - that is the semantics - of the data, and this is only discovered by extensive and careful analysis of the data. Automation of the normalisation process still requires this information to be supplied.

An important concept for normalisation is **functional dependency**, which is often referred to as **determinacy**. Two important properties are needed to define normal forms. One property concerns dependencies between attributes and consequently the facts in the system. The goal of the design is to ensure that no fact is stored more than once. The other property is the relation key (primary key). Relation keys are dependent on the attributes in a relation and the dependencies between these attributes. Non-redundant relations only store facts about the relation keys.

There are three stages of normalisation:

- *First normal form:* Ensure that all the attributes are atomic (that is, in the smallest possible components). This means that there is only one possible value for each domain and not a set of values. This is often expressed as the fact that relations must not contain repeating groups.
- *Second normal form:* Ensure that all non-key attributes are functionally dependent on (give facts about) all of the key. If this is not the case, split off into a separate relation those attributes that are dependent on only part of the key.
- *Third normal form:* Ensure that all non-key attributes are functionally independent of each other. If this is not the case, create new relations which do not show any non-key dependence.

The process of normalisation is only made possible by an understanding of the real relationships in the organisation, otherwise assumptions have to be made which may be incorrect. This is probably best demonstrated by the use of an example from the video shop case study.

Consider as an example an unnormalised relation as follows:

HIRE (<u>member-id</u>, customer-name, customer-address, customer-phone, date-joined, {tape-id, tape-title, date-borrowed, date-due, tape-certification, certification-description}*)

(Note that * indicates a group of items that are repeated).

In first normal form we must remove the repeating group. This results in the following:

CUSTOMER (<u>member-id</u>, customer-name, customer-address, customer-phone, date-joined)

HIRE-DETAILS (<u>member-id, tape-id</u>, tape-title, date-borrowed, date-due, tape-certification, certification-description)

In second normal form we check HIRE-DETAILS to ensure that the non-key attributes are dependent on the whole key. We can see that tape-title and other tape details only depend on the tape-id and not the member-id. This means that we have to create another relation called TAPE-DETAILS as follows:

CUSTOMER (<u>member-id</u>, customer-name, customer-address, customer-phone, date-joined)

HIRE-DETAILS (<u>member-id, tape-id</u>, date-borrowed, date-due)

TAPE-DETAILS (<u>tape-id</u>, tape-title, tape-certification, certification-description)

Finally for third normal form we check non-key attributes for the existence of functional dependencies. We can see in TAPE-DETAILS above that the certification-description of a tape is not dependent on the tape-id but on what the tape-certification is. We therefore have the following relations in third normal form:

CUSTOMER (<u>member-id</u>, customer-name, customer-address, customer-phone, date-joined)

HIRE-DETAILS (<u>member-id, tape-id</u>, date-borrowed, date-due)

TAPE-DETAILS (<u>tape-id</u>, tape-title, tape-certification)

CERTIFICATION (<u>tape-certification</u>, certification-description).

Through entity-relationship modelling, relational modelling and normalisation, we have a model of the data aspects of the application area. We now turn to modelling process aspects.

6.6 Data flow diagrams

Process-oriented techniques focus on the processes that the system must perform. A process must have data input to it and must produce some output. The major process-oriented techniques are:

- Data flow diagrams
- Functional models.

Techniques associated with the detailed descriptions of processing include:

- Decision trees
- Decision tables
- Structured English.

We look first at data flow diagrams which are used to show the following:

- Data flows into the system from the environment
- Data flows out of the system into the environment
- Processes which change the data within the system
- Data storage within the system
- The boundary and scope of the system.

When constructing a data flow diagram an appropriate boundary must be identified. External entities are positioned outside the boundary. Input and output data and physical flows (that is actual objects for example, goods purchased or videos loaned) cross over the boundary.

The diagram must be clear and easy to read. External entities are normally positioned along the edges of the diagram. One method is to place external entities on the left hand side of the data flow diagram and data stores down the right hand side. However, if there are a number of accesses to and from data stores, a clearer layout may include the data stores in the centre of the data flow diagram. One of the main purposes of a data flow diagram is to improve communication. Legibility and clarity are therefore as important as the content of the data flow diagram.

The symbols for the elements of a data flow diagram are shown in Figure 6.23, they are:

- *Data flows:* A data flow is a kind of pipeline. This represents the movement of data into, out of and within the system. Data flows must start or end at a process. A separate flow for each distinct packet of information should be shown and each flow should have a distinct name except flows into and out of files which do not need to be named. Data flows between external entities or between two data stores are invalid. Data flows between processes must be traced back to an external entity.

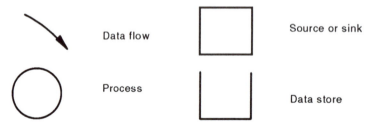

Fig. 6.23: Data flow diagram notation

- *Processes:* These show transformation of data flows. A process takes some input data, performs some processing on the data and then outputs some data to another process, data store or external entity.
  - Each process must have at least one input data flow and one output data flow.
  - Processes should be given logical names which should not be the names of people or places or departments. The process name must describe the process performed on the data.
  - Processes must be numbered.

- *Data stores:* This is where data is held within the system. They can be likened to files. A data store may represent a filing cabinet, index card or a computer file. A file is a temporary data store. A data flow from a file leaves it unchanged. A read and write operation will need a double arrow on the data flow. Data flows to files do not need to be named. Data stores are numbered and labelled. If it becomes necessary to repeat a data store on the data flow diagram, a vertical line is added to show that the data store is repeated. A data store in the data flow diagram must be related to one or more entities in the entity model but an entity may not appear in more than one data store. Data items specified on data flows should be represented in an entity.

- *Sinks:* This is either an external source of information or an external recipient of information. The external entity exists in the environment of the system. Information passed between the external entity and the system crosses the boundary of the system.

The example used to illustrate the use of structured analysis and design is that of a small video library. The shop lends out video cassettes. Mr. Williams owns the shop, Tracy, Sarah and Vincent work in it.

Tracy: 'When a film is returned I check it out in the register and then put it on the shelf. When a film is borrowed, I get it from the store and give it to the customer, after marking it down in the register. I also take the fee from the customer.'

Sarah: 'I do the same as Tracy, except I have to check the cash at the end of the day and deposit all except £5 in the night safe at the bank on my way home. I make a note in the cash book and Mr Williams checks it every couple of days against the till rolls. Old till rolls are put in the drawer under the counter.'

Vincent: Vincent works Friday evenings and weekends. 'I have two jobs. One is to check the damaged tapes. When a customer returns a tape which he says is no good, the girls give him his money back unless he is going to borrow another straight away. They note his membership number, each customer has to have his card to borrow a tape, and they put the film on a special shelf for me. I run it through and if it is no good, I scrap it and cross it off in the catalogue. If it is OK I return it to the shelves, I also note on the customer's card "refunded/OK" or "refunded/DAMAGED" depending on whether the tape is damaged or not. My other job is to look through the diary where each booking out is written and see which films are overdue. I ring up and nag them or I write a postcard and put a note on the customer's card. I have to tell Mr Williams if anyone is over a month overdue. I also help the girls if there is a rush in the shop, or if a customer gets nasty.'

If we take the first part of Tracy's statement about how a returned film is dealt with - 'When a film is returned, I check it out in the register and then put it back on the shelf....' and consider how we would build up an appropriate data flow diagram, this would follow the steps shown in Figures 6.24, 6.25, 6.26 and 6.27.

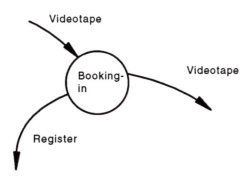

Fig. 6.24: Identifying data flows and processes

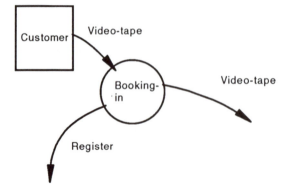

Fig. 6.25: Adding the external entity customer

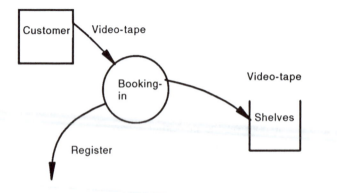

Fig. 6.26: Adding the data store 'shelves' where video-tapes are stored

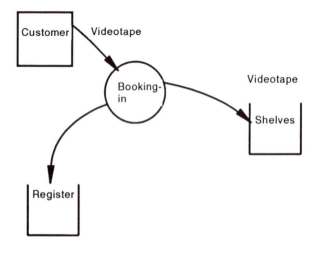

Fig. 6.27: Adding the data store 'register' (details of loans)

Figures 6.28, 6.29, 6.30 and 6.31 show how we would continue to develop the data flow diagram as a result of Tracy's second statement - 'when a film is borrowed, I get it from the store and give it to the customer, after marking it down in the register. I also take the fee from the customer.'

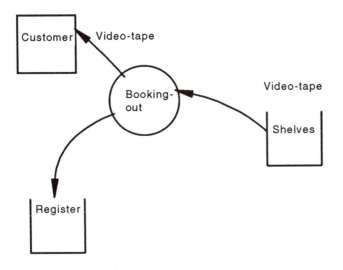

Fig. 6.28: Building up the data flow diagram for the booking out process

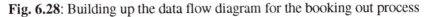

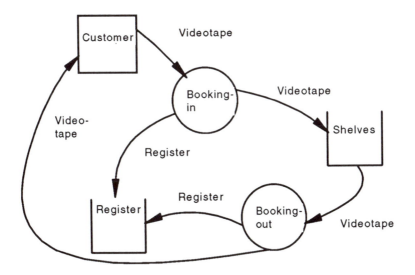

Fig. 6.29: Integrating the booking in and booking out processes

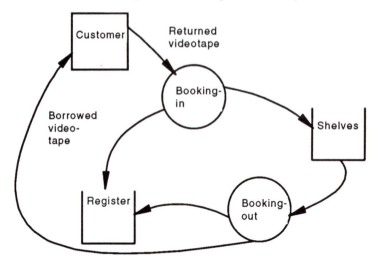

Fig. 6.30: Uniquely naming all data flows

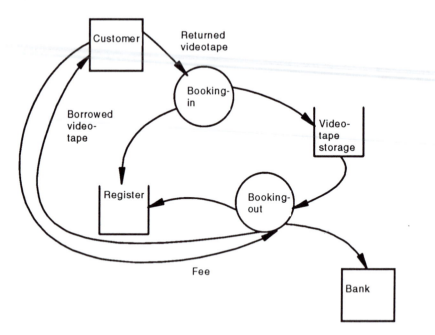

Fig. 6.31: Adding further detail to the data flow diagram

Context diagram

A context diagram shows the system environment. Only external sources and sinks are shown on it. All processes are summed up into one bubble.

Figure 6.32 shows the processing for booking videos in and out and this can be described in the single context level data flow diagram of Figure 6.33. All data flows to external sinks and from external sources must appear as such on the context data flow diagram.

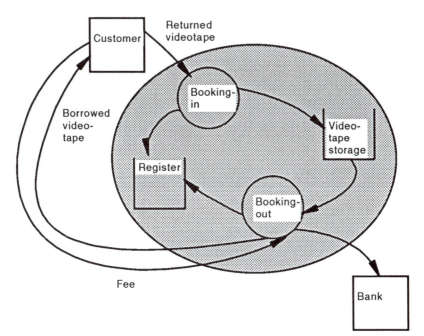

Fig. 6.32: Identifying the context of the processing

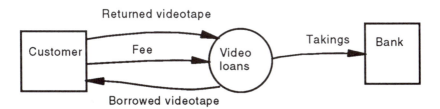

Fig. 6.33: Context level data flow diagram

To reduce the complexity of a data flow diagram, it might be limited to around six items per diagram. Each diagram should be restricted to one side of A4 paper. Levelled data flow diagrams should be used where each level shows the detail within a bubble at the higher level. Each process on a data flow diagram may be decomposed into a number of other processes. This is called **levelling**. Levelling occurs until the bottom level processes cannot be reduced to any further detail.

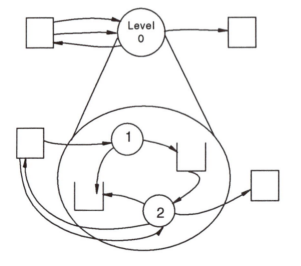

Fig. 6.34: Video library levelled data flow diagram

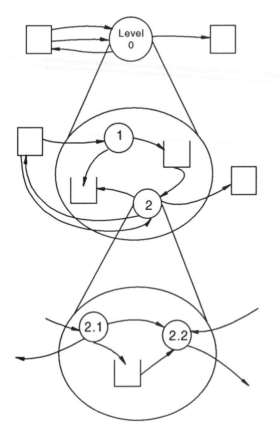

Fig. 6.35: Further levelling of video library data flow diagram

Some important points concerning levelling are:

- Lower level processes are prefixed by the process identifier of the higher level process. For example, process 2 is decomposed into processes 2.1, 2.2, 2.3 and so on.
- The boundary of the lower level process is the boundary of the process which is being decomposed.
- All data flows to and from the higher level processes have to be included on the lower level data flow diagram.
- New data flows added to the lower level data flow diagram must be added to the higher level data flow diagram.

Figure 6.34 shows the first level data flow diagram for the video library and its relationship to the context diagram of Figure 6.33. Figure 6.35 shows the second level data flow diagram for the video library and its relationship to the context data flow diagram of Figure 6.33 and the first level data flow diagram of Figure 6.34.

Specifying processing in detail

The data flow diagrams that we have produced so far provide us with a high level description of the processing. To complete our specification we need to produce a description of the lowest levels of data flow diagram. The final specification should be:

- Clear
- Concise
- Unambiguous
- Confirmable by the client
- Sufficient for designing a final system.

The process description is made up of four elements:

- Levelled data flow diagrams
- Structured English
- Decision trees
- Decision tables.

Learning Resources
Centre

Complex processes

When we are describing complex processes, such as that shown in Figure 6.36, we reduce (by levelling) the data flow diagram to a suitable level of detail. We then describe the resultant low level processes using techniques other than data flow diagrams. In developing data flow diagrams we will eventually reach a point when the level at which we are trying to describe the processing is too detailed to be represented by a data flow diagram. When this stage is reached then other techniques should be used to describe the processes. Two examples of processing detail going beyond that representable by data flow diagrams are given below.

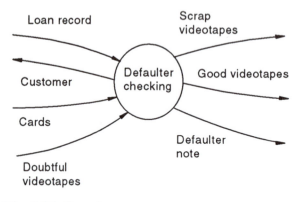

Fig. 6.36: Complex process

- *Processes with decisions:* Where we are trying to show the processes that are carried out on the outcome of a decision, then a data flow diagram is inappropriate. An example is seen in Figure 6.37. Here, an attempt is made to use a data flow diagram to show the processing to do with whether a customer has a membership card or not. We have gone down into a level of detail that a data flow diagram is not intended to show. We need to use another technique to show this detail. Decision tables and decision trees are suitable documentation techniques where a complex set of decisions need to be documented.

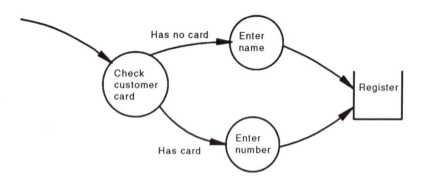

Fig 6.37: Incorrect data flow diagram attempting to show decision logic

- *Processes with control information:* Similarly, if we get to the stage where we are using the data flow diagram to show control information, such as the processing required at the beginning of a new day (see Figure 6.38), then again we have taken our data flow diagram to too great a level of detail. Again, it should be described in the higher level process logic using an appropriate technique, such as tight English or structured English.

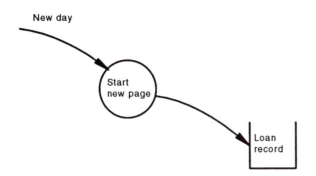

Fig. 6.38: Incorrect data flow diagram showing control information

6.7 Tight English

Using tight English involves replacing complicated words in narrative by simple ones wherever possible. It involves using a restricted vocabulary. In tight English, compound sentences are reduced to simple ones in which only imperatives are used. It only uses a limited set of conditions and logic structures and uses simple punctuation (only full stops). It excludes out of line comments, footnotes etc.

An example of a tight English description of a process from the video library example is shown in Figure 6.39.

```
Accept cover and membership card from customer.
     If the customer has his membership card then find
the cassette on the stock shelves enter the title of
the film and customers name in the loan record.
     If the customer has not returned a faulty cassette.
Look up the charge in the table and collect the fee.
Put the fee in the till and give the customer the
receipt and the loan cassette.
     Otherwise, if the customer has returned a faulty
cassette, give the customer the loan cassette.
     Mark the cover with 'out'.
     Whether or not the customer has his membership card,
return the cover to the display shelves.
```

Fig 6.39: An example of tight English

6.8 Structured English

An alternative to tight English is structured English and this is used more by systems analysts. The purpose of structured English is to produce a description of the process that is sufficiently 'tight' to be the basis for implementation, sufficiently 'natural' to be acceptable to the client, and at the same time sufficiently 'logical' to give freedom to the implementer. This is a narrative documentation tool which uses simple, concise sentences to describe procedures and specifications.

It is used to describe bottom-level processes in a data flow diagram. The aim of structured English is to overcome the ambiguities arising from the use of natural language. There is no accepted standard, but the idea is to use simple logic using the structured programming concepts:

- Sequence
- Selection
- Iteration.

These are expressed in simple language which consists of a simple vocabulary and syntax. Decision constructs are used of the form shown in Figures 6.40 and 6.41.

```
IF (condition)
        THEN
                do block 1
        ELSE
                do block 2
    ENDIF.
```

Fig. 6.40: Decision construct in structured English

```
CASE (variable)
        CASE 1 (value 1)
                do block 1
        CASE 2 (value 2)
                do block 2
    ENDCASE.
```

Fig. 6.41: An alternative decision construct in structured English

Repetition constructs are of the form shown in Figures 6.42 and 6.43.

```
DO WHILE (condition)
        do block 1
    END DO.
```

Fig. 6.42: Repetition construct in structured English

```
REPEAT
        do block 1
UNTIL (condition).
```

Fig. 6.43: An alternative repetition construct in structured English

Structured English uses simple vocabulary, consisting of verbs which are only transitive verbs, for example, 'update the customer-file' or 'issue credit-note'. Vague verbs, such as 'check,' 'process,' and 'deal with' should be avoided. The nouns that appear in the structured English description should only be objects specified in the data dictionary, for example, 'customer' or 'video'.

The advantages of structured English are that it is an organised and precise method of documentation which is understandable by technical and non-technical staff. It is easy to maintain and is readily translatable into code. Further, it is a useful technique to express logic.

The disadvantages of structured English are that some programmers consider that it is so similar to code that there is no point in writing it. Further, it is difficult to use for systems where there are a number of decision points. It does tend to be more programmer-oriented than user-oriented. Documentation can be lengthy and difficult to validate by the user. An example of structured English is given in Figure 6.44 .

```
BOOKING-OUT
        IF not no-membership-card
                DO ISSUE-LOAN
        ENDIF
        return cover to display-shelves
END BOOKING-OUT

ISSUE-LOAN
        locate cassette on stock-shelves
        IF new-day
                start new-page in loan-record
                enter date on top-of-page
                advance overtime-marker
        ENDIF
        enter title-of-film and customer-name
        in loan-record
        IF customer not returned-faulty-cassette
                DO EVALUATE-FEE
                collect fee from customer
                give customer receipt
                mark cover with 'out'
        ENDIF
END ISSUE-LOAN
```

Fig. 6.44: An example of structured English

6.9 Decision trees

A decision tree models the sequence of decisions or conditions in an information system. Each decision depends on the current value of some variable and previous decisions made. The root of the tree is placed on the left and possible outcomes of the decision are shown as horizontal branches from this root. Further decisions have to then be taken through the tree. An example of a decision in the video library scenario is shown in Figure 6.45. This shows that if a customer complains about a faulty video, we check to see whether the video is returned late. If late, then we compensate the customer by giving a free loan which is marked onto their card, otherwise a refund is given. If there is no complaint by the customer on the return of the video, then we again check if the return is late. If it is late, this is indicated on the customer's card.

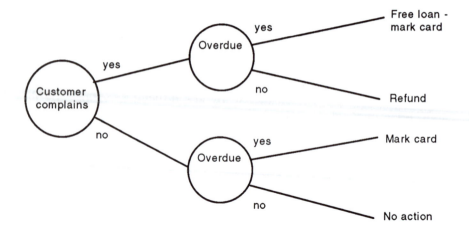

Fig. 6.45: An example of a decision tree

There are a number of advantages of decision trees. They provide a graphical view of variables tested, decisions made and the order that decisions are taken. They also help to focus on the sequence of decisions to be made and the cumulative effect of the decisions. They are easy to use, verify and construct. Probability scores can be added to branches, so that alternative strategies can be evaluated.

The disadvantages of decision trees are that they are difficult to maintain and the greater the complexity to be modelled, the more difficult the set of rules to follow. It can be quite difficult to appreciate full systems functionality from a set of complex decision trees.

6.10   Decision tables

This is a matrix of rows and columns to show conditions and corresponding actions to be taken. The table corresponds to the IF (condition) THEN structure. Figure 6.46 shows the basic format of a decision table. The table can be considered to be in four main parts consisting of the different conditions that need to be considered, possible states for those conditions, possible actions that can take place depending on the condition states, and the actions that result from those for a given set of conditions.

Possible conditions	Condition states
Possible actions	Resulting actions

Fig 6.46: Basic structure of a decision table

Figures 6.47. 6.48, 6.49 and 6.50 build up an example from the video library. We need to make a decision about whether we can loan a video to a person who has requested it and we need to decide how much they are to be charged. We can only loan videos to those who have a valid membership card. If the customer has a valid membership card and they have a complaint about a video that they are returning because it is faulty then we do not charge them for the replacement video. On the other hand if they have a valid membership card and have returned with a working video then they are charged according to the colour of the disc stuck onto the video's case. From this processing of the decision we identify the condition possibilities as being:

- That the person has a valid membership card
- That the person has complained about the video they are returning
- That the disc has a certain colour.

These are used to specify the condition possibilities as shown in Figure 6.47.

The possible states for these conditions are identified. In this case we can identify the following possibilities:

Has card Complained Disc colour	

Fig. 6.47: Specifying conditions

- *The person does not have a valid card.* In this case, once this state has been established then we are not interested in the possible states of the other condition possibilities 'has complained' and 'disc colour' so these are marked with 'X' to show that their state is irrelevant to the decision.
- *The person has a valid membership card and has complained about the video that he is returning.* In this case again we do not need to consider the colour of the disc on the video, as it is irrelevant since no charge is to be made for the loan of the new video. Again in this case we mark this condition with an 'X'.
- *The person has a valid membership card and has not complained about the video that they are returning.* In this case then we have to make a decision as to the charge for the video. There are three possibilities:
  - The disc colour is red which means that they are charged £2 for the video loan
  - The disc colour is green which means that they are charged £1 for the video loan
  - The disc colour is blue which means that they are charged 50p for the video loan.

Has card Complained Disc colour	N Y Y Y X Y N N N X X R G B

Fig. 6.48: Adding condition states

Has card	N Y Y Y Y
Complained	X Y N N N
Disc colour	X X R G B
No loan	
No charge	
£2	
£1	
50p	

Fig. 6.49: Adding possible actions to the decision table

These condition states could be used to build up the decision table as shown in Figure 6.48. The possible actions are put into the table as shown in Figure 6.49. Then finally the possible actions that result from the condition states across the top of the table are indicated by marking the resulting action with an 'X' at the relevant point of the table. Figure 6.50 shows the completed decision table for this decision of the video shop.

Has card	N Y Y Y Y
Complained	X Y N N N
Disc colour	X X R G B
No loan	X
No charge	X
£2	X
£1	X
50p	X

Fig. 6.50: An example of a decision table

6.12   Data dictionaries

One purpose of a data dictionary is to act as part of a complete structured specification. The data flow diagram needs supporting documentation to record further details. These are documented in a data dictionary. The data dictionary is an integral part of the requirements specification, it documents each and every element of the system's data. It enables consistency to be ensured. However the most important aspect of the data dictionary is that it is the place to look up definitions of data, that is, it is an index to all of the data of the organisation.

The data dictionary holds definitions of:

- Data flows
- Detailed structure of data flows, i.e. components of data flows
- Data stores
- Processes.

The data dictionary is also the basis for CASE technology, which is discussed in Chapter 10.

Describing the data in detail

A high level description of the data relevant to the organisation is provided by the E-R diagram. It is also necessary to provide a further lower level detailed description of this data. It is usual to do this using some appropriate structured notation, for example, Backus Naur Form (BNF). The definitions in the data dictionary represent top-down partitioning of data. This means that we describe the data in a hierarchical way. At the top level we show the overall data composition and then proceed down to further levels of detail for each of these components. In this way we are going smoothly from an abstract to a detailed description of our data. For example, we could have a data flow A which is made up of B + C. B in turn is made up of b1 and b2, and C of c3 and c4. c4 could itself be made up of cc6, cc7 and cc8. We could write the description of A as:

$$A = b1 + b2 + c3 + cc6 + cc7 + cc8$$

This however would be better described as the following hierarchy:

$$A = B + C$$
$$B = b1 + b2$$
$$C = c3 + c4$$
$$c4 = cc6 + cc7 + cc8.$$

BNF provides us with a number of constructs which can be used to describe the structure of data clearly and concisely. The basic constructs are as shown in Figure 6.51.

Operation	Notation
equivalent to	=
and	+
either-or	[......]
iterations-of	{......}
optional	(......)

Fig. 6.51: Basic BNF constructs

Consider the following verbal description of some data from our earlier example:

'The customer's card is made out when a new member joins. We put on it the customer's name, address and telephone number, if he has one, and we give him the next membership number.'

The following are some example BNF definitions of the data described in the above statement.

- Hierarchy

  customer-details = name + address + (telephone-number) name = surname + {initials}

  surname = {letters}

  customers-card = name + address + (telephone-number) + membership-number

- Equivalent to

  personal-number = membership-number

- And

  new-member-data = membership-number + joining-date + name + address + telephone-number

- Either-or [....|....]

  video-status = [on-loan|on-shelf|on-order|being-checked|deleted]

- Iterations-of {......}

  (note 0 or more occurrences of.....)

  catalogue = {video-details}limits   1{video-details}1000

- Optional (.........)

  (note instead of 0{....}1)

  customer-details = name + address + (telephone-number)

One of the aims of structured methods is to build a non-redundant specification. This means that care should be taken to ensure that there is no redundancy in the data dictionary. Each fact about the data should only be recorded in one place in the dictionary and in addition should not include facts documented elsewhere in the specification. Guidelines for avoiding redundancy should lead to the appropriate information being recorded in the correct place. The guidelines are as follows:

- Information about data composition (what are the components and how do they inter-relate) goes into the data dictionary

- Information about the content and processing of data goes into the process description

- Information about the routing of data goes into the data flow diagram.

Different aliases for data items must be recorded as a given data item may well be referred to by different names in different parts of the organisation. There may well be different user aliases as well as analyst aliases. Aliases may be at different levels of the system or in different parts of the system.

In some cases a component of a definition is not defined elsewhere in the dictionary. These are sometimes referred to as self-defining terms. This is in fact synonymous with undefined terms. A self-defining term is one that can be unambiguously understood from its name alone. For example:

```
video-details = title + genre-code + audience
genre-code = 'WES'|'THR'|'COM'
audience = 'U'|'15'|'PG'
```

Everyone knows what title is, so there is no point in including a definition of it. It is obvious that any definition process has to stop somewhere, it is recommended that this is done when everyone on a project understands what a term means without further definition. This may seem somewhat arbitrary but English (or any natural language) dictionaries contain many self-defining terms.

Data dictionaries can be organised in one of three ways:

- Totally manual procedures making use of index card files, notebooks and so on, and requiring considerable clerical support
- Totally automated procedures involving one of the commercial data dictionary packages
- Combined manual and in-house developed automated procedures.

Irrespective of the approach taken in implementing the data dictionary, the following are important:

- There should be no redundancy
- Definitions must be readily accessible by name
- Updating the data dictionary must be simple
- The convention adopted for defining data should be straight-forward and consistent.

We will consider further, both automatic data dictionaries and manual data dictionaries. The third method described above, which combines manual and automated procedures, will obviously consist of various combinations of these.

Automatic data dictionary

An automatic data dictionary should have the following features:

- Accept elements, structures, flows, files and processes
- Accept suitable formats for each

- Allow totally non-redundant input
- Be easy to update
- Include built-in consistency checking which should:
  - Identify duplicate occurrences of data
  - Identify disconnected aliases, where the same data is being described but by different names
  - Identify circular definitions, in which the definition of an element refers back to itself
  - Perform syntax checks, to ensure that the definitions conform to the required syntax
  - Produce listings in alphabetical order, so that all of the data definitions can be seen and easily searched
  - Produce cross-referenced listings so that connections between data and processes, the data items' hierarchical structure and undefined terms can be seen
  - Scan the structured English description of processes and compare with data flows in and out and identify processes which result in the updating of files
  - Maintain and draw the data flow diagrams.

Automatic data dictionaries can also be used for directly generating code from the descriptions contained in them.

Manual data dictionary

Although the availability of automatic data dictionaries is widespread, in this section we suggest the format for a potential manual data dictionary. This may be less costly and more appropriate for a small video shop. This approach uses index cards to record information about the data. The index cards should:

- Record name and definition of each item being defined
- Use the back of the card for physical details
- Include one card for each alias
- Cross reference all aliases of any item
- Keep all entries in alphabetical order.

Figure 6.52 shows the format of data about customers. Figures 6.53 and 6.54 show how the structure of individual data elements would be described. Similarly, Figure 6.55 shows how an individual data structure would be described. Figures 6.56, 6.57 and 6.58 show how information about data flows, data stores and process descriptions might be recorded in a manual system.

```
Smith    John ·Andrew     No 279
29/9/97

27 Gladys Road
Hays Heath

456-7890 (evenings only)

2/1/96 returned/us Police Academy
7/3/97 returned Airline 2


23/11/96 overdue Top Secret (phoned)
30/11/96 overdue Top Secret (phoned again)
1/12/96  returned
```

Fig. 6.52: Format of data about customers and their loans

Title-of-film			DATA ELEMENT

DESCRIPTION
 	
     The full title as appearing
     on the videotape box			

VALUES	DESCRIPTIONS	OR	RANGES
			Up to 50 characters

Fig 6.53: Data element description

Audience			DATA ELEMENT

DESCRIPTION
 	
     Shop's own classification
     of suitability			

VALUES	DESCRIPTIONS	OR	RANGES
u 15 pg x	Unrestricted over 14 parental guidance over 18 only		

Fig 6.54: Another data element description

Customer-details	DATA STRUCTURE

DESCRIPTION
 	
    Personal information
    about customer	

Name
Address
  Number and street
  Town
  (Postcode)
(Damage report)
(Overdue report)	

Fig. 6.55: Data structure description

Loan-record	DATA FLOW
DESCRIPTION Data flow generated when a film is borrowed	

VALUES 3.1	DESTINATION Loan-record

DATA STRUCTURES
  Customer-name
  Title-of-film
  Date-borrowed
	VOLUME
	  Approx. 100 per day
	  200 on Saturdays

Fig 6.56: Data flow description

Customer-card	DATA STORE

DESCRIPTION
 	
    Store of details of customer and
    borrowing activity	

IN-FLOWS Customer-register
          Damage-report
          Overdue-report
	OUT-FLOWS Overdue-report

DATA STRUCTURES
  Customer-details
  (Damage-report)
  (Overdue-report)
	VOLUME
	  Approx. 500 customers

Fig 6.57: Data store description

Booking-in	PROCESS DESCRIPTION
DESCRIPTION Process of receiving returned videos	

INPUTS	LOGIC SUMMARY	OUTPUTS
Videotape Loan record	Find video in loan record and delete it	Videotape

Fig 6.58: Process description

6.12   Functional modelling

Functional modelling is a technique used to understand the processes performed within an enterprise which enables it to achieve its objectives. Each process is described in precise structured sentences. It is necessary to model functions to ensure that we understand what the business actually does. The functional model acts as a communication vehicle with the user. The aim of the approach is to construct a complete list of processes into computer code or as clerical procedures. Modelling functions is also useful for cross-checking the entity-relationship model. It also provides a basis on which to drive detailed analysis, and will act as an aid in selecting implementation areas.

A function can be thought of as a type of business activity or process that is performed to enable the business objectives to be achieved. A function is what the enterprise actually does, not how it does it. An example of a function might be 'appoint an employee'. Each function is triggered by an event. An event is a stimulus or trigger which initiates one or more functions. When carrying out interviews it is important to identify events in order to recognise functions. It is important to find out what events cause the creation, deletion or loss of importance, change in attribute values and changes in relationships of specific entities. Similarly events linked to points in time, such as start/end of day/week/month need to be noted.

The main principles of functional modelling are:

- It is a top-down approach which is used to develop an increasing understanding of business processing
- It starts with a single statement for the business or business area, for example, course administration

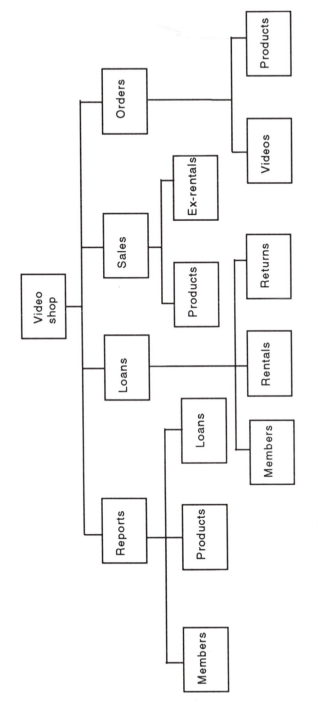

Fig. 6.59: Functional model for a video shop

- It continues with progressive hierarchical breakdown of the function into more detail
- Sub-functions are the result of the decomposition of higher level functions and are functions in their own right and are in turn decomposed into further sub-functions
- Higher level functions must be totally described by their sub-functions and nothing else.

Developing a functional model

The analyst should use the various interview notes and go through the following process:

- Write a single statement describing the activities of the business or business area being analysed.
- Break this top level function into 4-8 next level sub-functions, ensuring that all aspects of the top level function are covered by the sub-functions. Care must also be taken to ensure that each of the sub-functions actually belongs under the first function.
- Identify further functions from the interview notes and include them under the appropriate sub-functions, and so on, developing the hierarchy as appropriate. As functions are added it is important to check for completeness and consistency of the new function with other functions of the same parent function and also across the whole function hierarchy.
- Further interviews should be carried out to modify and extend the model as appropriate.

  Figure 6.59 shows an example of a functional model for a video shop.

6.13 Entity life histories

Data and process models are time independent. Time-dependent techniques represent time-critical sequences. An example of a time-dependent technique is an entity life history which is used to show the affect of time on an entity, in a way that the other techniques we have looked at do not do. This is particularly important in real-time systems, for example, monitoring the temperature in a furnace or controlling production lines.

Entity life histories describe the events in the life of an entity. They are the link between process models and data models and are a major part of structured methodologies such as SSADM.

Consider the events in the 'life' of an entity EMPLOYEE. These might be as follows:

- Recruited
- Paid
- Promoted
- Retired
- Dismissed.

The events will have various preconditions for each of these events, for example, employees cannot be paid unless they have been recruited. The representation for entity life histories used here is based on Jackson (1983) and the basic structure is shown as Figure 6.60.

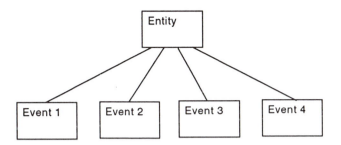

Fig. 6.60: Entity life history structure

An entity life history models the system from the viewpoint of information changes. An entity life history is prepared for each entity in the logical data structure. An entity life history must represent the birth, life and death of the entity. It represents the creation, life and deletion of an entity in terms of the events which cause the entity to change in some way. An event is the action which triggers a process to create, delete or modify an entity occurrence in some way. The basic elements of an entity life history are:

- Sequence
- Selection
- Iteration.

An important point to note is that component types cannot be mixed at the same level within the same part of the model.

Sequence
A sequence is a series of events which affect the entity, in a specific order. The sequence is a progression of events through time. The time interval between the events can be minutes, hours, days, weeks, months or years.

The notation that is used is a series of boxes read from top to bottom and left to right as shown in Figure 6.61.

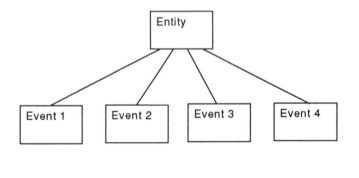

TIME

Fig. 6.61: Time dependency of entity life history

An example showing the sequential events in the life of an entity might be described verbally as follows:

'A video tape is ordered, received, catalogued, borrowed returned and eventually scrapped.'

We could represent this either as shown in Figure 6.62 or as a hierarchical structure as shown in Figure 6.63.

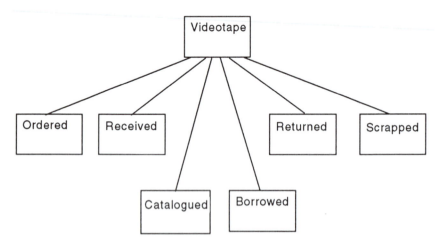

Fig. 6.62: A first approach to producing an entity life history for a VIDEO entity

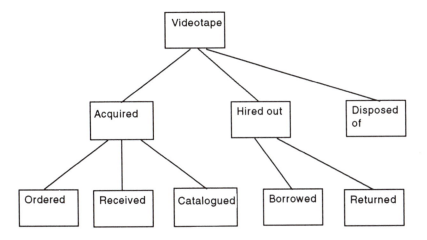

Fig. 6.63: Further development of the entity life history for a VIDEO entity

Selection
A selection models a number of alternative events which may occur at a particular point in the life of the entity. The notation for this is a series of boxes with a circle in the top right corner as shown in Figure 6.64.

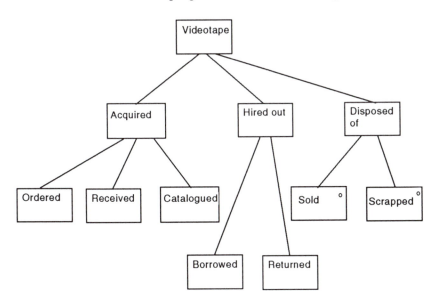

Fig. 6.64: Entity life history including selection

Iteration

Some actions are repeated during the life of the entity. An event may occur 0, 1 or more times at the same point within the entity life history. Each iteration must be completed before the next iteration begins. The notation for this is a box with an asterisk in the top right corner as shown in Figure 6.65.

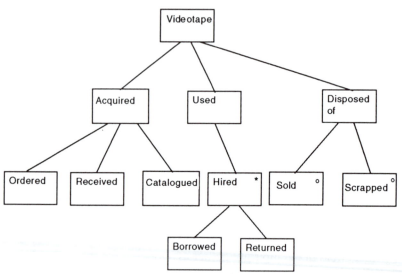

Fig. 6.65: Entity life history including iteration

This is a different view to that of the counter clerk who might view the entity life history as that shown in Figure 6.66.

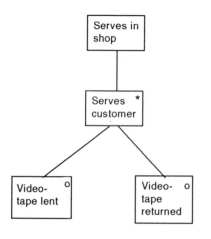

Fig. 6.66: Entity life history showing iteration and selection combined

Other structures

In addition to the three structures of sequence, selection and iteration already mentioned, the following structures are also useful:

- *Quit and resume:* Often there needs to be an 'error exit' from a life history which is shown using quit and resume. This component allows a quit from one part of the entity life history structure, that is, a break from the specified sequence. The sequence is then resumed at a different part of the entity life history. The notation for this is a Q followed by a number placed to the right of the event (where the quit may occur). R followed by the same number is placed to the right of the event where the structure is resumed. An example is shown in Figure 6.67.

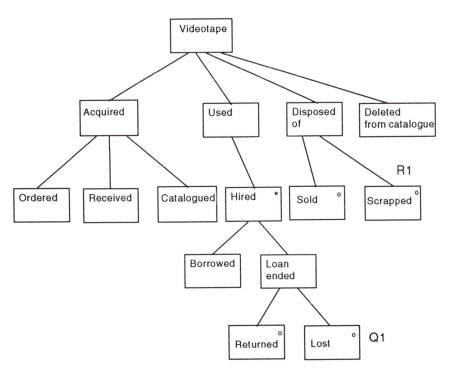

Fig. 6.67: Entity life history showing a quit and resume structure

- *Parallel structure:* A parallel structure represents the situation where events can occur in an unpredictable sequence or concurrently. The notation for this is a parallel bar joining the section of the entity life history as shown Figure 6.68.

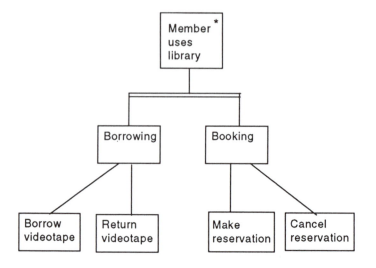

Fig. 6.68: Entity life history showing a parallel structure

Entity life histories make statements about the nature of the real world rather than particular ways of doing things. They describe events that change entities and show the link between processing and data. An entity life history is constructed for each entity in the E-R model. Each data item in the entity must be created, amended and deleted by events on the entity life history. Events in the entity life history trigger processes in the system. Events should therefore be shown in some way on the data flow diagram, for example, an event may be the arrival of an input data flow. The E-R model and entity life history are three views of the same system. The models should be consistent at all times and can be used to cross-check for consistency and completeness.

6.14   Summary

In this chapter we have considered the phase of systems analysis and how it is intended to lead to a better understanding of all the material we have been collecting about the system. We are trying to establish what is being done, why it is being done and when it is being done. If problems exist we are trying to establish their underlying causes and effects. Figure 6.69 provides an overview of the systems analysis stage of the information systems development life cycle.

We have discussed how we go through a series of models, physical current, logical current, logical new and physical new. We have discussed structured systems analysis and its goals. Also we have discussed the problems that might arise during analysis due to lack of communication between analysts and users, changing nature of requirements, lack of tools, difficulties in terms of the target document, allocation of work and organisational politics.

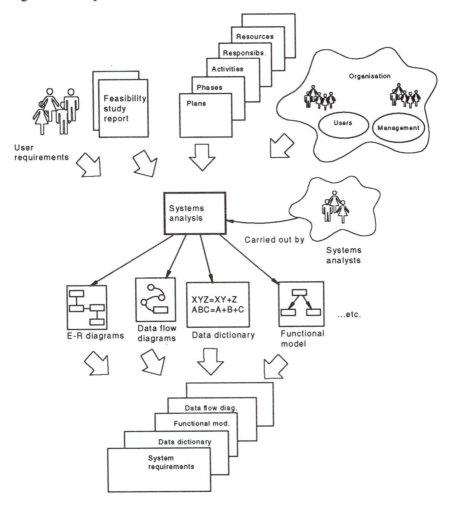

Fig 6.69: Overview of the systems analysis phase

We have identified various techniques from structured systems analysis and design approaches which are useful at this stage of information systems development. These techniques can be classified as data-oriented, process-oriented and time-dependent. In particular, E-R modelling, data flow diagramming, data dictionary generation, structured English, tight English, entity life histories, decision trees and decision tables have been described in detail.

Further reading

Batra, D. & Marakas, G. M. (1995) Conceptual data modelling in theory and practice, *European Journal of Information Systems*, **4**, pp. 184-193.
This paper discusses and compares the perspectives of academic and practitioner communities regarding the application of conceptual data modelling.
Chen, P. P. S. (1976) The entity-relationship model - towards a unified view of data, *ACM Transactions on Database Systems*, **1**.
A paper established as a classic in database literature, it discusses the early work on the entity-relationship model.
Codd, E. F. (1972) A relational model of data for large shared data banks, *Communications of the ACM*, **13**.
A paper established as a classic in database literature, it discusses the early work on the relational model and normalisation.
DeMarco, T. (1978) *Structured Analysis and System Specification*, Prentice-Hall, Englewood Cliffs, NJ.
Established as one of the classic texts for structured systems analysis. Further detailed information on data flow diagrams, data dictionary, process specification and system modelling are provided.
Jackson, M. A. (1983) *Systems Development*. Prentice Hall, Hemel Hempstead.
Some of the diagramming techniques are based on this text.
Mason, D. & Willcocks, L. (1994) *Systems Analysis, Systems Design*, McGraw-Hill, Maidenhead.
A useful text in the area of systems analysis.

Exercises

1. What is systems analysis?
2. List the questions that need to be addressed during systems analysis.
3. Explain the factors that have led to the development of structured systems analysis and design approaches.

4. What are the goals of structured systems analysis and design?
5. Discuss the difficulties that might arise during analysis.
6. List the three views which we might take of the problem situation in order to produce different models.
7. Discuss the main features of E-R modelling and explain why it is a useful conceptual modelling technique.
8. Describe the relational model and explain how an E-R model might be mapped to an equivalent relational model.
9. What is normalisation and what is it used for?
10. Describe data flow diagrams and discuss their usefulness in the information systems development process.
11. Discuss techniques for describing detailed processing.
12. Explain the importance of data dictionaries in information system development and discuss a suitable technique for describing data in detail.
13. Explain how functional modelling can be useful in the development of information systems.
14. What are entity life histories and what aspect of the information systems project do they enable us to model?
15. How do methodologies provide support for information systems development?

Areas to debate

1. Discuss the value of modelling during the systems analysis phase. Identify the different types of model that might be developed and their contribution to the systems analysis.
2. Consider the way in which E-R diagrams developed for Asifiori Salons would be presented to the management and staff and verified.
3. Identify and discuss the entities, attributes and relationships that are present in your college, university or other institution. Develop data flow diagrams and entity life histories for that organisation.
4. Search the literature and discuss the various extensions that have been proposed for Chen's E-R model. Discuss the reasons for their development. Do you think such extensions would be required for Asifiori Salons?

CASE STUDY

1. *Draw an E-R model for the following situation:* Each of the Asifiori Salons has many customers. The customers make appointments with the hairdresser of their choice in order to have their hair styled, treated, coloured or cut. The customer is charged according to the service carried out and who did their hair. Each salon has a number of hairdressers based there. The salon manager is responsible for the purchase of stock. This stock can be used in the salon or it can be sold to customers. The salons have a number of suppliers from whom they purchase their stock.

2. *Draw an entity life history for the following entities:* A person becomes a client of the salon when they first use the salon's services. They are asked for details, such as name, address and telephone number. This information is recorded. While they remain customers of the salons they may make appointments and purchase hairdressing products. The details of these are recorded. When they are no longer a customer of the salon then their details are deleted.

3. *Draw a data flow diagram for the following situation:* When a person wishes to make an appointment at one of the salons they usually telephone, though sometimes they visit the salon. The customer provides details of their name and address. If they are a new customer then their details are recorded on an index card which will be filed. The customer then books an appointment with a specific hairdresser for a particular date and time along with a brief description of what service they require. During the appointment certain hairdressing products from the salon's stock will be used, and exact details of this are recorded. After the customer's hair has been done, an invoice is provided detailing the service and products they have received. The customer then makes an appropriate payment.

Chapter 7

SYSTEMS DESIGN: A BETTER INFORMATION SYSTEM

7.1 Systems design

In this chapter we look in detail at the systems design stage of the information systems development life cycle. It is during this phase that we design the software component of the information system and we discuss in detail how this is done in the context of the information systems

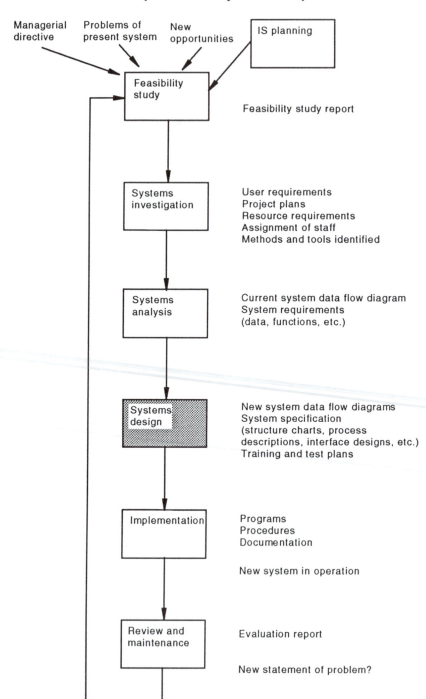

Fig. 7.1: Systems design stage of information systems development life cycle

development life cycle. We examine the use of techniques, and to some extent tools in this phase of the life cycle. Finally, we discuss possible alternatives for information systems, that is, the purchase of off-the-shelf packages or the development of tailor-made software, either in-house or by a third-party. Figure 7.1 shows the place of the systems design phase in the context of the overall information systems development life cycle.

Everything that has been done so far has been done with a view to understanding and improving the current situation. We have been carrying out the analysis activities so that we can get a good understanding of the activities in the application area and its environment. We understand how the present system works, but we must avoid being engrossed in the present way of doing things, otherwise we are unlikely to design a much improved system. But the understanding gained at the systems analysis phase should be the foundation of the design of our new information system and should therefore lead to the design of an improved information system. System design is a creative activity. It should result in the specification of the programs and procedures for the new system. It should produce programming specifications which are complete and detailed enough for programmers to proceed with minimal outside reference. During this activity, plans and procedures for user training, systems testing, acceptance testing and conversion to the new system need to be developed.

In this section we look in detail at the process of systems design. We suggest an approach which will involve development of a logical model of the new system. This will be derived from the logical model of the current system. We discuss the idea of a 'charter for change' to identify the things we want to change as a result of our project. We then produce data flow diagrams describing the logical representation of the new system.

An important aspect of the design of the new system is to identify the human-computer boundary, so that we can specify which parts of the new system will be automated and which parts are to be manual procedures. From the users' point of view, the interface represents the system. The design of the human-computer interface is therefore an essential and crucial part of this phase.

During systems design a hierarchy of system modules and their interfaces is developed. This is based upon functional specifications produced during the systems analysis phase. This activity is carried out by a team or individual who we will refer to as the systems designer. The systems designer uses the statement of logical requirements (the output from the systems analysis phase) and decides how best to fulfil these requirements. Whereas the systems analyst is user-oriented, the system designer is concerned with the overall system performance. The design activity requires a high level of skill, creativity, training and education in the face of evolving problems and rapid technological advances. The systems designer must carry out the following activities:

- Design the system output, input, files and/or database and processing methods
- Develop the specifications for programmers and procedure writers
- Present the system design to management and users for approval.

In many methodologies, during the systems analysis phase we will have built a model of the current physical system. Having built a model of the current system, the next process is the design of the new system. In some situations there may be no 'current' system as we might be developing a completely new application for a new aspect of the business. Even manual procedures might not exist. In this case we would construct a logical model of the new system based on the requirements that have been identified in the previous stage of the life cycle.

The main steps involved in the analysis and specification of the new system are identified by DeMarco (1978) as:

- Build a logical model of the current system
- Agree a charter for change
- Produce new system logical data flow diagrams
- Produce new system physical data flow diagrams by identifying the human-computer boundary
- Produce a structured specification for the new system.

The boundary between systems analysis and systems design is not as clear-cut as might be suggested by our discussions. For example, some of the earlier activities, such as building a logical model of the current system and agreeing a charter for change, are placed in systems analysis in some texts. The important issue is that they are important stages within systems analysis and design as a whole.

7.2 Logical model

In this section we discuss how we would go from a physical model of the current system to a logical model of the current system.

During this process, physical aspects inevitable in the higher levels of the data flow diagram should be systematically eliminated. We use the word **physical** to refer to a description that is in some sense implementation-dependent and **logical** to refer to a description that is implementation-independent. The logical description is purely a representation of user policy (that is, what is accomplished), while the physical description suggests one way of carrying out the policy (that is, how it is accomplished). The physical aspects normally arise due to the following reasons:

- *Political:* can give rise to certain destination names, for example, chairman's report
- *Procedural:* can result in particular document and department names, for example, P45 and E111
- *Historical:* can determine how files are structured
- *Tool-related:* can result in specific hardware or process names.

A data flow diagram can, like some other techniques, be used to show design as well as analysis processes. Figure 7.2 shows an example of physical aspects in a data flow diagram.

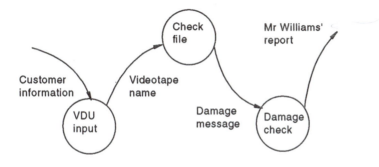

Fig. 7.2: A data flow diagram incorporating physical aspects

All physical elements will have to be revised during this logicalisation of the model. Logical equivalents can be derived by:

- *Expanding the data flow diagram to remove the highest-level physical characteristics:* There will be a concentration of physical characteristics at the top levels of the data flow diagram. These will mostly be due to political and tool-related aspects. Since bubbles at the higher level are representations of the networks of bubbles at the next level down, then the higher level bubble can be replaced by the next level network of bubbles that it represents. Doing this should result in a logicalisation of the model. It is usually sufficient to replace level one and two bubbles, by which time the physical aspects should be eliminated.
- *Using decomposition and normalisation to express data store (or file) structures in a logical form:* We must examine each use of the set of data stores and derive an appropriate data store structure from the

pattern of use. By removing physical considerations from each use of stored data, the structure of the data store that evolves from these logical requirements should, by definition, be the most logical file structure. One way of doing this is to ignore current physical file structures and consider the starting point to be a 'superfile' which is the union of all the data items that occur in the current physical files. This superfile is then divided into suitable component parts and reconstituted to:

– Reduce redundant references, so that only the data items needed are referenced

– Combine data items to minimise data flows

– Normalise the individual file structures to remove repeating groups.

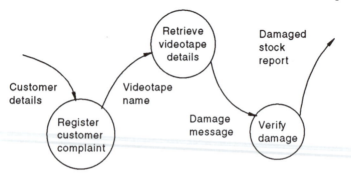

Fig. 7.3: A first attempt at modifying the data flow diagram of Figure 7.2, eliminating physical aspects

- *Eliminating procedural and historical characteristics by minimising data flow:* The previous two steps should eliminate most of the physical characteristics from the data flow diagram. The remainder will have to be removed simply by inspection. All flows should be examined, reducing them to their component (logical) parts. The question that must be asked is: 'does it have to work this way?'. We should be checking to ensure that the model describes what the policy is, not how it is carried out. As a result of the design activity, we are trying to produce a statement of the requirements of the new system. This is an implementation-independent statement of operational requirements.

It must to be recognised that logicalisation cannot be done completely, as there will be some situations in which it is impossible to separate the user policy from its implementation. Figure 7.3 shows a first attempt at addressing the physical aspects in the data flow diagram of Figure 7.2.

7.3 Domain for change

In order to help us focus on the areas of the logical model of the current system that are to be affected by the design activities, we need to agree a **charter for change** with the initiators or owners of the project. The charter for change refers to the things that we want to change as a result of the project. The earliest stage analysis activities involve concentrating on the current system and its environment. As a result of the project a new set of rules is to be applied to the future environment. This is the charter for change.

In terms of our video library example a question such as: 'Mr. Williams, what do you hope to get from the new system?' is likely to produce a response which corresponds to this idea of a charter for change. A possible response is given below:

'What I want is to improve the loan side of things, to make the system work better, and give better information. If someone rings in about a film we have to search the shelves to see if it is out and we do not know who borrowed it, or when it is due back. When a film is damaged we don't know who the previous borrower was. We don't know how often a film has been borrowed, nor can we find films with certain actors or producers, unless I happen to remember them. We cannot do renewals properly because we don't know if a film is wanted by another customer. I think that if we had a good system we could specialise in old or unusual films, as well as the current ones. I don't want the bookkeeping changed, my wife does that, and neither is there any need to improve the ordering of new films.'

The charter for change aids the analyst in focusing on the parts of the logical model that are to be affected by the user requirements. We need now to identify specifically the part of the logical model that is affected by the charter for change and refer to it as the domain of change.

A reasonable approach to selecting the context of the project will result in it including substantially more than the area likely to be affected by the change as specified in the charter for change. This will mean that part of the new logical model will be exactly the same as corresponding parts of the old logical model. By identifying and isolating this part, better progress can be made in constructing the new logical model.

The objective is to identify the area of activities to be affected by the new system, that is the domain of change. The method by which this is done is to check bubble by bubble to find if that activity is affected by the charter for change. This includes all activities affected, not just those subject to computerisation. Thus we can classify activities into two groups: those that are affected by the charter for change and those that are not.

It is possible that we identify more than one (completely disconnected) domain of change on the data flow diagram that has been developed. This should not be considered 'wrong' since it is a result of the particular data flow diagram that has been developed and the way in which it has been drawn. A single bubble should replace the entire domain of change. This is very useful technique as it results in a data flow diagram where all the unknowns lie inside the boundary representing our, as yet, undeveloped information system. Everything that lies outside the boundary is known. The interfaces between our domain of change and the outside world are completely and effectively defined since they are represented by known data flows which appear on our data flow diagram and for which there are detailed entries in the data dictionary.

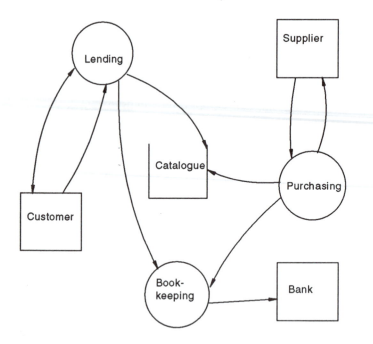

Fig 7.4: Domain of change will be part of data flow diagram that has been developed

Figures 7.4, 7.5 and 7.6 show how we examine the data flow diagram that we have developed so far, identify the domain of change and indicate it on our data flow diagram. From Mr. Williams' statements in the charter for change, we can see that he would like to see changes in the part of the process for lending out videos and the details that are kept about videos

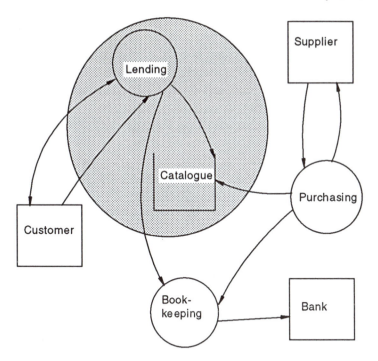

Fig. 7.5: Domain of change identified on data flow diagram

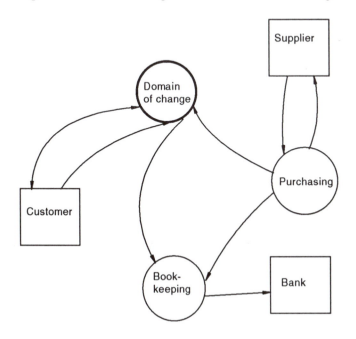

Fig. 7.6: Domain of change indicated as a process on data flow diagram

that are stocked, as this is where the difficulties lie. This part of the data flow diagram, the lending process and the catalogue, is identified as shown in Figure 7.4. It is indicated by the shaded circle as shown in Figure 7.5. This shaded bubble is replaced by a bubble representing the domain of change, as shown in Figure 7.6. From this figure it can be clearly seen that the data flows into or from any processes or data stores can be replaced as data flows into or from the bubble representing the domain of change.

Produce new system logical data flow diagrams
We now direct our energies into designing the new system. We want to build the logical model of the new system. So far, we have been studying how the business currently operates, we now want to concern ourselves with how the business ought to operate. We use the charter for change to target the areas for change. These will have been identified as the domain

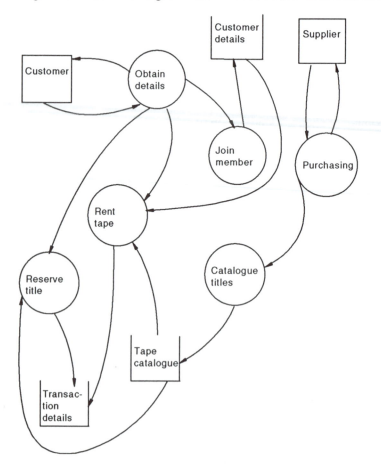

Fig. 7.7: A first approach to a new systems design

of change as explained above. The process of producing the new logical model involves top-down partitioning of the domain of change. The new context level data flow diagram is the domain of change with its inputs and outputs. The analyst should:

- Carry out top-down partitioning in order to reduce the number of interfaces by minimising data transfer wherever possible.
- Use the charter for change to determine what new functions, processes and data flows need to be added.
- Design data flows and processes in small sets, as these are much easier to deal with than larger ones. As a general principle there should be fewer than seven elements.
- Aim for completeness, by ensuring that all data flows are specified and labelled.
- Respect data conservation, that is, any data item that flows out of a process must flow into it in some shape or form. Data can only be produced by a process if appropriate data from which it is generated was an input to that process.
- Be guided by the old logical model in producing the new data flow diagram.
- Keep the data dictionary up to date.

This process of designing the new logical model is very much an iterative one. Figure 7.7 shows a first approach to a new system logical data flow diagram.

Identify the human-computer boundary

The next stage is to modify the new system data flow diagram to take into account physical considerations. The main one is to decide how much and which part of the system is to be automated. In order to address the issue we select the human-computer boundary. When this boundary is identified and marked on the data flow diagram we have our new system physical data model.

Figure 7.8 shows two possible human-computer boundaries for the video shop example. We need to know the position of this boundary so that the scope and extent of the subsequent development can be determined. It also ensures that the specification includes a definition of which parts of the model will be performed by the computer system and which by people. The scope of the automation is determined by a trade-off between costs and benefits. It involves the following steps:

- Selecting one possible human-computer boundary
- Adding any implementation-dependent features

- Identifying costs and benefits
- Repeating the above two steps until a sufficient number of options are available to choose from
- Selecting the best option.

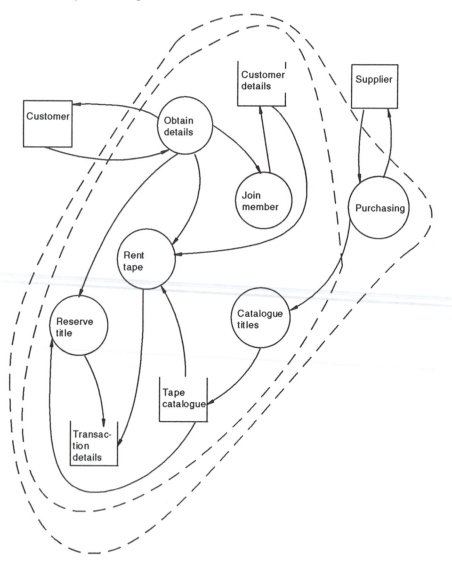

Fig. 7.8: Two possible human-computer boundaries

It is important that the analyst avoids presenting only one solution. This is likely to create difficulties for the analyst in the future. The system will be seen as belonging to the analyst. If it is too big or too small it will be seen as the fault of the analyst. The analyst should present a number of viable alternatives and allow the users and managers to be directly involved in the selection process. This is preferable, since it allows the users and managers to participate directly in the systems design. Figure 7.9 shows two further possibilities for the placement of the human-computer boundary. The costs will differ, and these differences may be as much as five- or ten-fold.

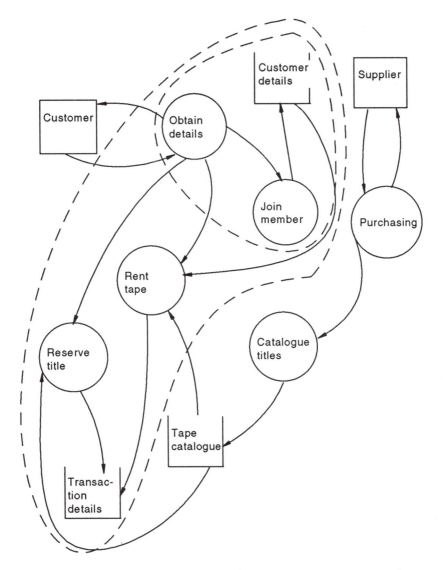

Fig. 7.9: Two further options for the human-computer boundary

7.4 Human-computer interface

At this stage we evaluate the importance of the human-computer interface design and consider the process that leads to the design. It is an extremely important aspect of the systems design process as a whole. This is the 'system' as far as the users are concerned. The rest of the system, which might actually be much larger, is invisible to the users. The quality of the human-computer interface will be an important factor in the success of the information system and users will tend to base their evaluation of the whole system on this aspect only.

The data flow diagram of the logical model of the new system, with its human-computer boundary marked on it, is used to identify the inputs and outputs of the new system. The design of the human-computer interface will involve designing the formats of inputs, outputs and dialogues through which these are fed into the system and produced by it.

Interaction design

We now look at the issues involved in designing the human-computer interface. The human-computer boundary, illustrated in Figure 7.10, represents the point at which the computer and its users meet. The interface is the means by which users can communicate with the computer system.

The design of this interface is concerned with:

- Input which the users enter into the system
- Outputs which the users receive from the system
- Dialogues through which the users and system interact.

Since the interface represents the most visible part of the system from the users' point of view, the quality and consistency of this will form the impression that users have of the total system. Even if the rest of the system is constructed on the basis of good design using all the latest techniques and consists of elegant code, this will not contribute to the users' evaluation of the system. Poorly designed interfaces will lead to a lack of easy interaction for the users and will ultimately increase the chances of inaccurate or incomplete data being entered into the system. This will lead in turn to correspondingly inaccurate 'information' being produced by the system. It can be seen that the design of forms, screens and reports is no less important than the of design of the various logical models of the system. Although over ten years old, the principles suggested in Macintosh (1987) constitute good interface design:

- *Concrete metaphors:* Most people who use computers are computer users not computer experts and use the computer as a means to an end.

They are domain experts not computer experts. The system should therefore try to take advantage of this prior experience by using metaphors which correspond to real-world actions.

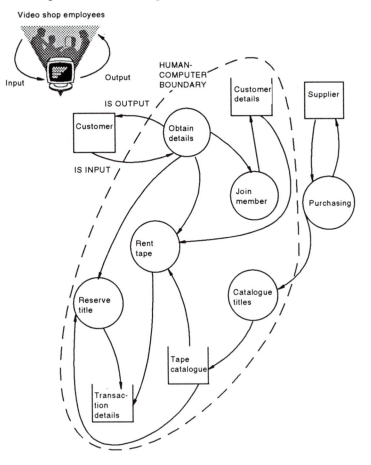

Fig. 7.10: Human-computer boundary and intervention

- *Direct manipulation:* When somebody presses a light switch they expect the light to come on. People expect their physical actions to have physical results, and they want their tools to provide feedback. This is true whether or not a computer is being used. The system should always give clues informing the user that a particular command is being carried out, or if it cannot be carried out, the user should be informed why not.
- *See-and-point (instead of remember-and-type):* The screen should provide an environment in which people can work effectively, taking full advantage of the power of the computer. The user should therefore

interact directly with the screen, choosing objects and activities they are interested in by pointing at them with a pointing device such as a mouse.

- *Consistency:* When using the system there should always be one coherent way by which the user can implement actions. Though alternatives may be provided, users should always be able to rely on familiar and straight forward ways to get things done.

- *WYSIWYG (What You See Is What You Get):* When using the system, the user should be in charge of both the content and the formatting of the screen. The system should display the result of the user's choices quickly and directly, so that the user does not have to wait for a printout or make mental calculations of how the screen version will be translated onto paper. WYSIWYG is highly consistent with the direct manipulation principle and is also in the spirit of using a computer as a thinking tool, as well as a production one.

- *User control:* People learn best when they are actively engaged. In many systems, however, the computer acts and the user merely reacts within a limited set of options. Alternatively, the computer may 'take care' of the user, offering only those alternatives that are thought by the original programmer to be 'good' for the user or that 'protect' the user. The idea of the computer as protector may be appealing, but this approach puts the computer rather than the user in the driving role.

- *Feedback and dialogue:* The user should always be kept informed about what the system is doing in order to remain in charge. When, for example, the user initiates a lengthy operation, the system should keep the user informed of its progress.

- *Forgiveness:* Users prefer trying to figure out how something works by exploration, with lots of action and lots of feedback. As a result, users sometimes make mistakes or explore further than they need. The system should be 'tolerant' and 'forgiving'. This means that the user should be allowed to do anything reasonable and be allowed to back away 'gracefully' or continue knowing the consequences .

- *Aesthetic integrity:* In many current systems, the visual appearance of the screen appears to have been of low priority. However, the use of graphics should not be merely cosmetic. When they are clear and consistent, they contribute greatly to ease of learning, communication, and understanding.

- *Modelessness:* Modes are contexts in which a user action is interpreted differently from the same action in another context. Put another way, the same action, when completed in two different modes, results in two different reactions. A mode typically restricts the operations that the user can perform. Since people do not operate in a modal manner in real life, dealing with modes when using a computer gives the impression that computers are unnatural and unfriendly. A mode is especially confusing when the user enters it unintentionally. When this happens, familiar objects and commands may take on unexpected meanings and the user's habitual actions cause unexpected results. This is not to say that modes should never be used. One instance when they are acceptable is when they emulate a real-life situation that is itself modal. For example, choosing different tools in a drawing application resembles the real-life choice of physical drawing tools.

7.5 Output design

We now look at the way we would design the outputs of the information system. The new system logical data flow diagram will have been used to identify the human-computer interface. In designing the output we are concerned with:

- The new system outputs which cross the system boundary on their way out of the system. As all data has been described in detail in the data dictionary then the relevant descriptions of the contents of these data flows can be obtained from the data dictionary.
- Having determined the content, the designer must select the appropriate method or technology to present the information.
- The designer needs to establish whether a display or printed copy of the output is required, the type of device required to produce it and the most appropriate layout to meet the users' needs.
- The method of presentation is determined by considering the following points:
  - Who is the output intended for?
  - When and how often is it needed?
  - What use will be made of the output by the target users?
  - Are there any environmental constraints on the technology which can be used?
  The two main alternatives when considering output devices are:
  - Printing using any of a variety of printers
  - Displaying the information on the screen of a terminal.
  Other less frequently used alternatives are:
  - Plotters producing graphs, diagrams and maps
  - Digital messages, speech, sounds, music or video images.

- Output for storage on magnetic media, optical disks, microfilm or microfiche.

Wu and Wu (1994) suggest that the purpose of system output is usually one of the following:

- *To provide information:* this is usually provided as
  - A response to a query for which existing organisational data is used
  - A report detailing all the activity linked to a certain organisational attribute or area
  - A recording of transactions which represent the organisation's activities.
- *To serve as a turnaround document:* that is, a document which is an output but later on will be an input into the information system. Such documents are usually created by the use of multi-part stationery.
- *To act as archival storage:* the firm may remove some or all records from a computer file to archival storage from time to time. It does this to keep access times of current data within reasonable limits.

Output design is concerned with:

- *Selecting the output medium:* the output medium is the physical material on which the data are recorded. It is possible that the user requires the output on more than one medium. The systems designer determines the most appropriate output medium by comparing costs and the requirements of the system being developed. Some possible media for output are:
  - *Computer screen displays:* outputs are shown on the computer screens of the users
  - *Printed documents:* this is the most common medium for computer output and is commonly referred to as hard copy
  - *Voice output:* this has been used successfully by telephone companies, in responding to directory enquiries, the requested telephone numbers are 'spoken' by the computer
  - *Magnetic tape or disks:* this will be readable by computer system only
  - *Optical disks:* these are suitable for large volumes of data which is computer readable
  - *Microfilm or microfiche:* this is photographic film which records information in reduced size.
- *Selecting the processing method:* this involves designing the way in which the system will produce the output for the user. It involves selecting between batch and on-line methods. In on-line methods the

system provides an immediate response to the user request while in a batch method processing is delayed until the required program has been executed, usually at a fixed point in time.

- *Designing the output format:* this is the way in which data is represented on the chosen medium. In terms of presenting information, three important principles need to be incorporated which are:
  - *Information content should be kept as simple as possible for the purpose intended.* Only that information which is needed by the user should be included. It is unhelpful to the user to include information that is not needed.
  - *The output should be uncluttered and easy to read.* Poorly designed outputs will have large amounts of detail crammed into small amounts of space. Blank spaces on outputs should be used to enhance its readability.
  - *Information should be arranged logically on the output so that it can be quickly and easily understood.* Headings should be used to identify the purpose of the report and to identify the various sections contained in it.

Output reports are typically arranged as tables containing the information. As seen in Figure 7.11, graphics can be used to present data in other ways such as pie charts, bar charts and line graphs, depending on the needs of the users they are intended for.

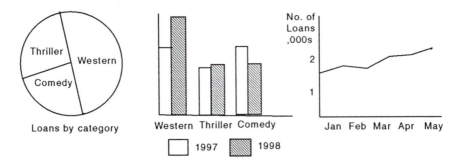

Fig. 7.11: Pie chart, bar chart and line graph

The layouts of printed and screen reports can be specified using appropriate documentation, such as a print layout chart or a display layout chart. Output may also be produced on:

- *Special pre-printed stationery:* where the system adds the details which are variable.

- *Multi-part forms:* which are used to produce more than one copy of an output for distribution to different places.
- *Turnaround documents:* which are outputs produced by the system, sent out to customers and are later re-input into the system when returned. They are then read automatically via special equipment. The processing of electricity bills provides an example.

7.6 Input design

We now consider the design of the inputs to the information system. The content of the inputs is indicated on the data flow diagrams and is described in detail in the data dictionary. In designing the input we are concerned with the following:

- The data flows that are of interest at this stage are those which cross the system boundary on their way into the system.
- The systems designer must identify suitable means of collecting and entering the required data into the system.
- As all data has been described in detail in the data dictionary, then the relevant descriptions of the contents of the data flows of interest to us can be obtained from the data dictionary.
- The systems designer must specify an input device to change the collected data into a form that can be read and processed by the computer system.

Yeates *et al.* (1994) identify the choice of appropriate method as depending on a number of factors, the two most important of which are summarised as follows:

- *Identify a method which will be most suitable to the needs of the users who have to enter the data.* For example, a keyboard is appropriate in many situations, but where speed and accuracy are important machine readable media might be more efficient.
- *Identify the method most suitable for the format and volume of the data to be entered.* For example, where copies of large numbers of documents are to be stored onto the computer then the most suitable method of input might be a scanner.

Regardless of the method chosen, Yeates *et al.* suggest that input will include all or some of the following steps:

- *Initial recording* of significant data by the user
- *Transcription* of data onto an input document

- *Conversion* of the data from a form that is readable by humans to one that is readable by computer
- *Verification* of the data conversion to identify any errors
- *Validation* of the data by the computer system to ensure that it is logically correct
- *Correction* of any errors that have occurred and have been picked up by the data validation program.

Data entry can be a costly process since it needs to go through some or all of the above processes. The objective for the systems designer trying to develop systems of a high quality will be to keep the process as simple as possible while minimising the opportunity for incorrect or incomplete data being entered into the system. The following need to be carried out:

- *Choosing the input medium:* this is the physical substance that contains the input data prior to it being entered into the information system. Examples of input media are:
  - *Paper forms and stationery*
  - *Computer screens* used in combination with other devices, such as keyboards, mice and light pens

  The most popular form of data entry is the keying of data on a conventional keyboard, cash register or specially designed keyboard. Input media also include:
  - *Magnetic ink character recognition*, which is used on bank cheques
  - *Mark sense recording*, which is commonly used for the marking of multiple choice examination papers. It is often a preferred option when a small amount of data is to be entered on a form
  - *Magnetic strips*, which are commonly used on the back of credit cards and cashpoint cards. They carry details of the account in computer readable form.
  - *Bar codes*, which are used in numerous applications, such as identifying products in supermarkets and for parcel tracking.
  - *Voice input systems*, which at present can recognise a limited vocabulary of words spoken by particular individuals.
  - *Magnetic tape or disks*, which can be used to transfer data between computers.
- *Choosing data entry mode:* this involves deciding whether the input data are sent to the computer immediately when they are created or following some delay.
  - *Delayed data entry:* this is commonly found in batch processing systems. In these applications data are collected and then grouped in

batches for processing. For example, applications for membership of a video shop could be made on paper forms which could be collected and then processed at the end of the day, when the relevant details are entered into the computer.

- *Immediate data entry:* this is commonly associated with on-line processing. In the video shop, for example, the information about the customer could be entered into the system immediately it is provided and used to update the relevant computer files or database.

- *Data format design:* this involves specifying the visual representation of the data and its associated data entry screens. Standard forms might be used to specify the screen design or a CASE tool might be used to produce a prototype of the form or screen. Screen design should aim to keep the screen as simple and uncluttered as possible and should minimise user input wherever possible.

Having considered input and output design we now need to consider the design of the dialogue between the user and the computer. The dialogue will transmit commands from the user to the computer and information from the computer to the user.

7.7 Dialogue design

Input is provided to the information system and output from it through an appropriate dialogue between people and the computer. We now discuss the design of the human-computer dialogue. The computer system will carry out the tasks specified by the user. The user will convey the tasks that require doing by specifying appropriate commands to the computer system. The user-issued commands and the responses produced by the computer make up the human-computer dialogue. This is the interface between the user and the computer.

The design of the dialogue is of extreme importance as it determines how easily the user is able to interact with the computer in order to carry out the organisational activities. Dialogue should be designed to enable user-efficiency and minimise potential for error. Designing the human-computer interface will be dependent on the users themselves. What might be a suitable dialogue design for one group of users might not be so for another. Therefore it is imperative that the potential users of an information system are considered in terms of the following characteristics (Wu and Wu, 1994):

- *How frequently they will be using the system:* users who perform the particular tasks repeatedly need a different dialogue to those users who only occasionally execute the task.
- *What computer skills they possess:* users with more IT skills and knowledge have more confidence in the use of computers than those users with little or none. The designer must take this into account.
- *What their educational level is:* a general rule is that the type of instructions and interface design should be geared to the average ability of intended users.
- *What training will be required for the use of the system:* the amount of training required for the use of a particular system depends on the tasks and the design of the system. While some systems are designed for users with no training, others require extensive training.
- *Whether the user is to be an active or a passive operator:* there is a considerable amount of difference between tasks that require the user to construct the dialogue as opposed to one that simply requires replies to pre-determined dialogue.
- *What environment the user functions in:* the environment that a system will function in is very important. Where responses to queries are required very rapidly this will be a factor in the design of the dialogue.

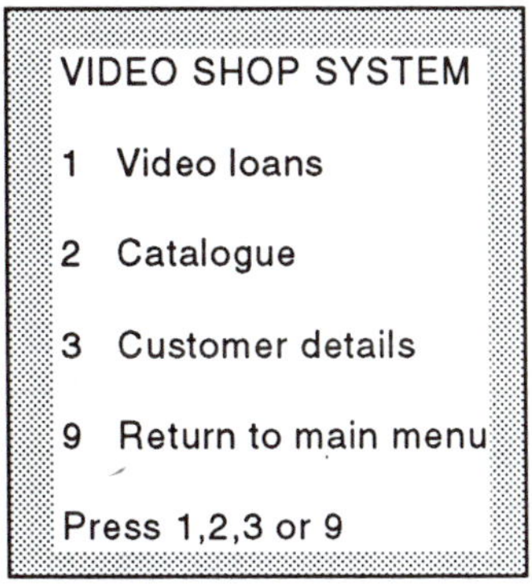

```
VIDEO SHOP SYSTEM

1  Video loans

2  Catalogue

3  Customer details

9  Return to main menu

Press 1,2,3 or 9
```

Fig. 7.12: A pull-down menu

Dialogue design will also involve deciding how the dialogue should be presented to users. The four options are:

- *Menu-driven dialogues:* these include:
  - *Pull-down menus:* which display the main menu choices. The list displayed as Figure 7.12 gives the user choice of system to access.

The list of film categories shown in Figure 7.13 could be obtained through clicking on 'film categories'. Clicking on one of these categories may lead to another list being displayed.

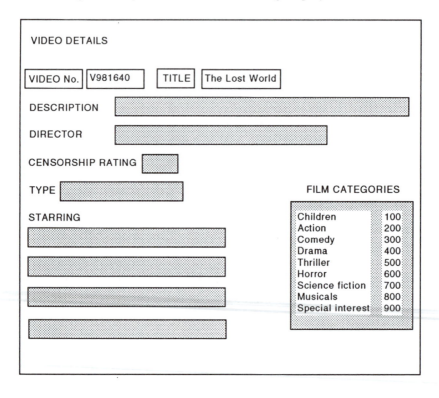

Fig. 7.13: A pull-down menu of film categories

— *Full screen menus:* a full screen style menu displays menu items in a vertical numbered list, with the identifying text that would appear as help text for a bar or pull-down menu. As the name indicates, this kind of menu consumes a lot of screen space. The menu shown as Figure 7.12 could be a full-screen menu.

   Menu-driven systems can be easy to use and are therefore useful for many applications.

• *Graphical user interfaces:* illustrated in Figure 7.14, these are program-controlled dialogues based around icons which are small graphical images representing some system function. The user interacts with the computer by pointing to the icons with a mouse and selecting specific icons by clicking on the icon with the mouse. The clicking of an icon will result in the display of further icons or menus displaying further choices or forms to be completed. The essence of such interfaces is that the visual display of information provides constant assistance to the users for performing their tasks.

VIDEO SHOP SYSTEM

Customers   Videos

Fig. 7.14: Graphical user interface

- *Form filling:* This is commonly used for the input of data from paper forms and the screen forms are designed to correspond with the paper form. An example is given in Figure 7.15. The parts of the form where the user is required to enter details is indicated by being highlighted in some way so that it stands out from the background. As data is entered into the form, the cursor moves to the following input area. This mode of interaction is useful when large volumes of similar data are to be entered into the system.

MEMBER

MEMBER NO.

SURNAME   INITIALS

STATUS   LIMIT   NO. OF TAPES
                                           ON LOAN

LOAN DETAILS

Catalogue No.   Title

Date out   Date due   Amount   Payment
                              payable   method

Fig. 7.15: Screen form for video shop application

```
C:\ format a:
Insert new diskette for drive A
and press ENTER when ready ....

Checking existing disk format
Formatting 1.44m
Format complete
Volume label (11 characters, ENTER for none)?
                            CUSTOMERS
1,457,664 bytes total disk space

Format another? (Y/N)? n
```

Fig. 7.16: Command language interface

ADVANTAGES	DISADVANTAGES

MENUS
Shortens learning
Reduces keystrokes
Structures decision making
Allows easy support of error
   handling
	Danger of many menus
	May slow frequent users
	Consumes screen space
	Error handling requires rapid
	   display rate

FORM FILLING Simplifies data entry Requires modest training Makes assistance convenient	Consumes screen space
COMMAND LANGUAGE Flexible Appeals to 'power' users Convenient for creating user macros Supports user initiative	Poor error handling Substantial training needed Great memorisation required
GRAPHICAL USER INTERFACE Easy to use Visual display of information No need to remember syntax of commands	Constant use of mouse tiring

Fig. 7.17: A comparison of interaction styles (modified from Schneidermann, 1987)

- *Command language:* in this type of interaction the user has to remember and enter exactly the specific instructions to get the computer to perform the required tasks. The commands have to be syntactically correct to be understood by the system. This type of interaction can be unfriendly and difficult except in the hands of very experienced users. Nevertheless, for experienced users these may well be a very fast and efficient means of communicating with the computer for their purposes. Typical command sequences are shown in Figure 7.16.

Major advantages and disadvantages of the four interaction styles are given as Figure 7.17.

We have described the main dialogue types. During this phase of the information systems development life cycle the systems designer has to evaluate the needs and characteristics of the users of the system and consider the available alternatives to determine the most suitable dialogue type for the different applications in the system.

7.8   Software design

An important aspect of the information systems project is the development of software. This software will correspond to the automated procedures within the information system. In this section we discuss the design of the software using appropriate techniques. As we use structured techniques in systems analysis and design, we also use structured techniques in software design. This approach to software design is generally referred to as **software engineering**.

Software engineering is the systematic application of an appropriate set of techniques to the design and construction of computer programs, including associated documentation required to develop, operate and maintain them. There are three aspects to software engineering:

- Several techniques are used with the aim of increasing quality and productivity
- The techniques are applied in a systematic way
- The techniques are applied to the whole process of developing software.

Software engineering is a very important part of the overall process of information systems development. Information systems development consists of a number of activities which include the development of software.

The objective of the design phase is to produce a structured design of the final software system. Structured design is an approach for producing an easily maintainable and easily tested **top-down design**.

Structured design is documented using a **structure chart**. In the design of software there are two aspects:

- *Procedural characteristics:* which describe the order of processing
- *Hierarchical characteristics:* which describe the rank of the various components, that is, the level at which they appear in the hierarchy.

In structured design we begin with the hierarchical characteristics by considering the different aspects of the system in order of their importance, as opposed to the order in which they are done. Subsequent levels of the structure chart add more and more detail. The top of the chart represents the underlying ideas behind the system, while the bottom levels provide the detail.

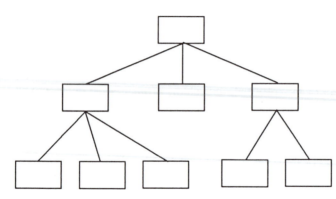

Fig 7.18: The general organisation of a structure chart

A structure chart is a graphical representation of the hierarchical decomposition of the system (Figure 7.18). It is made up of three elements:

- *Module:* this can be considered to be a named bounded contiguous set of statements. On the structure chart it is represented by a labelled box (Figure 7.19).

Fig 7.19: A module

- *Connection:* this is any reference from one module to another. It usually means that one module has called another. On the structure chart it is represented by a directed line between the two modules (Figure 7.20). Modules participate in the process of invocation, that is, a module is invoked by another.

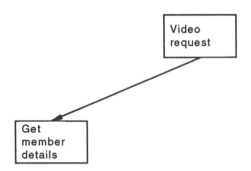

Fig. 7.20: Module invocation

- *Couple:* this is an item (data flow) that moves from one module to another. On the structure chart it is represented by a short arrow with a circular tail (Figure 7.21). A filled-in circle means that control information is being passed between modules (Figure 7.21). The fundamental difference between a data flow and a control flow is that the former has both an occurrence and content, while for the latter there is no content but their occurrence is of significance. The need for control flow is due to common situations in which the system needs to be made aware of something that has happened. Data flow could represent a value for data or a customer name on a receipt. Control flow could be, for instance, 'end of data' or a start signal.

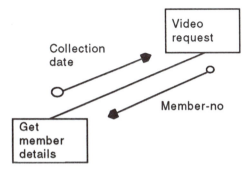

Fig. 7.21: Data flows between modules

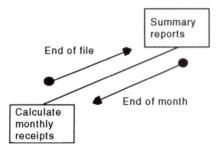

Fig. 7.22: Control information passed between modules

There can also be a linking between modules due to structure. These links between modules due to structure are called:

- Coupling
- Cohesion.

Coupling is the relationship between modules. **Cohesion** is the relationship within modules.

Coupling
This is concerned with the quantity of data transferred between modules. It is a measure of the degree of interdependence between modules. The systems designer will aim to make modules as independent as possible by minimising coupling. Low coupling indicates a well partitioned system. By minimising the connections between modules we are decreasing the chance of an error in one module causing a problem to appear in another. When making changes to modules, we want to reduce the likelihood of having to change another module, as in changing a given module we do not want to be concerned with the internal mechanisms of another. Low coupling can be achieved if two modules communicate exclusively by parameter passing. Each parameter is an item of data. High coupling occurs when

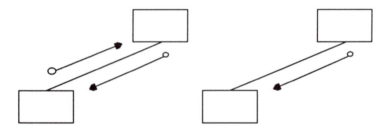

Fig. 7.23: Low levels of coupling - only data flows between modules

two modules refer to the same common data area. Figures 7.23 and 7.24 show low and high levels of coupling respectively.

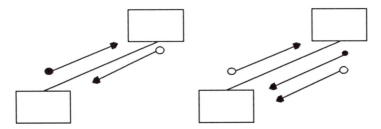

Fig. 7.24: High levels of coupling - control information as well as data flows between modules

Cohesion

Cohesion is a measure of how closely elements within a given module are related together. The systems designer will aim to produce highly cohesive modules, in which all the elements are related. Thus, all activity in a module should relate to the same data and the same purpose. We need to ask the question: 'What is the full purpose of this module?' If the answer has a single verb and a singular object then the module is probably highly cohesive. We need to ensure that the module is appropriately and concisely named. If we have trouble doing this, then it is likely that the module has unacceptable cohesion. Coupling and cohesion are interrelated. The greater the cohesion within individual modules, the lower the coupling between modules.

7.9 Structure charts

The data flow diagram that we have produced is a statement of our **requirements**. It specifies what needs to be done. The structure chart is a statement of our **design**. It says how we are going to meet those requirements. There is therefore a strong correspondence between the data flow diagram and the structure chart. Two techniques are used to assist in deriving the structure chart from the data flow diagram. These are transform analysis and transaction analysis. They deal with different types of data flow diagram (or different features of the same data flow diagram). They can be used as mechanisms for producing corresponding structure charts.

Figure 7.25 shows the general structure of a transform centre. In this type of application the data flow diagram can be divided into:

- Processes that can perform input and editing (shown as input processes in Figure 7.25)
- Processes that do processing, for example, calculations (shown as transform processes in Figure 7.25)
- Processes that do output (shown as output processes in Figure 7.25).

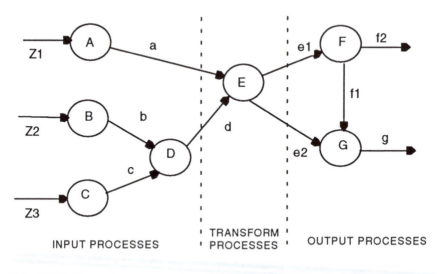

Fig. 7.25: General structure of a transform centre

In mapping to a first-cut structure chart, each of the three groups of processes are given a parent module. In Figure 7.26 we call this **input control, transform control** and **output control**. In this example we have considered processes A, B, C and D to be concerned with input, E with transformation and F and G with output. The structure chart shows the introduction of a special module called 'Do All' whose purpose is to handle the three input, transform and output control modules. The input control module receives the data flows a and d and passes them to the 'Do All' module which will pass them onto the transform control module. The transform control module passes the data flows a and d to module E which carries out the processing necessary to transform these into data flows e1 and e2. Transform control will then return the transformed data flows e1 and e2 to the 'Do All' module which will pass them to the output control module.

Transaction analysis aims to identify processes that are transaction centres. A transaction centre is a process that does not do any actual transformation on the incoming data flow, but routes the data to two or more processes. Recognising such processes on a data flow diagram is relatively easy, since it will be a process containing a single incoming data flow with two or more outgoing data flows to other processes. The process of updating a master file is an example of a transaction which the process has to route to the appropriate modify, add or delete process.

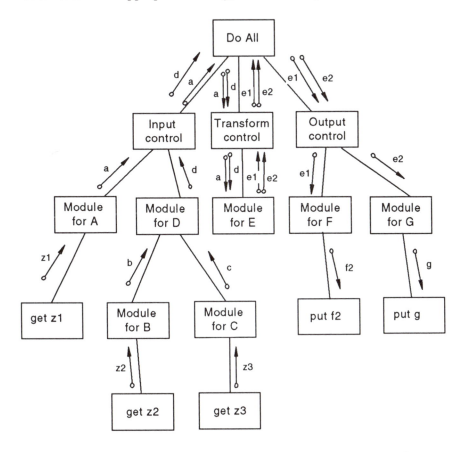

Fig. 7.26: The mapping to a structure chart of the transform centre from Figure 7.25

Figure 7.27 shows the general structure of a transaction centre. As with the transform analysis, the data flow can be used to produce a first-cut structure chart. Figure 7.28 shows one possible mapping to a structure chart for this transaction centre. In this figure we can see that the processes which constitute the transaction centre are converted into modules under the control of a transaction control module. These processes are concerned with transforming z into h.

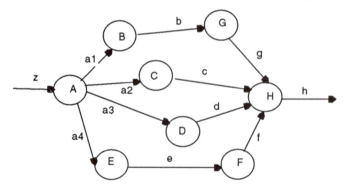

Fig. 7.27: General structure of a transaction centre

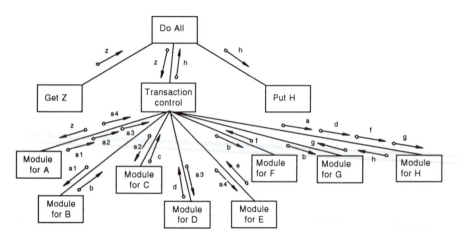

Fig. 7.28: The mapping to a structure chart of the transaction centre from Figure 7.27

7.10   Tools and techniques

Drawing tools, CASE tools and 4GLs, which are described in more detail in Chapter 10, prove of great help to the analyst in the systems design phase (as with the previous systems analysis stage). They do not alter the content of the phase, but they certainly can help the systems analyst and designer in carrying out the work. They help, for example, in drawing the diagrams, correcting them and in linking the content of one technique with another. For example, they might ensure that the contents of the E-R model and data flow diagrams are reflected in the data dictionary.

The techniques described in Chapter 6, such as data flow diagrams, E-R models, decision trees, decision tables and structured English, are also useful in the systems design part of the information systems development life cycle. As we have seen in this chapter, we need additional techniques to describe the software design aspects.

Another useful technique for information systems development, particularly useful during the design phase, is that of the structured walkthrough. This is discussed in the next section.

7.11 Structured walkthroughs

Structured walkthroughs are a series of formal reviews of a system or a program, held at various stages of the life cycle. This is an idea which has developed around structured systems analysis and design approaches, where the opportunities for such review are clearly identifiable. These are intended to be team-based reviews of a product, such as a program or design component and are not intended to be management reviews of individuals or their performance.

The basic idea behind structured walkthroughs is that potential problems can be identified as early as possible so that their effect can be minimised. The benefits of this approach are:

- The overall quality of the systems analysis and design of the information system is improved, since more than one person is responsible for it and the analysis and design are exposed to the scrutiny of others at every appropriate opportunity.
- There is the opportunity to detect errors earlier in the development cycle than might otherwise be possible, avoiding the errors propagating throughout the rest of the systems development process.
- All team members have the opportunity to be 'educated' in the total system, resulting in a much better understanding of the total system by a greater number of organisational personnel. This means that team members can more easily take over work from each other. Other personnel, outside the development team, such as production and operational systems staff also have the opportunity to familiarise themselves with the overall system as well as particular components.
- Technical expertise is communicated through discussion that is often generated as a result of a structured walkthrough. More experienced staff will spot common sources of potential problems and discuss these with other staff, thereby transferring their own knowledge and skills. This means that the technical knowledge is dispersed more widely than would otherwise be the case.

- Inherent in structured methodologies is that technical progress can be more readily and easily assessed, and the walkthroughs provide ideal milestones and opportunities to do this.
- If carried out in the correct spirit and atmosphere, structured walkthroughs can provide an opportunity for trainee analysts and programmers to gain experience and enable them to work on complex problems more quickly due to their participation in walkthroughs with other more experienced team members and also because of the opportunity of having walkthroughs on their work where they receive specific comments and feedback in a non-threatening environment.

Structured walkthroughs have been identified as being of considerable value in the development of information systems, and they should be held on completion of certain phases of the development as indicated. It is impractical to hold formal walkthroughs too often, as it causes unnecessary administrative overheads. The best approach is to maintain the spirit of the concept by team members discussing all decisions with others without necessarily calling formal meetings. It is intended that the approach will normally promote discussion and exchange of ideas within the team. As stated previously, formal reviews should be held on the completion of stages and certain phases within each of the stages of the life cycle and it is suggested that walkthroughs might be held at the end of the following:

- Feasibility study
- System investigation
- Systems analysis
- Systems design
- Program specification
- Program logic design
- Implementation
  - Test plan
  - Implementation plan
  - Operational system plan
  - User manuals
- Review and maintenance.

Formal walkthroughs should be attended by a number of team members because responsibility for the system is then placed on the whole team. All members of the team should be given the opportunity to contribute, from the most junior to the most senior. It might be appropriate to limit the number of people attending a particular walkthrough to around four.

For maximum benefit to be derived from the walkthrough, it is important that appropriate documentation is circulated well in advance of the walkthrough and that:

- Everyone attending is familiar with the subject to be reviewed
- Each attendee should have studied it carefully
- Minor points of detail are discussed before the walkthrough, so that valuable time is not wasted on trivial points.

During the walkthrough it is important that:

- All errors, discrepancies, inconsistencies, omissions and points for further action are recorded so that this can form an action list
- One person should be allocated the responsibility of ensuring that all points from the action list are dealt with.

It should not normally be necessary to hold another walkthrough for the same activity. Walkthroughs are a very powerful technique and are most successful where they are carried out in an 'ego-less' environment, that is, one in which the individual concerned with the particular activity does not feel solely responsible for it. It is important that all team members have responsibility for the system.

Even down to the level of individual programs, it is important that all team members have access to any code produced and feel responsible for the system as a whole rather than just that program. In practice, this means that a programmer should be able to accept criticism of the program design, code or test plan that has been produced. Equally, the programmer should not feel afraid to discuss code produced by someone else. This type of environment is encouraged by the use of structured walkthroughs because they are a formal introduction to an approach of communication. In some organisations structured walkthroughs are used extensively during coding. The idea is not to fault-find or criticise any individuals but to identify any potential problems and resolve them as early as possible in the information systems development process.

There are two specific types of walkthrough that are commonly used in programming, these are, code reading and dry running. These are not formalised procedures but entail team members critically examining each other's work:

- *Code reading:* This is performed both before testing and on completion of testing. It is normally carried out by someone other than the developer of the code being read. Again the idea is that work is exposed to outside scrutiny and comment as soon as possible. The aims of initial code reading are to:

- Detect any coding errors in going from the program design to the code of the programming language used
- Ensure that appropriate coding standards of the organisation have been adhered to
- Check that the coding is efficient in terms of the performance that the system will produce
- Cross-educate team members, as they all have the opportunity to learn from the code developed by others.

The aims of the final code reading, a task which is usually performed by the team leader, are to:

- Check that the code is of good quality and adheres to organisational standards
- Confirm that testing of the code has been completed according to the appropriate test plan
- Establish that the code is consistent with the specification that it was produced from.

Code reading is a difficult and time-consuming activity but it does have a number of benefits:

- Most minor errors are discovered before testing begins, preventing more time being wasted later
- Coding standards are maintained as programmers know that their code will be specifically checked for this and therefore they are more likely to conform in the first place
- Technical expertise is communicated by the code reader passing on their knowledge to the programmer as a result of the code reading activity
- An ego-less environment is created where the emphasis is continually on reviewing products rather than personnel.

- *Dry running:* This involves manually passing test data through the code. The start of the process involves the programmer listing all the variables and noting any initial values. As the test data is processed, variables are tested and updated as appropriate. This may seem a tedious task but it has the advantage that errors and discrepancies are highlighted and it can also verify that the test data is adequate. However, if previous reviews have been performed adequately, it is only necessary to dry run complex programs. This is because logical design errors will have been removed during the structured walkthrough of the design and clerical errors in the translation of design to code will have been found during code reading.

7.12 Package or tailor-made?

An important consideration in the information systems development process is whether to purchase an off-the-shelf package or to develop a tailor-made solution. Packaged software was discussed in Chapter 2, but the assumption thus far has been that an in-house tailor-made solution is to be produced. Nevertheless, there are many packages and much of modern information systems development is about integrating a variety of packages and in-house solutions as appropriate. Packages present the following opportunities:

- *Temporary solution:* packages can be bought off the shelf and installed as soon as a particular need is identified, without a long wait as would be necessary with a tailor-made solution. Further, it may be cheaper. This means that a package is suitable as an interim solution while further investigation is carried out or while a tailor-made solution is developed.
- *Advanced solution:* packages developed for specific applications for use by a number of organisations will have had a considerable amount of research and investigation reflected in their design. They should reflect requirements which have been well assessed. Their development should have been carried out by specialist developers, so that in many respects they represent a more advanced solution than might have been arrived at by a single organisation.
- *Building base:* packages can be used as a basis for further systems to be added. These add-ons might be either other packages or in-house developed software.
- *Strategic fit:* packages can be evaluated to ensure that they fit in with the strategic aims and objectives of the organisation.

Packages must be considered as an option since they present the following advantages:

- *Faster solution:* since the packages are already developed and available for purchase, this means that once requirements have been established and a suitable package identified, it can be installed far more quickly than a tailor-made package can be developed and installed.
- *Looser marriage - easier divorce:* since the package was 'easier' to obtain, it should also be easier to discard.
- *Growing market place:* the availability of packages is becoming more and more widespread, the likelihood of organisations finding off-the-shelf solutions is therefore increasing.

- *Growing sophistication:* packages are becoming increasingly sophisticated. As the length of time they are available increases, they are continually improved and developed by the issuing of new releases.
- *User support:* packages will have a number of users and these often collect into user groups who are available to provide each other with information and are able to approach vendors collectively.
- *Shared risk:* risks and costs associated with the use of a package are now spread across a number of users, whereas that for a tailor-made solution is totally on the organisation.
- *Learning/use services available:* these are often available from third party suppliers as well as vendors of the package. Such availability also means that the costs of such services tends to be reasonable.

Figure 7.29 suggests possible advantages and disadvantages of computer-based applications packages.

ADVANTAGES	DISADVANTAGES
Time savings for delivery and use	Self learning
Concentrate on function and use	Minimal support
Evaluate real products not design ideas	User must conform to package
Documentation evaluation	Design limits
Vendor upgrades	'Quirks'
User group pressures	Search/evaluation time
Possible custom changes	Constant learning curve as upgrades and new versions introduced
Portability across numerous hardware platforms	Securing vendors' attention/co-operation
Training aids	Politics may limit choices
Source code may be available	
Consistent with low cost hardware	
Increased capabilities require less skilled staff	

Fig. 7.29: Advantages and disadvantages of purchasing packaged software

In selecting packaged software it is important that they satisfy the basic functionality that is required. Multi-function packages should not be bought unless their capabilities have some present or near-future use. Packages should run on equipment that is already acquired and the model, memory size, operating system and peripherals should be appropriate. If the modifications needed are extensive then it is necessary to search for an alternative solution. The package should meet volume and performance requirements. It is important to look at maximum sizes of files allowed and limits to the number that may be open at any time. Packages must be clearly documented. This documentation should be reviewed before purchase. No commitment should be made to purchase a package that is not demonstrably working according to specifications.

Software packages present some extensions to the risk spectrum of the computer systems buyer or user including:

- *Multi-vendors:* the package may be developed by one organisation and actually sold through another. This chain is often quite long, particularly where packages are developed in one country and then distributed in others through different organisations.
- *Exit/demise of package vendor:* should the vendor go out of business the software package user may be left without support, maintenance and training.
- *Non-user standards:* the package will be developed according to the standards and conventions of the developers or vendors, rather than the user organisation.
- *Learning of hidden details:* since packages can be huge and complex, not all features will necessarily be documented and this requires the users to learn these hidden features over a period of use.
- *Design constraints:* The packages will have developed to be applicable to as many organisations as possible. This means that their design will be constrained to make the systems as general purpose as possible.
- *Lack of flexibility:* the packages will have been developed according to some predetermined criteria that may not necessarily be applicable to all purchasing organisations. Since the code of the package belongs to the vendors or their representative there is not the flexibility to modify the software or to customise it to the particular user.
- *Lengthy change processes:* changes now are outside the control of the organisation using the package. When problems are identified they must be reported back to the vendor, usually via some agreed route. These are only addressed at the convenience of the vendor and the software purchaser cannot control this process.
- *Lack of empathy with product since it was not developed in-house:* An in-house system is likely to include user participation during the analysis and design phase and users will be conscious of the system being designed for them. A software package developed by an outside organisation for general and wider use is not likely to be viewed in the same way.
- *Deters integration:* packages usually represent stand-alone one-off solutions which may not necessarily be conducive to integration.

- *Requires establishment of specialised internal support unit:* personnel with skills in the purchased software must be recruited or trained from within the organisation with the specific aim of providing expertise to support the use of the package. Had the system been developed in-house, then such a team would have arisen as a natural consequence of the development process.

- *Variable package quality:* since the software package is developed by a third party, possibly completely unknown to the organisation, it means that the purchasing organisation has no control over the quality of the process of producing the software or the quality of the product. This means that the quality of the packaged software cannot be guaranteed.

- *Packages require more computer resources:* Frequently packaged software requires additional computer resources, such as larger computer memory or hard disks. The software will not have been designed to optimise use of the resources of particular customers as it is intentionally a generalised solution suitable for many organisations.

It is important that there is preparation for addressing, evaluating and compensating for these and other risks that will exist in the packaged software process.

ADVANTAGES	DISADVANTAGES
Internal support	Long time cycles
Team product	High expectations
Fewer compromises	Frustration cycles
Better internal costs	Possibly phased releases
	Overall cost estimation difficult

Fig. 7.30: Advantages and disadvantages of building systems

ADVANTAGES	DISADVANTAGES
Vendor support	External risks
Higher activity level	Lack of customisation
Visibility	
Reliability	
Lower expectations	
Shorter time cycle to delivery	
Existing training programs	
Overall cost estimation easier	

Fig. 7.31: Advantages and disadvantages of buying packages

Consideration of software packages changes the nature of the systems and refocuses user satisfaction levels. We can compare these for building systems and buying packages. These comparisons are shown in Figures 7.30 and 7.31.

7.13   Structured specification

Having completed the activities to design the new system, we now need to collate all the various outputs together into the structured specification. During this phase it is necessary to add in the 'extras'. These include:

- *Error routes:* these describe the processing that is to take place on detection of erroneous or unexpected data and the error messages to be displayed.
- *Start up and close down procedures:* how to get the system up and running and how to shut it down.
- *Control information:* the data flow diagram deliberately does not show control information, and it is sometimes useful to add a small number of controls on key data flows at this stage to address user concerns, if any, regarding control information.
- *Format of certain reports:* the format of some reports is so important, for example, fixed by law or used as an input into another system, that users will be justified in insisting that it is explicitly defined in the structured specification.
- *Conversion from old system to new:* how the conversion from the old system to the new is to take place needs to be clearly specified.
- *Performance requirements:* a statement of the expected performance level of the system should be developed and included in the structured specification.

All key interfaces need to be defined and included in the top level data flow diagram. These cover:

- *Computer-computer interface:* which represents the data flows between different computers in the system. For example, in a chain of video shops, the local processing is carried out on a branch computer which interacts with the large regional computer at another site for some of the processing.
- *Human-computer interface:* which represents the data flows communicating between the manual and automated parts of the system.

By collating these outputs, along with the previous outputs, such as structure charts, structured English statements and the data dictionary, we form the structured specification from which software code can be developed during the next phase of the information systems development life cycle.

7.14   Summary

In this chapter we have looked at the systems design stage of the information systems development life cycle. Figure 7.32 provides an overview of this stage. Our aim is to develop a better information system. We have proposed an approach to systems design based on developing a logical model of the current system, agreeing a charter for change, producing new system logical data flow diagrams, introducing physical aspects to the data flow diagram by identifying the human-computer boundary and then producing a structured specification of the new system.

Having identified the human-computer boundary, we must specify the design of the human-computer interface. This involves designing the interaction which consists of input design, output design and dialogue design. During this stage we must also specify the design of the software and we discuss techniques that can be used to do this. The process of developing high quality software systems is commonly referred to as software engineering. The relationship between this and information systems was outlined.

We discuss the two main alternatives available to organisations concerning how to proceed with the information systems project. This is either to develop a tailor-made solution or to buy an appropriate package. We discuss the advantages and disadvantages of these. We describe how the various outputs produced are collated into the structured specification.

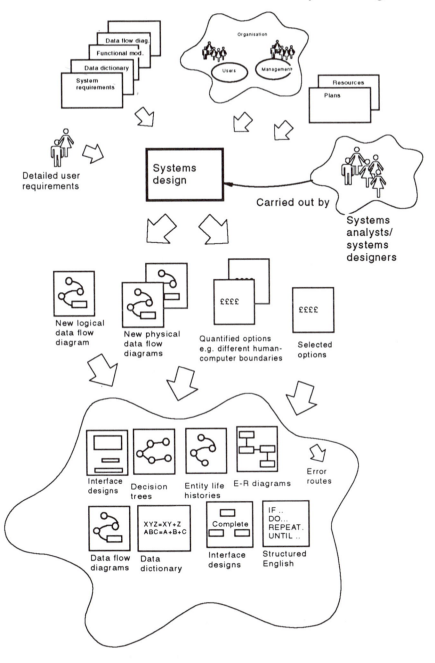

Fig 7.32: Overview of the systems design phase

Further Reading

DeMarco, T. (1978) *Structured Analysis and System Specification*, Prentice-Hall, Englewood Cliffs, NJ.
A classic text on structured analysis and design.

Hicks, J. O. (1993) *Management Information Systems: A User Perspective*, West, Minneapolis.
This is useful introductory text on information systems.

Macintosh Human Interface Guidelines (1987): *The Apple Desktop Interface*, Addison-Wesley, Reading, Ma.
Provides the standard principles for a graphical user interface.

Schneiderman, B. (1987) *Designing the User Interface: Strategies for Effective Human-Computer Interaction*, Addison-Wesley, Reading, Ma.
An excellent introduction to human-computer interface design.

Whitten, J. L., Bentley, L. D. & Barlow, V. M. (1994) *Systems Analysis and Design Methods*, Irwin, Boston, Ma.
Systems design is dealt with thoroughly in this text.

Wu, S. Y. & Wu, M. S. (1994) *Systems Analysis and Design*, West, Minneapolis.
Another excellent book on systems analysis and design

Yeates, D., Shields, M. & Helmy, D. (1994) *Systems Analysis and Design*, Pitman, London.
A very thorough and readable description of systems design.

Exercises

1. List the activities that must be carried out during systems design.
2. State the main steps involved in designing the new system.
3. Explain how physical aspects are often included in data flow diagrams.
4. In what way are logical equivalents derived?
5. What does the charter for change refer to?
6. What is the domain of change?
7. How are the new system data flow diagrams produced.
8. List the steps involved in identifying the human-computer boundary.
9. What does the design of the human-computer interface involve?
10. Discuss the principles that have been suggested for good interface design.
11. What questions need to be asked to determine the method of presentation of output?

12. List the three important principles that should be incorporated when designing the presentation of information.
13. In the design of inputs and outputs of a system where can we expect to find the detailed description of their contents?
14. List the characteristics of users which must be considered when designing the human-computer interface.
15. What are the four options for dialogue design and what are their advantages and disadvantages?
16. Discuss the use of structure charts in the design of software.
17. Explain what coupling and cohesion are.
18. Discuss the two main techniques in deriving structure charts from data flow diagrams.
19. What is software engineering and what is its relationship with information systems?
20. Discuss the purpose, organisation and use of structured walkthroughs in information systems development.
21. Organisations can go for packages as opposed to tailor-made solutions. Discuss the advantages and disadvantages of these two options.
22. List the further information that must be included in the final specification.
23. Using the data flow diagram of figure 7.4 and the requirement that we also wish to improve the purchasing side of things at the video shop, what might the new system data flow diagram then look like?

Areas to debate

1. Identify an organisation with which you are familiar due to everyday contact. Discuss what might be an appropriate charter for change for this organisation. Suggest what the domain of change of such a charter might be.
2. For the organisation discussed above, what alternative human-computer boundaries can you suggest and what are their advantages and disadvantages?
3. Consider some regularly-used information system that you use or are aware of and discuss changes to the human-computer interface that would make your interaction with the system more effective. Suggest input and output design details where appropriate.
4. In some organisations there may be resistance to the idea of introducing walkthroughs due to individuals being wary of exposure to their work

to 'criticism'. Discuss the contents of a report which you would produce to allay such fears and enable the organisation to do whatever is necessary to create a climate conducive to using walkthroughs.

5. The organisation is about to commit to a major in-house development which you are convinced is unnecessary due to the availability of appropriate packaged software. Discuss how you would go about convincing appropriate personnel in the organisation of this.

CASE STUDY

Given the rich picture of Figure 7.33 try to produce a suitable charter for change and domain of change for Mr. Asifiori.

Using the form shown in Figure 7.34 which is used in the Asifiori Salons for recording the information about the work done on clients' hair, suggest a form-based dialogue design for entering this information into the system.

Mr. Asifiori of the Asifiori Salons is considering the two options of purchasing a package or having a tailor-made system developed for the salons. Produce a report for Mr. Asifiori discussing how these two options might be considered for his salons and the advantages and disadvantages of these.

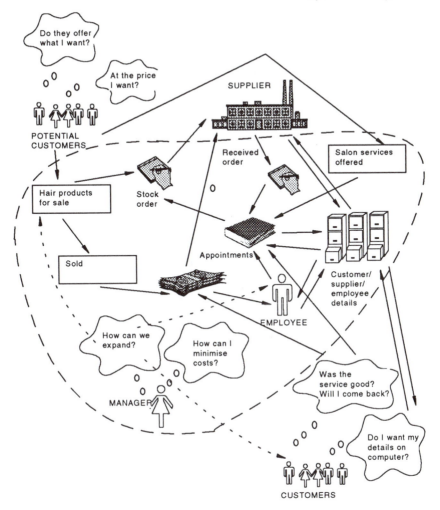

Fig. 7. 33: Rich picture of Asifiori hair salon

CUSTOMER RECORD CARD

Name of client _____ Telephone _____

Address _____

	PERMANENT WAVING				TREATMENT		
Date	Brand used	Strength	Development time	Remarks	Date	Treatment	Remarks

Fig. 7. 34: Customer record card for Asifiori hair salon

Chapter 8

IMPLEMENTATION: PRODUCING THE GOODS AND GOING LIVE

8.1 Implementation phase

With the systems design having been completed, the physical system can now be constructed. This phase constitutes the construction of the new system and the delivery of that system into day-to-day operation. The main task in this construction is converting inputs, outputs, files and their interactions into program code. This chapter looks at the process of constructing the system and delivering it into operational use. Figure 8.1 shows the context of this phase in the information systems development life cycle. Many organisations will be purchasing application software packages to meet these business needs rather than developing the system in-house. In this case the material in this chapter can be used to help evaluate such software.

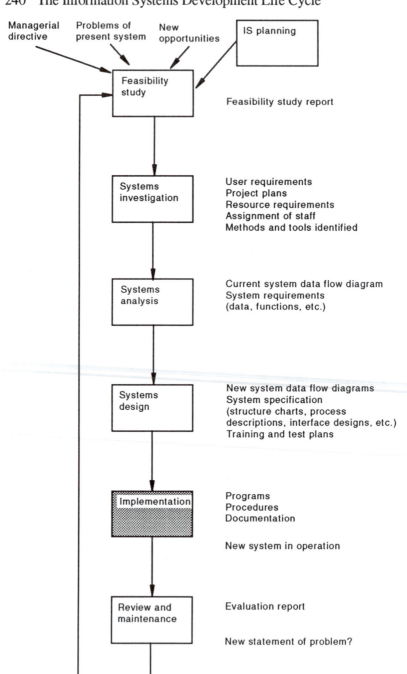

Fig. 8.1: Implementation stage of information systems development life cycle

8.2   Software development (programming)

The low level design must be converted into programs using a programming language. This is called coding, and the code produced should accurately fulfil the business process requirements. There is considerable complexity in the programming of information systems. Nevertheless, DeMarco (1978) argues that it is more straightforward than analysis. He makes a number of distinctions between programming and analysis which are summarised in Figure 8.2.

PROGRAMMING	ANALYSIS
Straightforward, since software sciences are relatively new and not as highly specialised as, say, medicine or physics.	A complex task, needing diplomatic skills, involving a large community of users with different and conflicting requirements.
Interpersonal relationships are not very complicated nor numerous	Interpersonal relationships can be very complicated and hostile.
Work is very exact and known. Code either works or does not work and it is very obvious when it is incorrect.	The analysis activity is not definite. It is not obvious when any phase is complete.
Work can be very satisfying because it is obvious when it is working correctly or if the cause of an error has been correctly diagnosed.	Work need not be so satisfying because in complex systems many compromises have to be made so that no person is entirely happy with the result.

Fig. 8.2: Distinction between programming and analysis (adapted from DeMarco, 1978)

This phase needs to be planned so as to guide the development and testing of new or revised computer programs. This implementation plan is developed when the design is complete.

- The plan needs to consider how changes to the design specifications are to be handled
- Programming team organisation needs to be planned
- A detailed development plan needs to be produced.

The process definitions need to be expressed in computer code. It is widely accepted that structured programming techniques will assist in the production of good code. That is:

- *Code that is easy to read and understand:* this will enable people other than those who produced the code to modify it later if necessary
- *Code that is easy to maintain:* to support changes in the system after it is built
- *Code that uses the computer resources in the most efficient manner.*

Structured programming uses standard control structures to improve program clarity and maintenance. The control structures encourage top-down program development by systematic and orderly expansion of program blocks. Programmers specify each top-level function by one program block, and the block is then expanded into more detailed components. Each block of code should implement some well defined function. This top-down development is made possible by the use of four main constructs shown in Figure 8.3. These are

- *Sequence:* enables the sequential flow of program statements.
- *Selection:* enables the selection of a path based on the single condition stated and is expressed using an IF-THEN-ELSE statement.
- *Iteration:* enables the repetition of a set of statements until a particular condition becomes true.
- *Multiple selection:* enables several conditions to be tested in the order of appearance using a CASE construct.

Readability of code can be improved by the sensible use of comments to annotate the code.

The starting point for the program code is the process specification. As has been seen, the process specification uses very similar constructs to that used in structured programming. This effectively means that the conversion from the process specification to the structured code is relatively straightforward. Essentially the keywords are replaced by the appropriate keywords of the programming language. The transformation and arithmetical statements of the process specification are replaced by appropriate statements of the programming language.

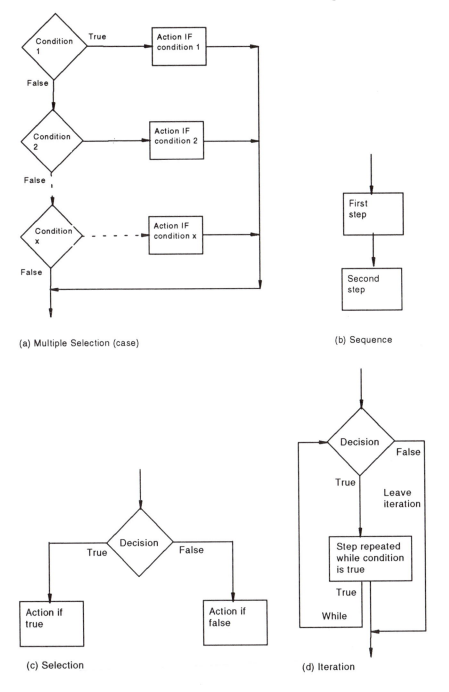

(a) Multiple Selection (case)

(b) Sequence

(c) Selection

(d) Iteration

Fig. 8.3: Four main control structures for structured programming (adapted from Wu and Wu, 1994)

8.3   Use of tools

CASE tools, which will be discussed further in Chapter 10, can be used to generate code automatically (see Figure 8.4). The input to such tools will be the program structure diagrams or structured English. From this, code in either a third generation or fourth generation language is produced. While it is obviously beneficial to be able to produce code automatically from higher level design documentation, it is commonly found that in practice the code generated will need to be modified in order to fine tune the system for a particular set of requirements. Obviously these modifications to the code will be lost when the system code is regenerated after any redesign of the higher level documentation. Previously added in code will need to be re-integrated into the newly generated code and this may not necessarily be straightforward.

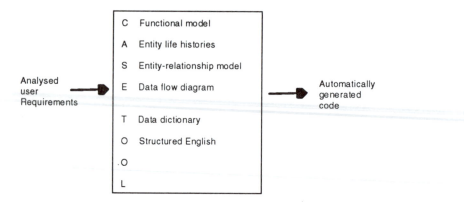

Fig. 8.4: Automatic code generation using CASE tools

Definitions for database management system input of the structure of tables can also be automatically produced as well as automatic production of some of the data dictionary entries from the E-R model. These automatically generated definitions can be modified as appropriate. Database management systems are also discussed in Chapter 10.

8.4   Testing software

Testing includes verification of the basic logic of each program and also verification that the whole system works according to plan. A test can be considered to be the execution of a program in order to detect the existence of a defect in the program. Such defects are called 'bugs' in software. Debugging is the process by which defects are identified in the program and removed by modifying appropriate parts of the code. After the suitable modifications have been made, the testing needs to be repeated to ensure that the defect was successfully removed and that no additional defects have been introduced into the code as a result of the modifications made.

The programmer must create sample test data to test the various paths of the program. The main points to consider in creating sample test data for the video shop example are:

- The upper and lower limits of a loop should be tested, as well as values which fall within a loop. For example, a customer having 0, 1 and the maximum of 5 videos out.
- Values which generate error messages should also be tested, such as having 20 videos out, which is not permitted at the store.
- Other valid values should be used, and the output should be checked to verify that these valid values produce the expected output.
- The analyst needs to be satisfied that erroneous test data was suitably rejected by the software.
- Where the test data produces erroneous output or causes the program to terminate unexpectedly, then the bug needs to be located and the code suitably modified.

Small programs can be tested as a single unit. A large program will have been designed as consisting of several subsystems, these subsystems will consist of program segments and these in turn will consist of modules. Testing at all levels needs to be carried out. Figure 8.5 provides a classification of software testing.

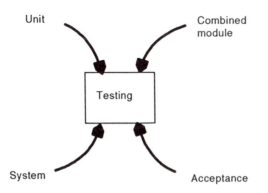

Fig. 8.5: Classification of testing

- *Unit testing:* Testing needs to be performed on individual modules to ensure that each functions as designed.

- *Combined module testing:* Testing needs to be carried out on integrated units (made up of individual modules) to ensure that they work together. The purpose of this type of testing is to test the interfaces between programs in the same functional area. Each program must be linked to all the other programs with which it interacts. Here we are not just concerned with producing the correct data in terms of content and format, but also the sequence in which it is produced and the amount of time taken.

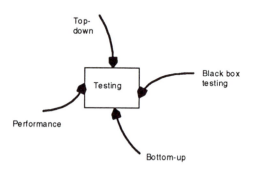

Fig. 8.6: Approaches of testing (adapted from Wu and Wu, 1994)

- *System testing:* Testing must be carried out on the system as a whole. Application programs written in isolation must work properly together when they are integrated into the total system. This will ensure that individual programs will accept the output of other programs as their input data where appropriate.
- *Acceptance testing:* This validates the performance of the system for the user. Actual production data is used to prove that the system is ready to go into operational use. The users usually submit the data and they will examine the resulting outputs to satisfy themselves about the capabilities of the system. In addition, the users investigate the human-computer interfaces, training manuals, clerical procedures and also verify the performance of the system to establish that it does meet their requirements.
- *Top-down testing:* Testing is performed incrementally from the top down. Program modules are integrated gradually as shown in Figure 8.7. The main module, which is called the control module, is executed during all of the testing. Modules that have not yet been integrated and tested are substituted by what is called a 'program stub'. This is a piece of code acting as the module it is replacing. It does the bare minimum for that module in that it is able to accept the input data and produce the appropriate output data that will be done by the actual

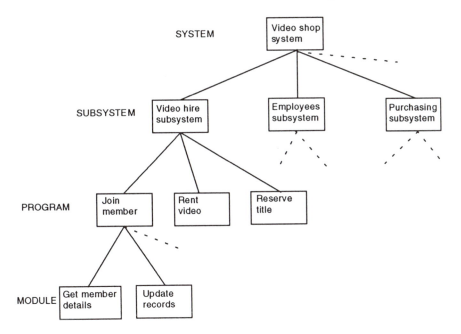

Fig. 8.7: Top-down structure of a large system

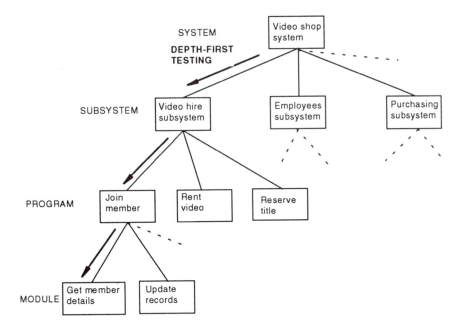

Fig. 8.8: Depth-first top-down integration testing

module it is replacing. The program stub does not perform any other activities. As modules are tested, they are included in the testing of further modules. The integration can be:

— *Depth-first:* in this approach modules are integrated top down to the lowest module in the hierarchy. This is shown in Figure 8.8.

— *Breadth-first:* in this approach modules are integrated by moving across an entire level horizontally. This is shown in Figure 8.9.

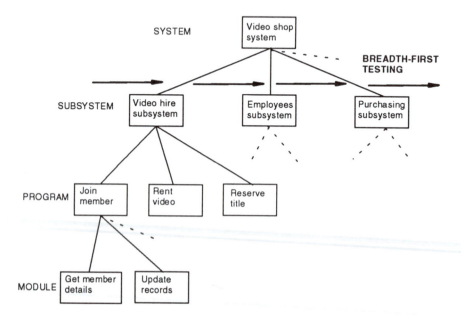

Fig. 8.9: Breadth-first top-down integration testing

Since program stubs only simulate the behaviour of a module, their use in top-down testing can impose considerable limitations. This is particularly problematic for lower level models, since the stub will not accept the full range of data that will be accepted by the actual model because it has only limited functionality.

• *Bottom-up testing:* in this approach modules are tested and integrated from the lowest level upwards until the complete system has been constructed. Program stubs are not necessary in this case as modules will have been tested before any modules that call them. However, a module called a test driver is written which controls the execution for each set of modules to be tested. This driver simulates the environment of any module by obtaining the input data for the module and receiving the output data. This is illustrated in Figure 8.10.

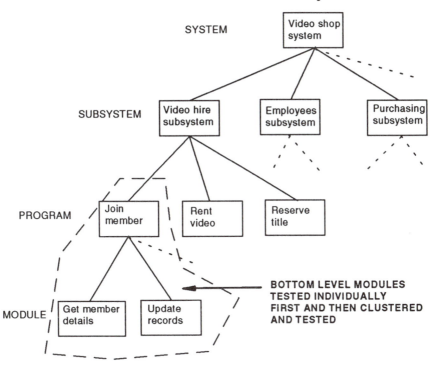

Fig. 8.10: Bottom-up integration testing

- *Performance testing:* this involves additional testing of a system for its level of performance. It may be necessary for a system to deal with thousands of transactions. The system must be tested to ensure that it is able to meet the performance levels required. Systems can be 'stress tested' to determine the maximum performance levels. When these are known, procedures can be put into place to prevent the system failing due to overload.

- *Black box testing:* in this approach, the code is passed to another person after it has been tested and debugged to the satisfaction of the person who originally developed the code. The idea behind this is that the original developer will naturally introduce bias into the testing of that software. This bias will be introduced due to the programmer's intimate knowledge about the internal structure and logic of the program. The second person does not study the program logic, but focuses on the tasks that the code has been written to perform. This approach is called black box testing because the code is treated as a black box that receives input and produces output, and knowledge of its internal structure and operation is unnecessary. Test data is produced and supplied to the code to ensure that the expected output is produced. Black box testing is illustrated by Figure 8.11.

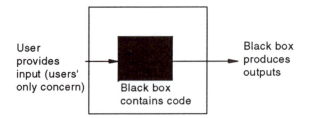

Fig. 8.11: Black box testing

8.5 Going live

This implementation phase is often called installation. Once the system has been constructed and tested successfully, then the final system needs to be delivered to the users and made operational. The main objective of this phase is to replace the existing system by the newly-constructed system. This transition needs to be done smoothly, so that users are not unnecessarily inconvenienced. The main activities that constitute this phase are:

- Capture relevant data
- Convert existing files into appropriate formats
- Train users
- Install the new system.

If the new system requires new computer-based data then this data must be captured and recorded in the files or database by suitable means. This may involve clerical staff typing in the data directly or it may be captured by some other means, such as scanning.

Alternatively, or in addition, different file formats may be required by the new system. In this case it will be necessary to convert this data to the new formats. Any programs to perform the file conversions must be written and tested in the same way as the other software. The conversion of files can be scheduled for a time when the system is halted for the new system to be installed. This will mean that the files are not out of date when the existing system updates the files. If the existing system continues to run beyond the time when the files are converted, then it is important that arrangements are made for both existing and new files to be updated until the new system is installed.

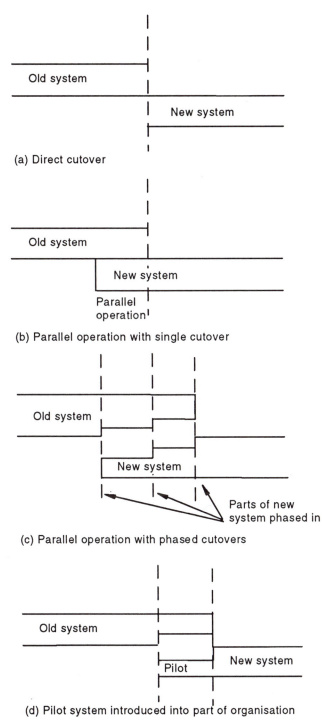

Fig. 8.12: Types of cutover to new system

As part of the documentation process, appropriate system documentation for the users must be produced. User training manuals and reference guides will be part of this documentation. Training will involve both formal training sessions and on-the-job training. All these should have been incorporated into the plans. Timing of the training is an important issue. If this training is scheduled too soon before the system is installed, the users are unlikely to remember all the important details, especially as they will be interacting with the existing system at the time. There is also the possibility that subsequent changes to the system prior to installation may require training to be modified, and the user may well become confused by having been given conflicting information. Training is therefore often done in parallel with data capture and file conversion, but this may put a heavy burden on staff.

The proposed new information has now been analysed, designed and produced. We now look at how that system can become operational so that it can be used to support the activities of that part of the organisation for which it was developed. As shown in Figure 8.12, there are four possible ways in which the new system can be installed:

- Direct cutover
- Parallel operation with single cutover
- Parallel operation with phased cutover
- Pilot system operation.

- *Direct cutover:* The direct cutover installation is simple in concept. It involves stopping the use of the existing system and replacing it immediately with the new system. At a given point in time, use of the old system ceases and the new system starts. This method presents a very high risk, and there is no protection in the event of failure. If problems are encountered with the new system, it is very difficult to revert to the old system. The problems in the new system must be worked around until they can be resolved. The cost of returning to the old system is high, and an organisation is only likely to do this in very extreme circumstances, and this is therefore a relatively rare occurrence.
- *Parallel operation with single cutover:* This approach avoids the risks of direct cutover. Both the old and new systems are operated simultaneously for a period of time. Since all the processing is performed on all files, both in the old system and new system, this means that the data files are up to date and so the switch to the new system can be made at any time. The decision is usually made to cutover to the new system at a predetermined time, although it can be

made when users indicate that they are happy with the new system. The advantages of parallel operation are that problems with the new system can be dealt with without disruption to normal operations, and this approach presents a considerable amount of security to the organisation. The disadvantage of this approach is that considerably increased effort is required from the users to operate both systems. This will therefore be an important consideration in planning the length of time for parallel operation.

- *Parallel operation with phased cutover:* This approach is similar to the one described above, except in the way that cutover to the new system is implemented. Again, the old and new systems operate simultaneously, but the removal of the old system and its complete replacement by the new system are phased in steps. The new system is phased in over a period of time. Changeover is carried out on the basis of functional area, or physical location or other selected criteria. For example, in the case of the video shops example, this could be done on a shop-by-shop basis or by the different functions, such as loans processing or purchasing.

  Again, the advantage of this approach is the opportunity to test the new system in operation, while minimising the consequences of problems with it. If any major problems arise, and it is necessary to revert to the use of the old system, then only a limited part of the organisation is affected. The potential disadvantages concern difficulties that might arise due to the concurrent operation of two different systems to do the same thing. Another problem is that this kind of approach cannot be used if the new system is not able to interface with the old system in other functional areas. Other disadvantages concern the high costs incurred in operating both systems and the increased possibility for confusion.

- *Pilot system operation:* This method involves installing the entire system at one location, for example, at one department or division, while the rest of the organisation continues to use the old system. The pilot system may be installed by direct cutover at this given location while the old system continues to operate in the other parts of the organisation as normal. This provides an opportunity for the system to be thoroughly tested while operational. When any problems that might arise with the software have been sorted out and the reliability of the software has been established to be of an acceptable and appropriate level, then the system can be installed for use throughout the remainder of the organisation. Again, there might be incompatibility between the new pilot system and the existing system still installed and operational in most parts of the organisation and this might be a problem if this approach was attempted.

As the project heads towards completion, the users may now find that some features that they required have been either completely left out or not designed very well. These aspects will become apparent to users at this stage because the system design is now in a visible form. If they now request changes and attempts are made to include them, then the system will be delayed. Care is needed, because if a project is always undergoing change, then it cannot be installed as the operational system. Rather than constantly postponing the completion date of the project to include such modifications, the requested modifications would normally be deferred for consideration until after the system is operational. There will be exceptions to this rule, but generally it is better to defer changes and avoid situations where the system might never be ready for completion.

The information systems development process has involved interaction between users and developers. While in development, the system has 'belonged' to the developers, when it is operational, it will 'belong' to the users. Having trained the users in the everyday operation of the system, the ownership of the system must be transferred to them. The system's developers may well be involved in future maintenance activities to do with the system, but it is the users who are now owners of the system.

An agreement must be reached as to when the old system is to be closed. Difficulties may be caused by user reluctance to master the workings of the new system. This may cause delay to the operational use of the new system and may perpetuate the old system. The old system needs to be clearly and categorically eliminated. This can be done, for example, by removing from user shelves all documentation related to the old system and archiving it. These steps should be a part of the installation procedure thereby making installation of the new system clear and explicit.

8.6　Summary

In this chapter we looked at what happens when the systems design has been completed. The physical system is constructed at this implementation phase and the new system is delivered into day-to-day operation. Figure 8.13 provides an overview of this stage of the information systems development life cycle.

We have described the software development process. When the system has been constructed it must be thoroughly tested to prevent problems occurring when the system is operational. We have identified the different parts of the system that need to be tested and discussed a number of approaches to testing.

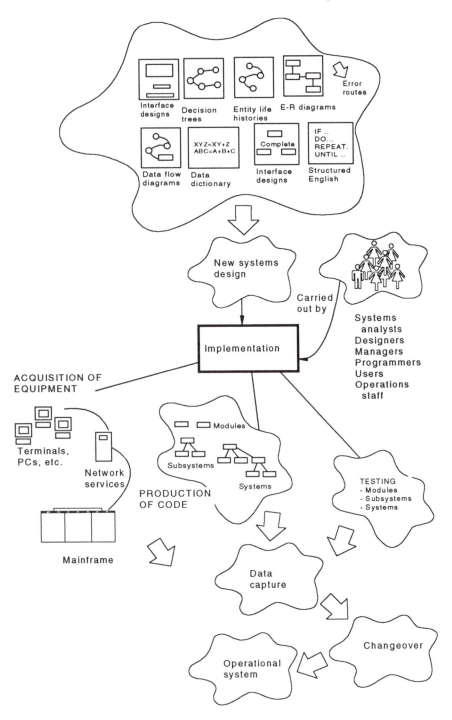

Fig 8.13: Overview of the implementation phase

Once the system has been successfully constructed and tested, it needs to be delivered to the users and become operational. The activities involved include the capture and conversion of relevant data, the training of users and the installation of the system. We have described four possible ways in which the new system can be installed. These are: direct cutover, parallel operation with single cutover, parallel operation with phased-in cutover and pilot system operation.

In the next chapter we consider what happens when the system has become operational. This is the maintenance and review phase of the life cycle.

Further Reading

CACM. (1997) Special feature on the debugging scandal and what to do about it, *Communications of the ACM*, **40**, 4.
Spotlights the software debugging controversy, that the trial-and-error scenario for debugging software remains the prime industry practice. It includes a series of articles depicting approaches for improving the process.
Wu, S. Y. & Wu, M. S. (1994) *Systems Analysis and Design*, West, Minneapolis.
Detailed discussion of this phase of the life cycle.
Yeates, D., Shields, M. & Helmy, D. (1994) *Systems Analysis and Design*, Pitman, London.
Testing and code generation are discussed fully.

Questions

1. Explain the purpose of the implementation stage of the information systems development life cycle.
2. What is coding?
3. List the characteristics of code that structured programming techniques help to produce.
4. State the constructs that enable top-down development of programs.
5. What is the starting point for program construction?
6. In what way can CASE tools be useful for coding programs?
7. Explain the purpose of testing.
8. What are the main points to consider in creating sample test data?
9. Explain the following terms: top-down testing, bottom-up testing, performance testing and black box testing.

10. What is system installation? Discuss the three main activities that constitute this phase.
11. Describe the type of documentation that needs to be produced.
12. There are four possible ways in which the new system can be installed. Briefly explain each of these.

Areas to debate

1. With the advent of CASE tools, it has been anticipated that for future information systems, programmers would not be required or would have a much reduced role as code would be generated automatically. Explore relevant literature and discuss the extent to which this has happened. Attempt to identify the reasons why the situation is as you have revealed.
2. Debate the different changeover strategies and the different characteristics of situations to which they might be suited.
3. Suggest structures for documenting the system, in particular the users' guide.

CASE STUDY

Discuss the different types of testing that must be carried out on the system developed for Asifiori Salons. What might be appropriate mechanisms for the system becoming live in such an environment? Discuss your ideas in detail. Draft a users' guide for the users of the information system.

Chapter 9

REVIEW AND MAINTENANCE: THE JOB IS NOT YET FINISHED

9.1   Review and maintenance phase

In this chapter we look at the post-implementation activities. We discuss the process of evaluating the information systems development project from the point of view of the product that we have developed. We also evaluate the process of development, since this information will be useful to us for future projects. We discuss the potential problems that must be considered in the evaluation of the system and we examine how a new life cycle might result from problems identified with the now existing system.

The information system has now been successfully installed and is in operational use. However the job is not complete. It is necessary to carry out a post-implementation audit and review of the system. Figure 9.1 shows this phase in the context of the complete information systems development life cycle.

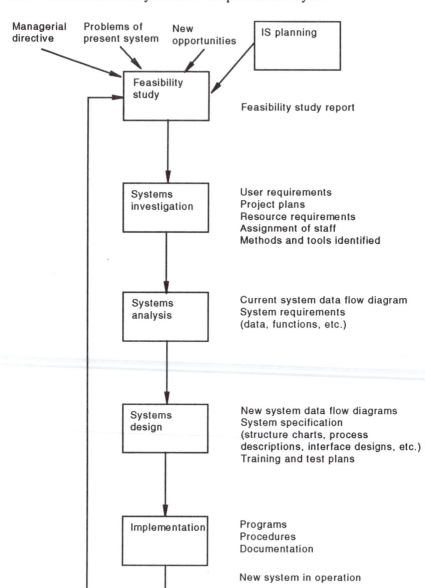

Fig. 9.1: Review and maintenance stage

9.2 Evaluation

This post-implementation audit and review, is normally carried out by a team composed of representatives from the management of the organisation, the department or part of the organisation where the system was implemented, the systems development project manager and selected systems developers.

The review is an opportunity for the organisation to reconsider the development of the information system so as to learn from the experience. Organisations that learn from experience are likely to be more successful in the long run. Management may learn from any mistakes that were made, so that future practice can ensure that the same mistakes are not repeated. In addition, any best practices that are identified can be recognised and highlighted for inclusion in other and new projects.

During this phase the knowledge acquired during the project is summarised and recorded so that it is available for future reference. The causes and effects of parts of the project going over time or over budget and any technical problems that were encountered need to be examined in detail. It is also an opportunity to see how effective the use of any new tools or techniques was and analyse experiences of team interactions. Comparisons need to be done between the planned schedule and estimated person-months for systems development and the actual figures. In this way, the experiences of completed projects can have a beneficial affect on future projects.

9.3 Potential problems

After the new system has been operational for, say, three to six months, a review of the system is required. This time-lapse enables the users to familiarise themselves with the system and also allows statistical information concerning system usage and performance to be obtained. This review process should be systematic in addressing the following issues:

- *Does the system do the job it was intended to, that is, does it meet management and user objectives?* This question is essentially addressed to users. It is only they who can comment on whether the system meets their original specification. Where requirements have now changed with respect to the original specification, these should be collated as system modification requests. The system is also reviewed to establish whether management objectives have been met. The cost/benefit analysis that was carried out for the project is also examined to show how accurate the cost estimates were. It needs to be considered whether the anticipated benefits have actually been realised.

- *How well does the system do this job, that is, how well does it achieve its objectives?* One aspect of this is the overall performance of the system. The ongoing daily operations are reviewed to determine whether the projected benefits have been achieved. Where it is recognised that the projected benefits are not being realised, then modifications need to be proposed to improve the system. The user interfaces need to be reviewed to ensure that users' interaction with the system is not being constrained in any way. Figures regarding error rates for manual processing where data is input to the system using a keyboard also need to be reviewed so as to ensure that these are within acceptable limits. As a result, modifications to the system might need to be proposed. During the operational period prior to the review, figures should also have been collected to do with bugs in the software. These should record date of occurrence, type of problem, its severity and the time that it took to rectify. These figures should be evaluated to determine the quality of the software delivered, as well as result in suggestions as to how the current development methods in the organisation might be improved.

- *What modifications have been identified as necessary?* From the moment that the system is installed and operational, there will be many occasions on which modifications will be demanded. The system will need to be maintained on an ongoing basis throughout its lifetime to incorporate enhancements and remove programming and design anomalies. The sheer size of some systems will mean that they take many person-months or even years to complete. Organisations are dynamic by their very nature and their needs are continually developing. This will mean that when the system is implemented changes will be required almost immediately to meet these new needs.

Addressing these issues should result in a comprehensive coverage of potential problems so that nothing is overlooked.

9.4   Change...a new life cycle?

During this review phase, different user requests can be collated and prioritised. Indeed, these modifications may be so drastic as to require the building of a new system rather than to perform maintenance on the present one. There will be reluctance on the part of management to build a new system so soon after the installation. What generally tends to happen is that authorisation is given for selected groups of modifications to the system to be made and these will then be scheduled according to the priorities identified.

This phase should result in a report which records the findings of the review team and the actions identified.

9.5 Summary

In this chapter we have shown that it is necessary to carry out a post-implementation systems audit and review. Figure 9.2 provides an overview of this stage of the information systems development life cycle. The development process must be scrutinised during this audit as well as the information system itself. We have described the organisation and content of this audit. A full review of the information system needs to be carried out after a few months of it being operational. Changes required may lead to demands for another new information system.

In the next chapter we look at tools which may be used to assist the systems analysts and designers develop the information system.

Further Reading

Frenzel, C. W. (1992) *Management of Information Technology*, Boyd & Fraser, Boston, Ma.

Provides a good coverage of the implementation phase.

Taylor, M., Moynihan, E. & Wood-Harper, T. (1997) Knowledge for software maintenance, *Journal of Information Technology*, **12**, 2, pp. 155-166.

This is concerned with the 'knowledge' factor affecting maintenance of systems. It splits this into two categories, arguing for the importance but difficulty on acquiring both. It incorporates case study research in 31 IT departments in the UK.

Questions

1. Explain why, although we have installed the information system into operational use, the job is not yet finished.
2. Discuss the way in which this review phase is carried out.
3. Why is it possible that this phase could result in the initiation of a new life cycle?

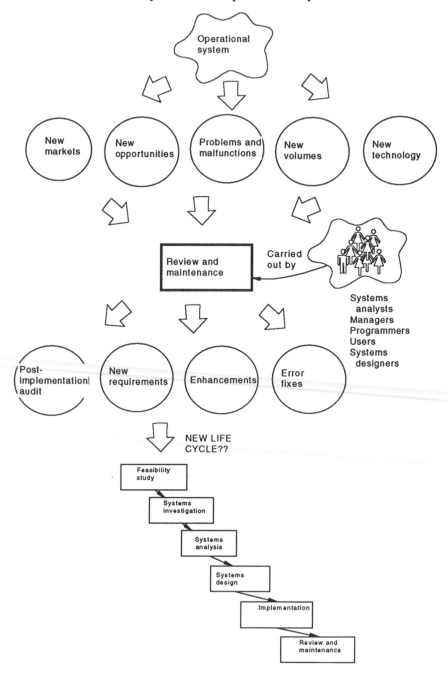

Fig 9.2: Overview of the review and maintenance phase

Areas to debate

1. Discuss possible reasons for the unpopularity of the systems maintenance task. Why is this task necessary? Do you think that it will be as necessary in the future?
2. Discuss the view that as soon as a system requires any maintenance it should be scrapped and replaced by a new system.
3. Consider how a system, though technically successful, might be inappropriate for an organisation.
4. Search the literature for further information on post-implementation audit and identify and discuss the purposes and mechanisms for this activity.

CASE STUDY

Assume that a computer-based information system has been developed for the Asifiori Salons. Discuss any areas where there might be problems in such a system and identify the actions that might result from this.

Chapter 10

TOOLS

10.1 Tools

It will be clear from the description of the information systems development life cycle found in Chapters 4-9, that it can be a long, complex and difficult process. Information systems failures are commonly reported in the press. While the causes of many of these difficulties are either not clear or are very difficult to address, one area in which there has been some progress in terms of providing help in the information systems development process, lies in the availability of software tools.

Research has been aimed at producing computer-based software packages which assist the information systems developer in the various activities involved in information systems development. These software tools can be broadly classified as consisting of:

- *Tools supporting cross-cycle activities,* such as planning and controlling of projects. We have already looked at these in Chapter 3.
- *Data dictionary tools* for managing data about the data. We have already looked at these in Chapter 6.
- *Repositories* which are essentially extended data dictionaries.
- *Drawing and documentation tools* which are either stand-alone or integrated into CASE tools.

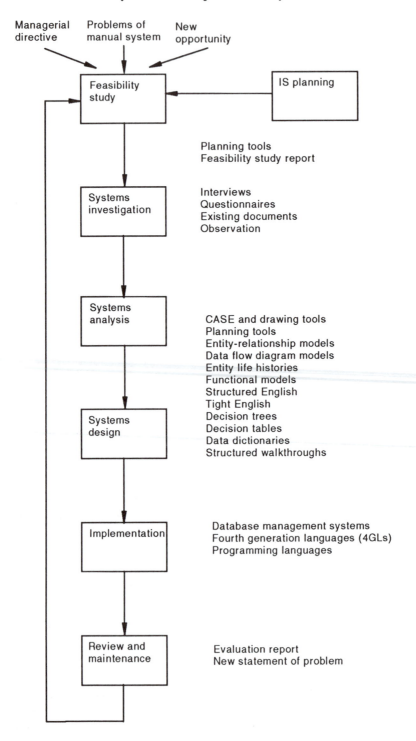

Fig. 10.1: The role of tools and techniques

- *Computer Aided Software Engineering (CASE) tools* providing support for the various stages of the life cycle.
- *Database Management Systems (DBMS) tools* to automate the management of creating, accessing and deleting data items in a database, normally through fourth generation languages (*4GLs*).
- *Object-oriented CASE tools* supporting this particular approach to information systems development
- *Client-server development tools* again supporting this particular design.

We will look at CASE tools, database management systems and fourth generation languages (4GLs) in this chapter in particular because they have had most impact on the systems development process. We will look very briefly at other support tools. In Figure 10.1, we show where particular tools are emphasised in the information systems development life cycle. We also show where particular techniques are emphasised because tools are often used to support the use of techniques.

10.2   CASE tools

Due to the scale and complexity of information systems development, various computer-based tools have been produced to assist the process. Computer Aided Software Engineering (CASE) refers to an integrated environment containing a collection of tools which supports the work of analysts and/or programmers. CASE products fall into three categories supporting different sections of the systems development life cycle:

- *Front-end tools:* which provide features to support and document analysis and design. These tools are used to define system requirements and system properties. The outputs of front-end case tools will typically be:
  - *Process specifications:* in the form of data flow diagrams, structured English descriptions, decision tables, decision trees, structure charts and module specifications (described in Chapter 6).
  - *Data structure specifications:* in the form of entity-relationship diagrams, data dictionaries and entity life histories (also described in Chapter 6).
  - *Screen and report definitions* (described in Chapter 7).
  These will require support from the CASE tool in terms of diagram editors, screen painters and dialogue prototyping aids.
- *Back-end tools:* which provide support for constructing systems, that is, producing software. The outputs of these are typically:

- *Program source code and program object code*
- *Database structure definitions and file definitions.*
- *Re-engineering tools:* which take existing code and re-engineer it to improve its efficiency and ability to integrate with other programs as well as producing the following outputs:
  - *Diagrams representing the existing system*
  - *Data dictionary entries for existing systems.*
- *Integrated CASE (I-CASE):* attempts to encapsulate tools covering the entire process of planning, systems analysis, systems design and implementation; in other words providing full information systems development life cycle support.

CASE use has increased over the last decade, and predictions are that its use will continue to increase for some time in the future. Some of the benefits claimed for CASE tools include:

- *Increased productivity:* This is due to a reduction in the human effort required to produce systems, as more of the work is carried out by computer. Time spent on producing diagrams and charts is reduced and this is particularly pertinent when it is considered that each diagram may have to go through several versions before completion. Automatic generation of source code, object code and database structure also contributes to productivity.
- *Increased opportunity for control and consistency:* CASE tools can assist in keeping track of the development process. These tools can keep notes of the developers, versions of models and schedules. They can help in ensuring consistency and completeness by cross-checking across models and across stages of the development process.
- *Increased systems quality:* This should result from the opportunity for more complete, accurate and consistent design specifications presented through the use of integrated computer-based specification tools and a central information repository, since most errors in the development of a new system occur in the systems specification stage. Without tools, such problems may not be identified until acceptance testing by users takes place and then putting things right may delay the project so that this may not be done.
- *Reduction in systems maintenance:* This should result if the use of CASE tools leads us to developing the systems that are required, when they are required and to the quality standards demanded. Changes should be less frequently necessary and easier to do when they are necessary.

- *Development of systems aligned with corporate strategy:* This is more possible because of the integration of all aspects of information systems development. It is becoming widely recognised that the development of a particular information system is not only a technical issue arising from where an organisation currently is, but from where an organisation wants to be. Information systems development is an activity that should concern itself with the translation of corporate information systems requirements into operational systems.
- *Interactive systems development ensures systems are accepted and meet requirements.* CASE tools allow the production of system prototypes where the users can see what the likely outputs and user interfaces will be like. Users have an opportunity to comment on these so that changes can be made. The information systems eventually implemented should thereby be in line with user requirements.

A limitation of CASE is that benefits only apply to new systems developed and that it cannot assist in the maintenance of existing systems unless they are re-engineered. This can cause difficulties for most organisations in that they have a great deal of investment in 'legacy' systems (that is, systems already operational, many for some time) which need to be changed to keep pace with the changing organisation, but which do not warrant the investment of wholesale replacement.

Further, introducing and incorporating CASE technology into organisations is a difficult and complex task that needs to be handled with care, since many complex factors determine its success. The issues that need to be considered are:

- *Cost and risks associated with CASE tools are relatively high:* Costs will be incurred for purchasing the CASE software along with appropriate additional hardware, so that teams of information systems professionals have access to the CASE tools. The use of CASE may well help to solve some problems, but needs a considerable learning curve to absorb new concepts and techniques. It will take a considerable amount of time to determine how best to use CASE and mistakes will inevitable occur at first.

- *Training is still vital for effective use of CASE tools:* This training must be timely for it to be of any significant use. There is also a need for awareness of the new roles introduced and of the difficulties that might arise because of CASE adoption. In addition, the move to CASE should be seen as a move towards a better range of tools and techniques, but not as a solution to all existing problems. Training clearly needs to allow for changes in mind sets (programming in a third generation language compared to using CASE is not a matter of a change in degree, but a change in type). In other words, there needs to be allowance for an education as well as a training function.

There also needs to be training in user-analyst communications. In a CASE environment, systems designs, human-computer interfaces, outputs and so on, can be debated and changed with the user, even in 'real time'. Good communication skills are as much a requirement as good technical skills. Further, as users are likely to come across CASE systems or other computer tools themselves, they also need to be included in training in their use.

- *Standards, including documentation standards, need to be agreed and used:* This will enable the use of the CASE tools to be widespread within the organisation.

- *Resentment from programmers:* In making impressive productivity claims, there is an assumption that developers will be enthusiastic and more positive about the new development environment. However, some problems may well arise because of a distinct lack of enthusiasm for it. Programmers may prefer to use the more traditional third generation languages, such as COBOL, that they have been using previously. Even when there is a positive view taken of the new approach, when unexpected difficulties are encountered, these may well result in disillusionment. There are many difficulties which are due to individuals being asked to put aside what they are familiar and comfortable with. By introducing new concepts and techniques, they may feel uncomfortable as they are having to start afresh. They may find that newer and relatively inexperienced staff know, or appear to know, more than them, and this in itself can cause difficulties.

- *The use of a structured methodology will be required:* Most tools are methodology-driven and the implementation of both CASE and a new methodology at the same time compounds risk of failure. Training in the appropriate methodology will also be required. Of course the approach propounded in this book does combine a structured approach to information systems development with CASE where appropriate.

The approaches to information systems development based on CASE and the previous non-tool based approaches have some fundamental differences. Whereas non-tool based approaches tend to concentrate on the coding and testing of systems, the use of CASE tools has led to more emphasis on the analysis and design stages of the life cycle. There are two main reasons for this.

- *The tools are able to provide considerable support for developing and diagramming the analysis activities:* therefore more energy can be invested in creatively thinking about analysis. Where tools are not used, much energy is oriented towards documenting and modifying existing documentation, which can be largely handled by the CASE tool.

- *The documentation of the non-tool based approach is paper-based and not easy to maintain.* When using CASE tools, documentation can be produced and maintained more easily.

The differences between the two approaches are summarised below:

- *Non-CASE tool based approach:*
  - Effort invested on the development tends to be focused on the coding and testing phases of systems.
  - Documentation is largely paper based and not easily maintained, since even small changes will require considerable effort to modify the documentation.
  - The programs that need to be developed require coding manually, which can be a long and difficult task.
  - Once the programs are designed and written, they must be tested. Designing test data, using it to test the programs, finding the errors, and then correcting the errors, is a very tedious and time-consuming process.
  - Paper-based specifications can be difficult to modify and the ripple-through effect of resulting changes can also be difficult to carry out.
  - There is the possibility of re-use at the level of code, rather than at the level of systems design as is the situation when using CASE tools.
  - The maintenance of software can be difficult.

- *CASE-based approach:*
  - Effort tends to focus largely on the analysis and design of systems, since the CASE tools provide considerable support in terms of the other aspects of information systems development (particularly production of documentation and code generation).
  - The maintenance of the design is easier and its associated documentation can be generated automatically. When it needs to be modified, the changes can be incorporated easily and efficiently and diagrams redrawn rapidly.
  - Many of the programs that are needed can be generated automatically. However, they often require further code to be included to customise them, and if changes are made to the design

from which the code was automatically generated, then these customisations will be lost and the newly generated code will need to be recustomised. This is a potential cause of difficulties.

- The automatic checking of design is possible since the complete systems design is now computer based.
- It might be possible to carry out the reverse engineering of existing systems using the CASE tool so that although the systems were not originally designed using CASE, a design can be produced for which appropriate documentation can be automatically generated.
- Since the design is held in a CASE tool on the computer, it can then be used again as a component in the design of other systems.
- The reporting of the impact that changes will have on the system can be produced more easily.

Using CASE for information systems development is not simply a matter of providing better tools, but is an inherently more complex problem introducing organisational change. The fundamental problems with information systems development are caused by the difficulties in managing the development process. The lack of tools can be an excuse to cover for the lack of management and engineering discipline. The benefits of CASE will not be realised in the context of any projects which are undisciplined and chaotic. This often means that appropriate documentation is not being produced nor is the project carrying out essential reviews of its activity. Often organisations purchase CASE tools or other technologies and then try to employ a process that fits the new tools. Without an explicitly defined process for developing their software, it will be difficult to identify:

- How to design an information systems development environment in which the activities of all these involved are well co-ordinated
- All of the tools needed that will enable support for the whole process
- The appropriate integration of these tools and the process of producing the information system.

This can only be done effectively by recognising the need to focus on defining the processes used in information systems development, and only then selecting carefully the tools and methods to support those processes.

Implementation of CASE requires the introduction of new:

- Techniques
- Equipment
- Methodology

- Working practices
- Approach to development.

Each individual change has potentially high risks associated with it. Although the cumulative benefits of change may be great in the long term, the cumulative risks are also great and there will inevitably be problems in the short term.

As well as CASE tools supporting conventional information systems development, there are a huge number of client-server development tools. Client-server architecture is discussed in Section 13.3. Selecting an appropriate tool can contribute to the success or failure of a project. In general, most of the available tools can create applications for the client side, some are capable of spreading the processing of the application across a number of computers as well as generating applications to run on the server. Most client-server tools provide an integrated development environment, which includes screen painters, object browsers, integrated debuggers and code editors. The integrated development environment enables the developer to build the interface and define its behaviour. Many of the tools are able to link to a variety of databases, because appropriate middleware has been built into the tool enabling this link. Some have database servers included that run locally on the client. This enables developers to build their applications before linking to a remote database server. Included with all tools is a programming language which allows the customisation of applications.

In general client-server development tools support the object-oriented development model and they enable developers to build applications quickly, supporting rapid application development (RAD) and prototyping.

10.3   Database management systems and fourth generation languages

A database management system (DBMS) is a large piece of software which is used for defining, creating, accessing, updating and deleting data. Any interaction with the data is done through the DBMS. Organisations are modelled in terms of their data using conceptual modelling techniques, such as entity-relationship modelling described in Chapter 6, and this model can then be mapped onto the DBMS.

Process modelling and data modelling are separated in this approach. Data is much less likely to change and therefore is more stable than the processes which operate on that data. By separating these two models we have the 'data independence' which leads to greater flexibility. Changes can take place in the processing of the data that do not require corresponding changes in the storage of that data on the database. Conversely, changes can take place in the way that the data is stored, and this will not require any corresponding changes in the processing of that data by the applications. The DBMS is able to provide different views of the same data for different users. DBMS often have an integrated data dictionary partly to manage and control their data.

An important part of the database environment is a fourth generation language (4GL). Each development in computer languages has had the objective of reducing the amount of time required to write programs. This has most often been achieved by making programs easier to write through increasing their human understandability.

All computer programs are developed in order to solve a problem or to carry out practical tasks. Computers have become more powerful while their costs have decreased. As a result, computers are more widespread and there is an ever greater pressure to increase programming productivity to meet growing demand. 4GLs are another step in the process of de-skilling computer use in order to make programming feasible for a wider range of computer users who want to be able to program their computers with the minimum of specialist skills. This is even more apparent now with the widespread use of personal computers by people not trained in computing.

Following the earlier stages of machine level and assembly languages which were very difficult to use, came high level or 'third generation' languages. They are so called because they are far from the level of the machine. High level languages, such as COBOL, Basic, Pascal, and PL/1, represented a major leap forward for the computer industry. Through their use, programs could be written more quickly and by less 'expert' users.

The central factor in distinguishing the various levels or 'generations' of programming languages would seem to be the level of abstraction that they offer. Abstraction can be considered as the process by which the essential properties required for the solution of a problem are extracted while hiding the details of the implementation of the solution. As the level of abstraction increases, the programmer needs to be less concerned about 'how' a task must be carried out and more concerned about 'what' needs to be carried out. At present, 4GLs offer the highest level of abstraction to the programmer.

Underlying the progression through the generations of programming languages have been several fundamental trends. The key aspect has been the astounding increase in power and flexibility of computer technology. This has resulted in reductions in the cost per unit of power and storage which even ten years ago were difficult to contemplate.

Partly inspired by this trend, but also by increasing pressures for more complete and up-to-date information, users have demanded increasingly sophisticated and comprehensive computer systems. The accelerating demands for new or modified systems have been difficult to satisfy and many organisations now have a large backlog of development and maintenance work.

All high level languages have their advantages and disadvantages, but the handicap that they all share is that of syntax. The programmer is confined to a strictly-defined set of instructions which are sometimes cumbersome and verbose. This means that third generation languages need vast numbers of lines of code for typical commercial systems and they are still intended to be used by computing professionals rather than by users. They are time-consuming to debug, awkward to modify and consequently they do not produce programs which are as responsive to changing business needs as they need to be. Fourth generation languages were created in response to these problems and to meet the following objectives:

- *To decrease the time taken to develop software* in order to reduce the 'applications backlog' present in many organisations.
- *To make applications easy and quick to change* so reducing the time and money dedicated to maintenance. Many organisations are now devoting as much as 80% of their information systems resources to maintenance.
- *To minimise debugging problems.*
- *To generate code from high level expressions of requirements.* Using non-procedural mechanisms which allow the programmer to specify what is required rather than how it is to be done, results in more correct programs.
- *To make programming languages user-friendly* and accessible to users so that non-programmers can develop their own computer systems.

It was thought that 4GLs would bring programming capability to users, but it has been recognised that this is not feasible with most 4GLs. It is now generally accepted that 4GLs are more of a professional programmer's tool than a user's tool. However, certain types of 4GL, especially those developed specifically for personal computers, do lend themselves more to user application.

Given that 4GLs were created with the above-mentioned aims in mind, any 4GL should have the following characteristics:

- *High productivity:* 4GLs were developed first and foremost to increase programming productivity, and therefore any 4GL has to improve on the productivity of a typical third generation language. Some early estimates were for ten-fold increases in productivity over development in third generation languages like COBOL.

- *User-friendly:* A 4GL should be user-friendly and users should be able to use it effectively to obtain the results that they desire. It has been suggested that non-professional or non-specialist users should be able to learn a subset of the language in a two-day training course.

- *Non procedural:* This is one of the main differences between all earlier languages and a 4GL. The latter are non-procedural language solutions. Using a 4GL, the programmer should be able to state what needs to be done rather than how it is done. This implies that the 4GL software formulates the procedure. The programmer merely 'decides' the requirements.

- *Prototyping capability:* A 4GL should facilitate prototyping, since the speed and ease with which one should be able to write a program and, more importantly, the ease with which it can later be altered and improved, should allow sample solutions (prototypes) to be developed, demonstrated to the users and then gradually refined and modified to their precise requirements.

- *Interactive:* 4GLs should be programmed interactively, to ensure that programming errors are detected at an early stage.

Everything about 4GLs leads to the conclusion that they tend to be more of a concept than a specific product, nevertheless it is possible to outline the general features of a 4GL.

It should be pointed out that '4GL' describes a very wide range of systems, from 'query languages' to 'report generators' and 'application generators'. We will consider the ideal, a 'full-function' 4GL which embodies the entire spectrum of 4GL capabilities. Such a 4GL is capable of building complete applications. Many 4GLs are more specialist and can only carry out one or more specific tasks.

A typical full-function 4GL will consist of the following components:

- *Database management system:* at the heart of any 4GL should lie a database and its database management system. A vital element is the provision of a user-friendly query language. This should provide the user with a non-procedural means of retrieving information from the database. The standard query language for relational products is presently SQL.

- *Data dictionary (see also section 6.7):* The data dictionary ensures that commonly used information will be defined in one form, irrespective of where it appears within the application. Whenever a program needs to handle data which is held on the database, the

programmer uses the standard data dictionary data names and the 4GL will consult the data dictionary and obtain the correct information. Therefore, it is no longer necessary for the programmer to give explicit instructions to:
- Read data from the database
- Check whether or not the record exists
- Update the data within the record
- Write the record back to the database.

These are all part of the data dictionary function.

- *Screen painter:* An important requirement of a 4GL is the ability to enter data into the system easily. A rapid means of describing the input document to the computer system without going through the process of writing a procedure in considerable depth is required. Most 4GLs have some sort of screen painter to allow the programmer to design the screen layouts. Using this tool, data-entry screens can be designed quickly and easily. The design should normally take place as an interactive dialogue.
- *Report generator:* A 4GL should also offer a quick means of extracting information from the system and, since printed reports still form the backbone of commercial computing, the provision of a report generation facility is essential.
- *Interactive interface/dialogue manager:* this component controls both the user interface of the 4GL and that of any applications created using the 4GL. A consistent interface throughout the system is essential. This should be designed to support novice users and to offer flexibility to more experienced users. Many will employ a graphical interface as found on modern personal computers.
- *Development tools:* this is the component with which programs are created. It should provide both non-procedural and procedural facilities.
- *Integrated development environment:* all of these features are accessed from a common core. The user does not have to return to the operating system to move between components.

Figure 10.2 illustrates the basic architecture of a typical full-function 4GL.

4GLs are so far removed from high level languages in terms of their characteristics and architecture, that many people feel that 'language' is not the correct term to use, especially since a traditional programming language might be one of the many components of a 4GL. The alternative terms of fourth generation tool, fourth generation system and fourth generation environment are often used.

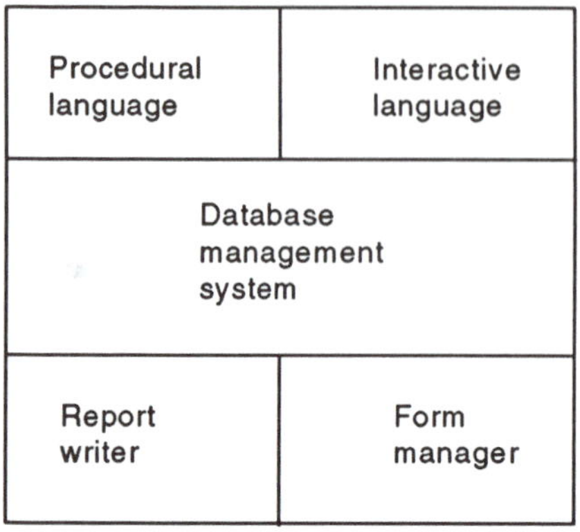

Procedural language	Interactive language
Database management system	
Report writer	Form manager

Fig. 10.2: Basic architecture of a full-function 4GL

10.4 Other tools used in systems development

Data dictionaries
These are software tools which manage information about the data resource, the meta-data, that is, data about data. The data dictionary is often integrated with a database management system. The data dictionary is a central store of the definitions and usage of the data an organisation. It is an important mechanism for data sharing. The data dictionary is also a useful documentation aid for the data. Data dictionaries have now developed to include information about processes in a similar way to that of data. This provides a useful opportunity for cross-referencing between the data and the processes which use that data.

Repositories
The original idea of the data dictionary has since been expanded to include information to support the wider aspects of information systems development. The inclusion of information about processes is one such development. In view of this expansion, the term data dictionary is no longer appropriate to describe this tool, and the terms, 'system repository' and 'system encyclopaedia' have become synonymous with this expanded form of data dictionary.

Drawing and documentation tools
Detailed documentation, which accurately reflects the objects it represents at all times and includes the various diagrams showing the different models produced, is important throughout the development and maintenance of information systems for the following reasons:

- Documentation may be the only tangible deliverable to show that a phase of development has been completed. Such documentation includes interview notes, draft reports and data flow diagrams.
- Larger projects sometimes take as much as three to five years to complete in entirety, so it is essential to ensure that good documentation is maintained. This will aid continuity of the project phases over this time and support good communications between the many staff that will be involved in such projects.
- Staff may leave during the development of the information system. New members of staff may join the development team part way in the project (particularly if the project is behind schedule). Detailed documentation is therefore needed to enable someone else to continue with the development.
- Documentation is needed to ensure that an accurate understanding of the user requirements has been obtained. Some companies ask users to sign-off documentation, to confirm that the system to be developed will meet their requirements.
- Documentation is needed to maintain the system after implementation. Many companies divide systems development staff into project and maintenance teams. In this environment, the staff who developed the system are not the same as those who will be maintaining the system. Companies may be using information systems which were developed 30 years ago. Documentation is needed to understand what the programs are actually doing and to show why certain changes were made.
- Documentation is sometimes considered to be boring and many developers put off producing the documentation. The low priority given is often reflected in documentation that is of poor quality, inaccurate and incomplete. Drawing tools will make good documentation more likely.
- Many methodologies encourage documentation to be produced during the systems development process rather than at the end. Various forms and reports need to be completed during the development. A phase of development is not complete until the required documentation has been produced.
- Documentation produced on paper is difficult to maintain. The addition of a process on a data flow diagram, for example, may require a number of changes to be made at other levels in the diagram. Models such as entity-relationship models and data flow diagrams also require the data dictionary to be maintained to ensure that all participants in the development have a common understanding of key concepts.

All the above tools - data dictionaries and repositories, drawing and documentation tools - along with database management systems, 4GLs, report writer, form manager, screen painter, and languages, can be incorporated into a CASE tool.

10.5   Object-oriented CASE tools

Object-oriented based CASE tools are intended to support object-oriented software development (see section 13.5). As with other CASE tools they are based on the idea that software tools could be used to automate aspects of the software development process.

At the heart of a CASE tool is the repository in which all the components resulting from analysis, design and coding are stored. The repository is responsible for keeping track of all the interdependencies between elements produced during different phases of the development process, for example a change in one diagram should be reflected in all other relevant parts.

In the late 1980s, IBM launched its AD/Cycle repository project whose aim was to provide a single repository that all CASE products could use. The idea was that such a repository would allow diagrams created in one CASE tool to be used to generate those in another CASE tool used for a subsequent stage of development. In 1991 IBM cancelled the AD/Cycle project. The demise of the project was for a number of reasons:

- The project was begun when CASE tools were being used to create standard COBOL applications for mainframes, such as accounting and transaction processing systems.
- The shift was towards new types of applications such as client-server and CASE tools were required for these.
- Another shift was away from traditional procedural programming languages towards object-oriented ones.
- The number of different tools, approaches, data types, analysis and design constructs was far too much to be able to be accommodated in the AD/Cycle project.

A more popular term for describing such software tools is Application Development Environments (ADEs) or AD tools, but this includes the conventional idea of CASE and graphical programming tools like IBM's VisualAge and the graphical 4GL tools like PowerBuilder.

The application development tool market is moving towards distributed, scaleable, object-oriented products. They help to produce object-oriented, on-line transaction processing applications using a client-server architecture. Products include Forté, Dynasty and Composer. These products have dynamic partitioning capabilities, which allow developers to drag and drop object classes onto a client or a server machine. Some of the tools allow:

- *Object sharing:* enabling multiple tasks to access an object concurrently and change its data.
- *Object distribution:* enabling the object to be sent to a remote partition.
- *Object transaction participation:* enforcing the basic rules of a transaction (atomicity, consistency, isolation and durability).
- *Object monitoring:* enabling display and mapping of object to a window.

High-end tools are appearing on the market. These are defined to be those tools which are expensive and risky, and require a longer learning cycle than a 'low-end' tool. They require senior management approval and more time to consider, and are more challenging for IT management. It is necessary to analyse return on investment and justify payback, because they are expensive.

However, they can considerably reduce the development time of applications and can reduce the cost of applications development and maintenance. Vendors claim that they are reliable, open, portable to many platforms and high-performing. Nevertheless, there is still a need to perform rigorous analysis in terms of requirements and design.

Ideally, tools should be selected after deciding on a methodology to be used. In practice, however, the two tend to be done concurrently. Investing in a concrete product such as a CASE tool is easier than investing and understanding an abstract concept such as a methodology.

The ideas of Booch (1994), Jacobsen (1992) and Rumbaugh (1991) have been merged into the Unified Modeling Language which is likely to become a *de facto* standard set of object-oriented modelling semantics.

Some object-oriented modelling tools also generate code which accelerates the transition from analysis and design to construction. The disadvantages of object-oriented tools are that they have limited capability for mapping the object model to a relational schema (the standard model for database management systems). Current relational databases do not support inheritance and this represents a design challenge. The organisations that use high-end object-oriented tools effectively are finding the process a non-trivial undertaking. Issues such as learning the tools' object framework, maintaining the models, concurrently undertaking business process reengineering (BPR) with customers ensuring that business-driven applications are being built, addressing training issues and standardising, all present challenges.

Examples of object-oriented CASE tools are, TI Compose from Texas Instruments, Usoft Developer from Usoft, Forté from Forté Software Inc., Natstar from Natstar International, Sapiens ObjectPool from Sapiens, Object Star from Antares Alliance Group and Visual Age from IBM.

10.6 Summary

In this chapter we have looked at the ways in which computer tools can assist the process of information systems development. We have stressed the use of CASE tools, fourth generation languages and database management systems, but other tools, such as those for object-oriented methods and client-server technology have also been briefly described. We have also discussed the importance of good documentation in the successful design, development and maintenance of information systems. By using automated tools, that documentation should be more easily and cheaply produced, according to the standards of the organisation.

Further reading

Avison, D. E. (1992) *Information Systems Development: A Database Approach.* 2nd edition, McGraw-Hill, Maidenhead.
A detailed discussion of databases and database environment is discussed along with 4GLs.

Clifton, H. D. & Sutcliffe, A. G. (1994) *Business Information Systems*, 5th edition, Prentice-Hall, Chichester.
This contains a discussion of DBMS and 4GLs.

Curtis, B. (1992) The CASE for Process, In K. E. Kendall., K. Lyytinen. & J. I. DeGross. (eds.), *The Impact of Computer Supported Technologies on Information Systems Development*, North-Holland, Amsterdam.
Discusses the apparent lack of success of CASE and the reasons for it.

Iivari, J. (1996) Why are CASE tools not used?, *Communications of the ACM*, **39**, 10, pp. 94-103.
Examines attitudes towards CASE usage in a wide variety of organisations.

Iivari, J. (1995) Factors affecting the perceptions of CASE effectiveness, *European Journal of Information Systems*, **4**, 143-158.
This paper studies the impact of a number of variables in the perceptions of CASE effectiveness. It reports the findings of a survey of 105 individual CASE users.

Linthicum, D. S. (1997) Driving development: a look at the reasoning behind today's application development tools, *DBMS*, April 1997.

Mathiassen, L. and Sorensen, C. (1996) The capability maturity model and CASE, *Information Systems Journal*, **6**, pp. 195-208.
This paper reviews software process maturity as a framework for CASE introduction, trying to identify the strengths and limits of this approach and to identify the most important supplementary issues.

Questions

1. What categories of tools can be used in the information systems development life cycle?
2. Discuss the different types of CASE tools.
3. What benefits are claimed for CASE?
4. What are the issues that must be considered when introducing CASE into organisations?
5. Distinguish between a DBMS and a fourth generation system/fourth generation language.
6. List the reasons for the development of 4GLs.
7. Discuss the main characteristics of a 4GL.
8. List the components of a 4GL.
9. What are data dictionaries and repositories?
10. Explain the importance of documentation in information systems development and explain how tools might support documentation products.

Areas to debate

1. A senior executive in an organisation thinks it a good idea to introduce CASE technology into an organisation for information systems development activities. How would you construct a report detailing how the organisation should go about this change.

CASE STUDY

Which tools described in this chapter might be relevant to Asifiori Salons? Describe how they might fit into the organisation. Would other aspects be relevant if the organisation was much bigger?

Chapter 11

SSADM

11.1 What, Why, When....?

As we have seen, structured systems methodologies provide an appropriate framework within which information systems development can be carried out. These methodologies try to provide control over areas where there are potential problems. Information systems development involves cost, delay and quality problems. There is therefore a need for a better way of carrying out such projects. One approach to dealing with this has been the development of appropriate methodologies for managing the design and development of information systems.

In our description of the information systems development life cycle (Chapters 4-9), we described a generic structured approach. In this chapter, we describe a commercial methodology, Structured Systems Analysis and Design Method (SSADM). SSADM is a methodology developed originally by UK consultants Learmonth and Burchett Management Systems (LBMS) and the Central Computing and Telecommunications Agency (CCTA) which is responsible for computer training and some procurement for the UK Civil Service. SSADM has been used in a number of government applications since 1981 and its use has been mandatory for many Civil Service applications since 1983. It is said to be a data-driven methodology because of its history and emphasis on data modelling and the database, but in its later versions it has become more balanced, with, for example, importance attached to the role of the users. It is an important methodology, particularly in the UK, and version 4 was released in June 1990. A description of the methodology can be found in Downs *et al.* (1988), Weaver (1993), Eva (1994) and in its complete form in NCC (1995). The following represents only an outline of SSADM and is based on the much more detailed description found in Weaver (1993).

The methodology provides project development staff with very detailed rules and guidelines to work to. It is highly structured. Another reason for its success has been in the standards provided (often exercised by completing pre-printed documents). Documentation pervades all aspects of the information systems project.

SSADM version 4 has seven stages (numbered 0 to 6 in section 11.3 below) within a five 'module' framework (the first set of bullet points in that section) with its own set of plans, timescales, controls and monitoring procedures. The activities of each stage are precisely defined as are their associated end-products (or deliverables), and this facilitates the use of project management techniques (the project management method PRINCE is recommended, see section 3.4). Over the years the approach has been continually developed and improved as a result of practical experience and the incorporation of new ideas and techniques.

SSADM is a typical structured approach. It uses systems analysis and design techniques to help structure a project into units of manageable size, where the activities making up those units are well defined and the sequence and interaction of these activities are clearly specified. It uses diagrammatic and other modelling techniques to produce a structured definition that is both precise and understandable by users and developers. The use of structured methods helps in producing a clear statement of requirements that is understandable and is also an appropriate foundation for the subsequent design and development of the required system.

The use of this structured approach allows for improved project planning, management and control. The decomposition of the project into appropriate stages and steps allows better estimation of time and resources required to complete the project. This level of detail also allows problems to be identified sooner rather than later. Using an approach such as SSADM is also considered to lead to better quality systems. The techniques ensure a comprehensive specification leading to this quality system. In addition, the use of structured techniques leads to systems that are flexible and easier to change. Structured methods include formal quality assurance reviews and informal walkthroughs which involve user participation. This ensures that the users' requirements are met in the system implemented.

SSADM works by building up several different views of the system. These different views are used to cross-check for consistency and completeness. The three views are:

- *The underlying structure of the data in the system.* This is the entity-relationship model (discussed in section 6.3), which is called a logical data structure in SSADM terminology.
- *The data flows into and out of the system and their transformation within the system.* This is the set of data flow diagrams (discussed in section 6.6).
- *The way in which the data in the system changes.* These are the entity life histories (discussed in section 6.13).

SSADM combines the various techniques into a framework which includes guidance on how and when to use them.

11.2   SSADM and the information systems development life cycle

Although SSADM is used in information systems development, it does not cover the entire information systems development life cycle. The diagram shown in Figure 13.1 shows a comparison of SSADM stages with the life cycle phases that we have established in the earlier chapters of the book.

SSADM does not provide any support for the information systems planning stage. It is therefore important that this activity is carried out before the start of an SSADM project. SSADM provides some guidelines for the project initiation activities. These include setting up the project, agreeing terms of reference, assigning team members and drawing up preliminary plans.

SSADM provides detailed guidelines for conducting feasibility studies. It gives details of the steps and stages required. For the systems analysis stage, SSADM specifies the means of recording and analysing the results of the investigation. This is dealt with by Stages 1, 2 and 3 of SSADM. Stage 1 is concerned with the analysis of the current system, stage 2 with producing outline systems design and stage 3 specifies the requirements of the new system.

In systems design, various technical solutions that meet the requirements are evaluated and one is selected. A detailed logical design of the new system is developed showing, in non-technical terminology, how the system will function within the organisation. SSADM stages 2, 3, 4 and 5 deal with the activities of this phase of the life cycle. During the physical system design activities, the logical design is mapped to the specific hardware and software selected. Further, file structures and/or

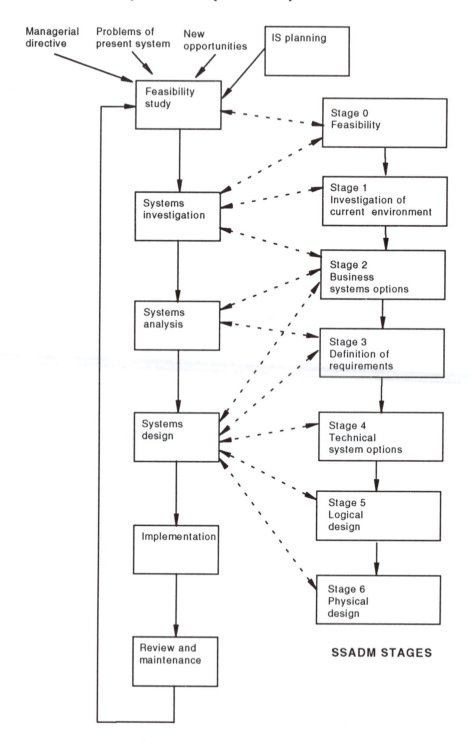

Fig. 13.1: The information systems life cycle and SSADM

database definitions are specified, as well as the specification of programs and detailed manual procedures. This activity is dealt with by stage 6 of SSADM.

SSADM does not provide any direct support for the construction phase, although there is indirect support through the planning activities carried out in Stages 4 and 6 of SSADM. Similarly, SSADM does not provide any direct support for the systems implementation phase which involves the transition from the old system to the new system. However, the plans for this activity are developed in SSADM stage 4. Finally, SSADM does not provide support for the production and review phases of the information systems life cycle.

As this section makes obvious, although SSADM is a structured approach to developing information systems, like other commercial approaches, it does not correspond exactly to the 'ideal' type proffered in this book.

11.3   SSADM overview

SSADM is essentially a data-based approach. The fundamental assumption is that the data structure is more stable over time than the process structure and less prone to change. Therefore, within this approach, data is modelled at an early stage. The final system architecture is based on the underlying data structures.

The SSADM framework consists of a number of modules made up of stages. Each of these stages is made up of a series of steps which use appropriate techniques for the tasks involved. The stages and steps have defined inputs and outputs. In addition, there are a number of forms and documents which are completed to record specific items of relevant information.

The SSADM modules are:

- Feasibility study (Stage 0)
- Requirements analysis (Stages 1 and 2)
- Requirements specification (Stage 3)
- Logical systems specification (Stages 4 and 5)
- Physical design (Stage 6).

The stages in SSADM are:

- Stage 0: Feasibility
- Stage 1: Investigation of current environment
- Stage 2: Business systems options
- Stage 3: Definition of requirements

- Stage 4: Technical system options
- Stage 5: Logical design
- Stage 6: Physical design.

The feasibility study stage is considered optional in the SSADM approach, as this is considered to be something that is carried out during the information systems planning activities. In addition, projects are sometimes considered to be such a fundamental requirement that it does not require an assessment of feasibility.

STAGE 0 - Feasibility study

- Prepare for the feasibility study
- Define the problem
- Select feasibility options
- Create feasibility report.

STAGE 1 - Investigation of current environment

- Establish analysis framework
- Investigate and define requirements
- Investigate current processing
- Investigate current data
- Derive logical view of current system
- Assemble investigation results.

The techniques used during this stage are observation, interviewing and others discussed in Chapter 5.

STAGE 2 - Business system options

- Define business system options
- Select business system option.

Data flow diagrams are widely used in this stage.

STAGE 3 - Definition of requirements

- Define required system processing
- Develop required data model
- Develop specification prototypes
- Derive system functions
- Enhance required data model
- Develop processing specification

- Confirm system objectives
- Assemble requirements specification.

STAGE 4 - Selection of technical options

- Define technical system options
- Select technical system options.

STAGE 5 - Logical design

- Define user dialogues
- Define update processes
- Define enquiry processes
- Assemble logical design.

STAGE 6 - Physical design

- Prepare for physical design
- Create physical data design
- Create function component implementation map
- Optimise physical data design
- Complete function specification
- Consolidate process data interface
- Assemble physical design.

These modules cover the life cycle from feasibility study to design, but not program design. Planning is therefore assumed to have been done, and the stages following design are presumably seen as installation-specific, and therefore not covered by the methodology. We will now look in outline at each of the seven stages of SSADM.

0 Feasibility

This stage is concerned with ensuring that the project which has been suggested in the planning phase is feasible, that is, it is technically possible and the benefits of the information system will outweigh the costs.

This phase has four steps: prepare for the study, which assesses the scope of the project; define the problem, which compares the requirements with the current position; select feasibility option, which considers alternatives and selects one; and assemble feasibility report.

Systems investigation techniques, such as interviewing, questionnaires and so on, discussed in Chapter 5, are used in this stage as are the 'newer' techniques of data flow diagramming (referred to as data flow models), drawn from an analysis of the flow of documents. The latter have different symbols (see Figure 11.2), but essentially the technique is the same as described in section 6.7. Entity models (referred to as logical data structures) similar to that described in section 6.4 are drawn. As one would expect at the feasibility stage, these are all done in outline and in not too great a detail. This detail will come in later stages.

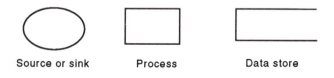

Source or sink   Process   Data store

Fig 11.2: Data flow diagram symbols in SSADM

The requirements of the new system, in terms of what the system will do and constraints on the system, are partly defined by considering the weaknesses of the present system. Once the problem has been defined in this way, it is possible to consider the various alternatives (there might be up to five business options and a similar number of technical solutions) and recommend the best option from both the business and technical points of view. All this information is then published in the feasibility report.

1 Investigation of current environment

The second module, requirements analysis, has two stages: investigation of current requirements and business system options. This module sets the scene for the later stages, because it enables a full understanding of the requirements of the new system to be gained and establishes the direction of the rest of the project.

The first of these stages repeats much of the work carried out at the feasibility study stage but in more detail. For example, at the feasibility stage, the data flow diagrams may not have included much of the processing which is not related to the major tasks nor decomposed to more than two levels of detail (level 3 diagrams would be the norm at this stage). Further, the conflicts and ambiguities of the entity model need to be resolved. Indeed, in some projects, the feasibility stage is carried out very much in outline and the investigation of current environment may have much less of a basis for the tasks of this stage.

The results of the feasibility study are examined and the scope of the project reassessed and the overall plan agreed with management. The requirements of the new system are examined along with investigating the current processing methods and data of the current system, again in more detail than that carried out at the feasibility stage. The present physical data flow model is mapped onto a logical data flow model and this helps to assess the present functionality required in the new system. Matrices might be constructed which, for example, show the relationship between processes and entities (that is, which processes access the information in the various entities). Catalogues will be created, such as the user catalogue, which lists the activities carried out in each job, and the requirements catalogue, which lists the functional and non-functional requirements. Again, there is a complete description of the results of this stage assembled and reviewed as the deliverable.

2 Business systems options

It is at this stage that the functionality of the new system is determined and agreed. The user requirements were set out in stage 1, but it is at stage 2 that only those requirements which are cost-justified are carried forward (using standard cost benefit analysis techniques) and these requirements are specified in greater detail. A number of business system options are outlined, all satisfying this minimum set of user requirements, and a few of these are presented to management so that one can be chosen (or a hybrid option chosen, taken from a number of the options presented). Each of these will have an outline of its cost, development time scale, technical constraints, physical organisation, volumes, training requirements, benefits and impacts on the organisation. The option chosen is documented in detail and agreed as the basis of the system specification which is the next stage of SSADM. Data flow diagrams and entity models are developed, but this stage is largely a specification in narrative.

3 Definition of requirements

This stage leads to the full requirements specification and provides clear guidance to the design stages which follow. Weaver (1993) describes this stage as the 'engine room' of SSADM where investigation and analysis are replaced by specification and design. For example, stress is placed on the required system design rather than the functionality of the current system. The requirements catalogue will be consulted and updated and the logical entity model extended followed by normalisation (section 6.6) of the relations (to third normal form). The data flow model is also extended and used as a communication tool with users, with the definition of user roles in the new system, but it is the entity model which is emphasised at this stage and is the essential basis of the logical design of the new system. Documentation forms for all the entities and attributes are completed.

Although the data model is emphasised at this stage, the components of each function (in terms of inputs, outputs and events or enquiry triggers) are defined. Each function is documented in detail and a form is used which includes space for function name, description, error handling, data flow diagram processes, events and input and output descriptions. Structure diagrams (section 7.9) are used to show the input and output structures. Further documentation shows other detail, such as the relationship between user roles and functions (via a user role/function matrix).

This stage in SSADM also has an optional prototyping phase. The methodology suggests demonstrating prototypes of critical dialogues and menu structures to users and this will verify the analysts' understanding of the users' requirements and their preferences for interface design. As well as verifying the specification, this phase can have other benefits such as increased user commitment.

Entity life histories (section 6.13) are also constructed during this phase. These document all the events which can affect an entity type and model the applicable business rules. Events affecting each entity may have been identified previously by constructing an event/entity matrix and entity/function matrix (see Figure 11.3). This is referred to as a CRUD matrix, where C=create, R=read, U=update and D=delete). Finally, at this stage, the system objectives are verified, the functions checked for completeness of definition and the full requirements specification documented.

The diagramming conventions used in drawing entity life cycles (called in SSADM 'entity life histories') are very similar to the entity structure step conventions of Jackson System Development (JSD), another 'brand-name' methodology for information systems development. In SSADM, the diagrams look like hierarchies, but they are meant to be read from left to right, and, in so doing, progressively suggest the different states of the entity. Using an example from the academic world, Figure 11.4(a) shows how the entity 'student' changes over time, as an applicant, registered student and graduate (there will be other intermediary states). Figure 11.4(b) shows the use of the selection construct, whereby the 'o' in the 'applicant with offer' and 'rejected applicant' boxes denote alternative conditions (these are mutually exclusive). Figure 11.4(c) illustrates the iteration construct, marked with an asterisk, which shows an event that may repeat (in this example, the possible repeated suspension and re-registration of a student who might regularly pay fees late).

Figure 11.5 presents an SSADM entity life history. The first level contains the events that cause an entity to be initiated into the system and those events that terminate the entity from the system. There is an iteration construct relating to whether the student is accepted conditionally or not,

Entity Name	Staff member	Group session	Location	Programme type	Patient
Function name					
Group session attendances	R	U	R		C/U
Programmes	R			R	R
Contacts traced	R				U
Assessments	R				R/U/D
Programme costing	R			U	R

Fig. 11.3: Entity/function matrix

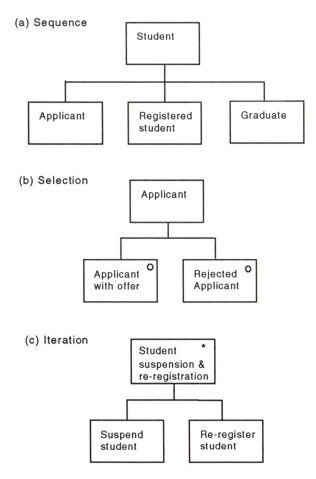

(a) Sequence

Student

Applicant | Registered student | Graduate

(b) Selection

Applicant

Applicant with offer | Rejected Applicant

(c) Iteration

Student suspension & re-registration

Suspend student | Re-register student

Fig. 11.4: SSADM entity life history constructs

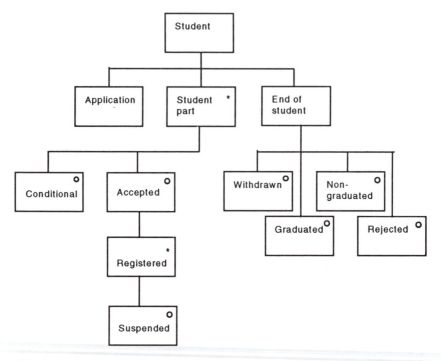

Fig. 11.5: Student entity life history

and to reflect suspended or registered states. There are four states for the end condition: withdrawn, graduated, non-graduated or rejected. These are all mutually exclusive (the selection construct). Notice that in this model it is not possible to show that 'graduated' can only happen from registered and that 'suspended' can only terminate with non-graduated. Thus, some information is lost in this representation of the entity life cycle.

4 Technical system options

This stage and the following stage are carried out in parallel. In the technical system options stage, the environment in which the system will operate, in terms of the hardware and software configuration, development strategy, organisational impact and system functionality, is determined.

The definition of technical options will be implementation specific, because there are so many alternative hardware, software and implementation strategies. The analysts need to identify constraints, for example, the hardware platform may be 'given' along with time and cost maxima and minima. System constraints might include performance, security and service level requirements that must be met and these will limit choice. Technical system options need to meet all these constraints and a chosen option has to be agreed with management.

5 Logical design

This is a statement of what the system is required to do rather than a statement about the procedures or program specifications to do it. The latter is the realm of the final stage 6, the physical design. In stage 5 the dialogue structures and menu structures and designs are defined for particular users or user roles. User involvement is recommended at this stage and the prototypes developed in stage 3 are referred to. Furthermore, following the entity life cycles designed in stage 3 (which are developed further), the update processes and operations are defined along with the processing of enquiries, including the sequence of processing. In other words, it is at this stage that further detail about how the system will apply and control of the operations following each event will be defined. Detail such as the rules of validating data entered into the system, will be specified. All the requirements to start designing the physical solution are now in place.

6 Physical design

It is at this final stage that the logical design is mapped onto a particular physical environment. A function component implementation map (FCIM) documents this mapping. The phase provides guidelines regarding physical implementation and these should be applicable to most hardware and software configurations. However, this stage will be carried out with the actual configuration in mind. The roles of the technologist, the programmer and database designers in particular, are stressed in this phase, although the analyst and user should be available to verify that the final design satisfies user requirements.

The logical data model will be converted into a design appropriate for the database management system available. The database mapping will be a key aspect of final implementation and include not only the way data and data relationships are held on the database, but also key handling and access methods. Much will depend on performance measurement so that database access is efficient, and again this will depend on the actual hardware and software configuration (including database management system).

The function component implementation map lists the components of each logical function and their mapping onto the physical components of the operational system. The principles of the FCIM are well specified in SSADM, although the form of the FCIM is somewhat ambiguously expressed. Presumably, this is seen as dependent on the standards of the particular organisation. Designs are optimised according to storage and timing objectives. From this stage it should be possible to design and develop the programs necessary to provide the required functionality. It is at this point that SSADM stops and detailed software design and testing starts.

The well-defined structure of SSADM make it teachable and many UK university courses in information systems have used this methodology for in-depth treatment and discuss other methodologies in overview only for comparative purposes. Its three basic techniques, entity models, data flow diagrams and entity life histories, are common to most methodologies and they ensure that there has been a detailed analysis of the target system. Along with the well defined tasks, and guidance with the techniques, the methodology defines the outputs expected from the stage, and gives time and resource management guidelines.

SSADM is expected to be used along with computer tools and there are many tools designed specifically for users of SSADM as well as those designed for other methodologies which are also useful to followers of SSADM. There are, for example, a number of CASE tools (section 10.2), supported by data dictionaries and systems repositories (section 10.4) which help analysis and design, some generating code from the SSADM design, and drawing tools (section 10.4), to help draw entity-relationship diagrams, entity life histories and data flow diagrams, and all these can be very supportive of the information systems development process.

The proponents of the methodology also recommend 'quality assurance reviews' based on structured walkthroughs (which were described in section 7.11). They are meetings held to review identifiable end products of the various phases of the methodology, such as entity models, data flow diagrams, entity life histories and process details. Usually, the end product is presented by the authors and reviewed by personnel from related project teams (helping good communications between project teams and ensuring a common standard of work), specialist quality assurance teams or groups of users. The purpose of the meetings is to identify errors in the product. Solutions are resolved outside the meeting. Post implementation feedback is also encouraged and there is an audit at this time.

The successful implementation of the methodology relies on the skills of key personnel being available, though the techniques and tools are widely known and the project team method of working, along with systems walkthroughs, encourages good training procedures and participation. SSADM emphasises good documentation standards, clear and detailed guidelines and thorough quality assurance.

11.4   Summary

The basic approach to information systems development presented in this text is based around the information systems development life cycle, using a variety of structured tools and techniques. In this chapter we have looked at SSADM, a 'brand name' methodology which is widely used to develop information systems. Although some of the 'ideal type' steps are missing in SSADM, and not all the other steps correspond, there is similarity between the two approaches.

Further reading

Avison, D. E. & Fitzgerald, G. (1995) *Information Systems Development: Methodologies Techniques and Tools*, 2nd edition, McGraw-Hill, Maidenhead.

Downs, E., Clare, P. & Coe, I. (1988) *Structured Systems Analysis and Design Method: Application and Context*. 2nd edition, Prentice-Hall, Hemel Hempstead.

Eva, M. (1994) *SSADM Version 4: A User's Guide*. 2nd edition, McGraw-Hill, Maidenhead.

NCC (1995) *SSADM 4+: Version 4.2*. Volumes 1 and 2, NCC Blackwell, Oxford.

Weaver, P. L. (1993*) Practical SSADM Version 4: A Complete Tutorial Guide*. Pitman, London.

Questions

1.   What is SSADM?
2.   Give a brief description of the stages and modules of SSADM. Give a brief description of each.
3.   Show how SSADM differs from the 'ideal' life cycle approach discussed in this book in Chapters 4-9.

Areas to debate

1.   'Using a systems development life cycle approach such as SSADM is a waste of time. More effort is expended on the approach rather than the information system'. Discuss.

CASE STUDY

Describe the development process using SSADM for Asifiori Salons? Is such a methodology necessary for developing systems for them? Would it be more relevant if the organisation was much bigger?

Chapter 12

THE INFORMATION SYSTEMS LIFE CYCLE REVISITED

12.1 People, politics and organisations

In this text we have proposed the use of the information systems life cycle as a means of understanding information systems development and demonstrated its potential to provide an effective means of planning, monitoring and controlling the complex and difficult task of information systems development. Readers should note, however, that we have been continually simplifying what is by its very nature a complex process which results in complex products.

In this chapter we discuss the criticisms of the information systems life cycle espoused in this book and offer arguments to counter some of them. We look briefly at some of the current ideas in information systems development in the areas of methodologies, techniques and tools.

One of the problems with developing any system is that of problem migration. Information systems development tends to take a long time and yet the real world in which the problem is set moves on and there is a tendency for specification drift to occur. In essence this means that the requirements of the clients do not remain static but evolve as the business evolves.

- *Environment drift:* these are the changes of the environment in the information systems project which alter the nature and needs of that aspect of the business for which the system is being developed.
- *Specification drift:* these are the changes which result from the actual process of the user discussing the problem with the systems analyst causing the user to re-evaluate the problem and its solution. There may be a change in emphasis or a realisation that the proposed solution is not what is required since it addresses the wrong problem.
- *Solution drift:* these are the changes that result from the clients' use of the delivered solution. In this case what changes is the clients' perception of what support is desirable, rather then the environment or the specification.

Problem migration can be the cause of problems in information systems development even when appropriate tools and techniques, such as those provided in structured approaches, are used.

It may have been assumed by our discussions so far that users are happy to adopt the new ways of working that might arise as a result of new information systems developed for them, but this is not always the case. Indeed, it is very likely that despite ostensible enthusiasm, there is always an of resistance to new systems because of the natural conservatism of employees in organisations.

Reactions to the new information systems will vary from enthusiasm through acceptance to outright hostility. This hostility, although often misplaced, could arise as a result of misunderstanding about the aims and consequences of the project. On the other hand, it could be fully justified as information systems sometimes result in a decrease in the quality and quantity of work. Even enthusiasm can be problematic, since excessive expectations can result in disappointment and non co-operation as the actual system is installed.

The process of introducing change can be seen as having three phases:

- *Unfreeze:* In the existing environment of the organisation the current processes are established, social structures have been built around them and users have created models which incorporate them. This situation could be described as stable, even cosy, in which change seems very negative. The first stage of introducing change involves the realisation that the present situation is in some sense not optimal, could be improved on, and possibly needs to be improved. During this unfreezing process people begin to accept the need for change.

- *Change:* The second stage is the change during which the new way of working is introduced. During this stage staff should get the chance to try out the new system, modify it to suit their own needs, and to assess its value. There needs to be substantial support to users in terms of explaining what the system is meant to do and training so that users can help it achieve that objective.

- *Refreeze:* It is not possible to live continually in an environment of change and the new way of doing things needs to be absorbed and set, so that it becomes the standard against which reference is made, not the exception which is continually referenced with respect to the 'old way'. This refreezing process marks the successful end of the innovation.

Because people do not tend to like change, successful innovation usually requires an active agent close to or within the group undergoing the change. This agent is usually referred to as a **champion** and that is the person who is likely to have identified the possibility of change and its potential value. The champion may well identify a new solution and adopt it first, operating within the change group and demonstrate the success of the new system. The champion can act as propagandist, constructive critic in negotiation with suppliers or developers, and can help train other users. An effective champion is important to the success of organisational change. In many organisations ambitious staff provide the champion function and expect to move on riding on the crest of the success of the project. For these reasons it is important that the refreeze phase is completed, otherwise the departure of the champion may lead to the group reverting to old practices.

12.2 Reflections on the life cycle

The information systems development life cycle discussed in this book has been the target of a number of criticisms. Some experts believe that alternative systems development techniques and methodologies have replaced the life cycle. However, many of these other approaches complement the life cycle rather than replace it. The life cycle is not obsolete since its purpose is to assist in the planning, execution and control of the information systems development project. Without such a formalised approach, the result is likely to be an information system developed which exceeds budgets and time constraints and if it does reach the implementation stage is likely to be difficult to maintain.

The information systems development life cycle describes the activities and tasks which are essential to systems development. For example, in our description of the life cycle, we have stressed the importance of studying and understanding the current system. This task would need to be carried out regardless of the approach being used, since we cannot hope to change what we do not understand. The life cycle will always provide a useful **framework** within which to consider various tools, techniques and methodologies. The detailed discussion of the life cycle that we have carried out in this text has drawn on these tools and techniques whenever appropriate.

The following are some of the criticisms that have been levelled at the information systems development life cycle:

- *Failure to meet management needs:* systems developed focus at the operational level of the company and not the needs of senior management.
- *Automates existing problems:* systems developed often encapsulate all the problems of the old system by simply doing the wrong thing faster.
- *Output-driven design:* the focus on deliverables of the system, such as reports, so early in the system design makes modification to those outputs difficult.
- *Failure to meet corporate needs:* systems developed are not flexible enough to meet the needs of the dynamic business.
- *Poor documentation:* documentation produced might be rushed and incomplete.
- *Application backlog:* systems are slow to develop and the waiting list of further applications grows.
- *Maintenance overload:* as the systems developed did not meet some user requirements, a high level of systems maintenance is required to modify the systems adding to the applications backlog.

Many of these criticisms concern how the information systems development life cycle has been applied, rather than the life cycle itself. For example, the second criticism that the systems developed automated existing problems, is due to poor systems analysis and design, not to the life cycle approach itself. The life cycle is in the hands of the analysts and designers. It provides a framework for planning, executing and controlling project development. It is not a substitute for the demanding skills of creativity and vision that are required of the systems analyst and designer (and the users).

The life cycle that we have presented includes many modern developments in tools, techniques and methodologies. It is very different from the 'systems development life cycle' that was presented in texts of the 1970s and 1980s. We have advocated the use of these at various points of the life cycle. For example, the use of the following would be either unusual or non-existent in any similar text of that earlier period:

- Rich pictures
- Entity-relationship modelling
- Structured programming
- Structured English
- Data flow diagrams
- Entity life histories
- Data dictionaries
- Systems repositories
- Fourth generation languages
- CASE tools.

There are many other approaches which may have aspects that can usefully be incorporated into a modern information systems development life cycle. Some of these will now be discussed.

12.3 Object-oriented analysis and design

In Section 10.5 we looked at object-oriented CASE tools and will look in more depth at object-oriented systems in Chapter 13. In this section we look at the methodologies for analysis and design that are based on object-oriented concepts.

Object-oriented analysis and design methodologies do not replace traditional approaches and can be considered as important new additions to the developer's toolkit. Object approaches require the developer to think in terms of objects and object classes. A class is any uniquely identified abstraction or model of a set of logically related instances that share the same or similar characteristics. For example, an object class 'Employee', might have attributes 'Name', 'Address'. It may also have methods amongst which are 'AddEmployee', 'UpdateEmployee', 'DeleteEmployee' or 'CheckEmployee'. The definition of the class 'Employee' will define the attributes and methods of the 'Employee' class. A real employee such as 'John Smith' is an instance of the class. If for example there are different kinds of employees, two new classes of employee which are descendants of the original employee class can be created. These descendants use inheritance to gain access to all of the Employee class attributes and methods. They also have the ability to override any of the ancestor's attributes and methods and can also contain any new attributes and methods that might be required.

In object-oriented analysis and design there are three types of relationships between classes which are:

- *Inheritance (generalisation/specialisation):* commonly referred to by the phrase 'is a kind of'
- *Aggregation:* commonly referred to by the phrase 'is part of'
- *Association:* if the relationship is not of the above two types but the objects are clearly related, for example, employee is related to the company that employs him, then the relationship is an association.

Classes are often categorised as:

- *Abstract:* this is a class that has no instances and is used for inheritance only
- *Concrete:* this is a class that can have instances, that is can be instantiated.

There are a number of different object-oriented analysis and design methodologies. However they have a similar fundamental view about objects, classes, inheritance and relationships. They will differ with respect to notation, features, cost of use, type of problem it is suited to, limitations and whether training is available. The methodologies which are becoming accepted (Gora, 1996) include Coad and Yourdon (1991).

This methodology focuses on analysis of business problems. It consists of five stages for analysis and four stages for design. The analysis stages are:

- *Subjects:* similar to levels in data flow diagramming
- *Objects:* specification of object classes
- *Structures:* organised into two groups, classification structures corresponding to inheritance relationships and composition structures corresponding to other types of relationships between classes

- *Attributes:* similar to attributes in the relational model
- *Services:* called methods or operations in other approaches.

The design stages are:

- *Problem domain component:* classes that deal with the problem domain, such as employee class and order class
- *Human interaction component:* user interface classes, such as window class and menu class
- *Task management component:* system management classes such as error classes and security classes
- *Data management component:* classes that deal with data such as database access method classes.

Rational Software employed three other 'names' in object-orientation, Grady Booch, James Rumbaugh and Ivar Jacobsen. They have been collaborating on what was originally referred to as a 'Unified Method' but is now known as the 'Unified Modeling Language' or UML. The idea behind UML is that it is a graphical modelling and documentation notation for describing the structure and behaviour of object-oriented applications, which can be used with any object-oriented methodology. This collaboration may result in establishing the object-orientation approach as an alternative to the relational approach that features in this book.

12.4   Client-server development

We will look in more depth at client-server systems in Chapter 13. Shimberg (1995) identifies a need for a client-server methodology based on the premise that traditional methodologies were not created to support modern technologies such as graphical user interfaces (GUIs), object-oriented concepts and rapid application development (RAD) methods which are associated with client-server computing. He recognises the essential differences between client-server and traditional applications as well as the extreme diversities in the developers' backgrounds and skill sets, and identifies a client-server methodology as involving the following components:

- *An integrated object-oriented model:* different to the relational model since it includes both enterprise entities and attributes as well as the methods associated with those entities which describe their interaction and behaviour in the system.

- *A good GUI design:* developed in close collaboration with users.
- *GUI consistency:* achieved through the use of standards.
- *Reusability:* achieved through a proper architecture and application layering.
- *A customisable architecture:* driven by user tasks
- *RAD techniques:* help deliver quality systems as quickly as possible.
- *Intensive prototyping techniques:* used in sessions with the users to gather the requirements and model the system.
- *Intensive database techniques:* used in sessions that address database issues specific to client-server applications.

The emphasis is on the methodology being customisable with respect to processes and components that might already be in place. However, these customisations should be overseen by a standards organisation or quality control group in order to prevent the quality of the product from being compromised due to unsuitable customisation.

12.5 Information engineering (IE)

Information engineering is a data-driven approach that is also process-sensitive. It is intended to be applied across the whole organisation, or some major part of it, rather than to individual projects. It emphasises, in particular, systems planning (lacking in SSADM), which it defines as the improvement of the organisation through information technology. It covers most of the life cycle. It is intended to be used to identify mission-critical data and functions that should be supported through technology. The approach involves the following phases:

- Strategic planning is carried out for the sector or organisation in question.
- The resulting strategic plan is used to identify appropriate business areas.
- A selected business area is further analysed using appropriate structured techniques.
- Subsystems identified in the selected business area are prioritised, designed and developed, again using appropriate structured techniques.
- The preceding two activities are repeated for other business areas.

The central component of the information engineering approach is the data of the organisation. Energy is directed into ensuring that the design, capture and storage of the data is satisfactorily.

12.6 Joint application development (JAD)

This technique places emphasis on people as opposed to data and processes. Its purpose is to bring together users, managers and information systems professionals, to specify user requirements, technical options and the design of inputs and outputs. By attaining greater management participation in the systems development life cycle, JAD aims to:

- Improve the relationship between users, management and information systems professionals.
- Improve the computer literacy of managers and users as well as knowledge of the business and application of the information systems professionals.
- Place the responsibility for resolving conflicts to the appropriate people, that is, the users and managers.
- Decrease the elapsed time spent on information systems development by combining multiple interviews into a structured JAD workshop.
- Lower the cost of the development and maintenance by defining and prioritising requirements the first time.

JAD workshops tend to be organised as three to five day workshops. In order to be successful, JAD requires that:

- Managers are willing to release their employees from their everyday activities to participate in sessions.
- Managers are willing to take part in the sessions themselves, and to help foster an environment of listening to subordinates and of co-operation.
- Leaders of sessions are well trained so that they are able to focus and redirect discussion as well as to mediate in conflicts and disputes.

12.7 Prototyping and rapid application development (RAD)

This is an engineering approach used to develop a small-scale working or simulated model of a product or its components. In terms of information systems, prototyping means building iterative working models of a system or some components of it. There are many benefits to using prototyping, including:

- Encouraging users to become more active participants in information systems development. This is helped by a concrete representation of some of their requirements which can stimulate discussion of other parts of the system as well.

- Providing assistance in the difficult process of defining requirements. The prototype will help in defining these in a detailed and unambiguous way. This should reduce the likelihood of rejection by the users.
- Reducing the development time, although there is some debate about the validity of this assumption.

The potential problems of prototyping are:

- The risk that analysis and design are carried out too quickly, and code produced without a proper understanding of the problem situation and its requirements.
- The tendency to discourage consideration of alternate technical solutions. The analyst is likely to adopt the first alternative that receives a reasonably positive response from the users.
- Information systems developed from prototypes might be inflexible and unable to respond to changing requirements, because the prototypes are developed in an *ad-hoc*, 'quick and dirty', manner. Sometimes the prototypes themselves are not easy to change.

Prototyping can be used at different stages of the life cycle, such as:

- *Feasibility prototyping:* This is used to test a specific technology that might be applied in an information system. An example of this kind of prototype might be as follows. An organisation's sales processing department currently puts all its information about sales into the database from paperwork submitted by the sales force. The sales director wishes to know whether this might be done directly by the sales team by the use of their own personal computer. A prototype (non-functional) can be produced very quickly to see what sort of response it draws from the sales force, and this feedback on the prototype can be used to decide whether or not this technical solution is worthy of further exploration.
- *Requirements prototyping:* This is used to stimulate users to think about their business requirements. The analyst can produce prototypes of screen formats and reports and obtain user feedback about them. Users see a concrete representation of their perceived needs and this should encourage them to think about what they want and also to convey their needs more easily to the analyst using the prototype as a point of reference. One possible problem with this type of prototyping is that users may become overly concerned with the format of screens and reports, when really the concern at this stage is with the content. Another possible problem is that users might consider the form of the prototype to be the form of the final system.

- *Design prototyping:* This focuses on the form and operation of the final information system, while requirements processing focuses on the content. Design prototypes should be evaluated by the user as if it were part of the final system. Users need to focus on how intuitive the system is to use and its 'look and feel'. Design prototypes can form part of the design specification or they might evolve into implementation prototypes.
- *Implementation prototypes:* These are produced as a result of the design prototype evolving directly into a production system. Details, such as security and help facilities, may well be missing initially and will need to be added if the prototype is to become a production system. The popularity of implementation prototypes has coincided with the increased availability of fourth generation languages (4GLs). These have provided tools for generating prototypes of screens, reports, files and database structures quickly.

Prototyping can be a useful approach appropriate for information systems development. However, prototyping is not a substitute for structured techniques nor for the life cycle. Prototyping should complement these and prototyping is not something that can be carried out without an appropriate specification.

Rapid application development (RAD) incorporates prototyping into information systems development, using its advantages and minimising its potential problems. RAD is a combination of structured techniques with prototyping and joint application development techniques. It involves:

- Using structured techniques to build preliminary data and process models to specify the perceived requirements
- Assisting analysts and users to verify the requirements using the prototype
- Using feedback on the prototypes to refine the data and process models
- Refining the prototype based on the modifications to the models
- Repeating this cycle of models and prototypes to result in the combined statement of business requirements and technical design.

12.8 Reuse

Considerable emphasis is being put on building software that is reusable. Many of the newer programming languages have this as an objective, indeed, this is an objective which could be extended to the process of design. The development of a new system can be made much easier and in less time if it can be constructed from existing reusable components. Such components will already have been tested and documented. It may be possible to build early prototypes of new systems very quickly from existing components. In terms of the information systems development life cycle, reusability means that we have to consider what might be appropriate points in the life cycle to consider available components that might be used. This will mean that mechanisms must be in place for reusable components to be classified, catalogued and readily available. Some systems repositories have this capability.

12.9 Outsourcing

In this approach, an organisation hands over a significant part of its information systems function to an external organisation. An IT facilities management organisation, for example, specialises in operating, staffing and managing computer-based information systems for other organisations. The work may include systems analysis and programming activities. Outsourcing is a long-term approach, contracts being typically of a five to ten year duration. It has become increasingly popular over the last ten years or so. Amongst the reasons for the popularity of the approach are:

- Businesses recognise that their expertise lies in their core business area (for example, telecommunications or food production) and not in information systems. They believe that an organisation which specialises in information systems will provide them with better management of that function.
- The cost to them of the information systems function can be reduced, since outsourcing has been found to be cheaper as well as more reliable, and the marketplace is very competitive ensuring that organisations opting for outsourcing are likely to get a good deal.
- In-house systems are more likely to become obsolete and incompatible with new technologies over time.
- The cost and time involved in recruiting and retaining information systems professionals is eliminated.

On the other hand, potential difficulties with outsourcing are:

- An important resource of any organisation is its information, and there may be risks attached with turning over information to an outside organisation.

- If only a part of the information systems function is outsourced, then the remaining information systems staff may be adversely affected, feeling that their past work is viewed as a failure.
- The organisation may choose an IT facilities management vendor on the basis of minimising costs, but once they are contracted to a particular vendor they may face price increases and it might be difficult to change vendors.
- There may be problems due to the quality of service provided by the outsourcing vendor. Even if the organisation is able to change vendors, it may be difficult to retrieve the situation.

The essence of a successful outsourcing relationship with an IT facilities management vendor is a good contract. Outsourcing will continue to be a significant factor in future information systems.

12.10 Business process reengineering (BPR)

This is a radical approach to information systems which aims to dismantle the way in which organisations are structured and to reorganise them in a new and more efficient way. A key enabler in this approach is information technology. The essence of BPR is that the old ways of working are no longer suitable. BPR is concerned with:

- *Fundamental change:* instead of asking questions about how to do something better, it asks questions about why these things should be done at all.
- *Radical change:* when it has been identified what the organisation needs to do, it must address questions about what is the best way to do those things, regardless of how they are done now.
- *Dramatic improvement:* is expected in terms of measures of performance, such as cost, quality, service and speed.

BPR is about using IT to do things that are not currently being done rather than to do faster what is already being done. However, enthusiasm about BPR should be tempered with the reported failure rate of 50-70% (Hammer and Champy, 1993). According to them, re-engineering projects fail primarily because senior managers lack the ambition for organisational change. Furthermore, many fail to comprehend the degree of change required, not only in business processes, but also in managerial behaviour and organisational structure.

12.11 Some conclusions

The approaches discussed in this chapter do not replace the information systems development life cycle which has been the subject of this text. They provide ideas, techniques and tools which might adapt it, in the same way that the life cycle discussed in the book has been adapted to include newer techniques, such as rich picture diagramming, entity-relationship diagrams, relational modelling and tools such as fourth generation languages, CASE tools and database management systems.

The environment of information systems development is forever changing. For example, the traditional information systems development activity would have been centred around a large mainframe computer in the 1970s and 1980s, whereas modern information systems development is more likely to concern itself with networks of smaller distributed systems. Again, it is as likely to be concerned with integrating different systems into this environment rather than developing complete and large systems from scratch.

In this text we have looked at information systems, given examples of different kinds of information systems and the human dimension and organisational aspects as much as the technology. Detailed consideration has been given to the need for a methodology and the requirements of an information systems methodology. We hope that we have provided the reader with an approach that satisfies the requirements of such a methodology.

However, information systems development is by no means a static area where there is one agreed approach. Indeed, many themes to information systems development are at present being widely discussed and are the basis of practical methodologies. These themes include:

- Systems approach
- Strategic information systems
- Business process re-engineering
- Planning approaches
- Object-oriented approaches
- Prototyping
- Participation.

Methodologies which reflect some of these approaches are:

- Structured Analysis, Design and Implementation of Information Systems (STRADIS)
- Yourdon Systems Method (YSM)

- Information Engineering (IE)
- Structured Systems Analysis and Design Methodology (SSADM)
- Merise
- Jackson Systems Development (JSD)
- Object-oriented analysis
- Information Systems work and Analysis of Changes
- Effective Technical and Human Implementation of Computer-based Systems (ETHICS)
- Soft Systems Methodology (SSM)
- Multiview
- Process Innovation
- Rapid Application Development (RAD)
- KADS
- Euromethod.

Further, the techniques and tools that have been introduced in this text have been further developed. Some are very sophisticated and complex and have the potential for considerable impact on information systems development. We leave detailed discussion of these advances to the second-level text on information systems (Avison and Fitzgerald, 1995).

12.12 Summary

In this chapter we have revisited the information systems development life cycle and considered some of the difficulties inherent in the complex world of organisations and their systems. We have discussed criticisms which are often levelled at the life cycle and we have countered some of these. In particular, we have discussed how problem migration difficulties complicate the task further. We have identified some currently important topics in information systems development.

Further Reading

Avison, D. E. & Fitzgerald, G. (1995) *Information Systems Development: Methodologies*, Techniques and Tools, 2nd edition, McGraw-Hill, Maidenhead.

Coad, P. & Yourdon, E. (1991) *Object-Oriented Analysis*, Prentice-Hall, Englewood Cliffs, NJ.

Shimberg, D. (1995) Following a client/server database methodology, *DBMS*, May 1995.

Shlaer, S. & Mellor, S. J. (1992) *Object Lifecycles: Modeling the World in States*, 1992, Prentice-Hall, Englewood Cliffs, NJ.

Willcocks, L., Fitzgerald, G. & Lacity, M. (1996) To outsource IT or not?: recent research on economics and evaluation practice, *European Journal of Information Systems*, **5**, pp. 143-160.
Reports findings from 26 longitudinal case studies of IT outsourcing.

Questions

1. What criticisms have been levelled at the information systems development life cycle?
2. Why is the life cycle not obsolete?
3. What arguments have been offered in defence of it?
4. How can other approaches be used with the life cycle?
5. List the modern developments in tools and techniques and methodologies that might be used at different points in the life cycle.
6. Describe one object-oriented methodology.
7. What are the components of client-server technology?
8. What are the main features of information engineering.
9. On what aspects of information systems does JAD place emphasis?
10. Identify the role of prototyping in information systems development.
11. What are the inherent risks of prototyping?
12. At what different stages in information systems development can prototyping be used?
13. What is RAD?
14. What is the significance of 'reuse' to information systems development?
15. Discuss outsourcing in the information systems context.
16. Explain BPR as an approach to information systems.
17. Contrast modern information systems development with traditional information systems development.
18. Discuss the people problems in information systems development.

Chapter 13

THE TECHNOLOGICAL INFRASTRUCTURE

13.1 Technology used by information systems

An important aspect of information systems is the technological infrastructure on which those information systems are based. The philosophy upon which this chapter has been written reflects a 'need to know' philosophy. We do not discuss technology for technology's sake, but attempt to give the reader sufficient understanding of the various technologies used to support information systems and information systems development. It is important to understand the underlying mechanisms which are used to deliver information and in this chapter we look at the various technologies for information systems. On the other hand, this chapter is not intended to be read from beginning to end. It is to be hoped that readers wishing to know about a certain technology will dip into that section. This need may also arise when readers find that the description of a technique or tool in earlier chapters refers to a specific technology.

Although this text is concerned largely with the non-technological aspects of information systems development, it is important for the reader to have some understanding of the technologies which are used as a basis for information systems. Amongst the most important technologies are: networks, open systems, client-server, object-oriented systems, AI technologies, multimedia and virtual reality systems, workflow computing, the Internet, intranets, and data warehouses.

Each of these is now briefly discussed. A number of references are given at the end to enable the reader to follow up any topics of interest in more detail.

13.2   Networks

A computer network is a collection of interconnected autonomous computers (Tanenbaum, 1996). Connections can be copper wire, fibre optics, microwaves and communications satellites. The word 'autonomous' is used to exclude those situations where one computer can forcibly start, stop or control another computer. Computers in different organisations, possibly at widely dispersed sites, may be linked via a network called a **wide area network** (WAN), or computers within the same site via a **local area network** (LAN). The computers in the network can range from mainframe systems to personal computers. It is through networking that many office automation facilities are provided, for example, electronic mail.

There are many reasons why organisations use computers but primarily they are used for:

- *Resource sharing:* making resources, such as data, programs or equipment, available to anyone on the network, regardless of the physical location of either the resource or the potential user.
- *High reliability:* having alternative sources of supply, for example, data files can be replicated on a number of machines on the network.
- *Reduced costs:* saving money since small computers have a better price/performance ratio than larger ones. Mainframe computers are approximately ten times faster than personal computers but can cost a thousand times more. A client-server model is often used. In this model

a request for something to be done originates from a client. The server carries out the work and then sends a reply back to the client. There can be many clients using a small number of servers.

- *Scalability:* being able to increase system performance in an incremental way as workload increases. This is done by adding more machines to the network as required. In the large, centralised, mainframe environment, when the system's capacity has been outgrown by the organisation's needs, it has to be replaced by a larger one. There is a significant cost to users both in monetary terms and in terms of disruption. With a networked system, based on the client-server model, new clients and new servers can be added as required by the organisation's changing needs but with the minimum of cost and disruption.

Tanenbaum (1996) believes that the motivation for building computer networks is essentially economic and technological in nature and that most companies would have continued to work by keeping all their data on mainframes with employees' terminals connected to it, if sufficiently large mainframes were available at acceptable prices. The basis for the success of computer networks has been the huge price/performance advantage over mainframe computers.

However, computer networks are now also being used to deliver services to private individuals in their homes. The motivation behind these has been different to that in organisational ones. In the case of these networks the motives are:

- *Access to remote information:* such as data from financial institutions, home shopping using on-line catalogues, access to the Internet, and information about hobbies, arts and business.
- *Provision of person-to-person communication:* via electronic mail (e-mail) which is now widely used and will increasingly include audio and video as well as text. Real-time e-mail, videoconferencing, newsgroups and discussion groups are features of this type of communication.
- *Access to entertainment:* as a result of a huge and growing industry, providing selective viewing with individual users being able to watch a film of their own choosing, new types of films which are interactive inviting the user to provide input to direct the story and interactive audience participation in TV shows.

The proliferation of networking technology will result in new social, ethical and political issues and problems. Laudon (1995) discusses some of these.

13.3   Open systems

Traditionally, computer systems communications companies had their own standards which catered only for their own computers, commonly referred to as 'plug compatible' systems. These systems were known as **closed systems** since it was not possible to communicate with computers with different standards. Open systems, on the other hand, are developed according to internationally agreed standards which allow for easy interaction and information exchange between the computer systems of different manufacturers. An open system is one that implements open specifications for interfaces and services so that appropriately developed applications software can be run on a variety of different systems with very little change being required. They should be able to interoperate with other applications on local and remote systems.

Open systems promote portability of applications, data and people between different hardware systems because they adhere to defined standards. This also provides the basis for interoperability of applications and systems. The result of this is that users are no longer dependent on a particular supplier or particular hardware and software systems. Open systems provide flexibility, enabling organisations to modify and enhance their information technology as the organisational needs change. They also enable integration of information, systems and applications from a variety of different sources. None of this was possible prior to open systems standards.

These factors allow organisations to preserve their investments and be in a position to take advantage of new technologies. The specific benefits provided by open systems identified by Isaak *et al.* (1994) are:

- Ability to support multiple hardware platforms
- Efficiency gains through consistent interfaces across different hardware platforms
- Opportunity to focus resources on developing application functionality
- Reduced development risk since choice of platforms is not an issue
- Reduced development and maintenance costs
- Explicitly stated standards guidelines enabling compliance checks with open systems specifications.

In order to facilitate networking and communications between systems, several standards have been developed. Network **protocols** attempt to ensure compatibility and synchronisation of data exchange throughout a network. A protocol defines how components of the network establish communications, exchange data and terminate communications. Protocols can be thought of as the rules which apply to information flow within a communications system. They determine the exact format, timing and order of data going out as well as interpreting data coming in.

The International Standards Organisation (ISO) has produced a reference model for **open systems interconnection** (OSI), intended to define protocols enabling different vendor's products to be interconnected. The model has a layered arrangement whose aim is to reduce complexity and to provide immunity to changes in one layer affecting another layer. Each layer tends to be relatively self-contained. The layers are as follows:

- *Physical layer:* this handles the transmission of raw data over the chosen communications medium
- *Data link layer:* this produces reliable communications by handling error detection and transmission speed conversion
- *Network layer:* this handles the routing of messages
- *Transport layer:* this handles addressing and flow control functions
- *Session layer:* this handles the setting-up and termination of communications between a sender and an addressed destination
- *Presentation layer:* this handles the formatting of data sent to and from the session layer
- *Application layer:* this handles the functions defined by the user, including input, output, processing and storage.

Standards are important for the efficient and effective use of networking technology. Open systems have made it easier for organisations to remain independent of a particular vendor and not get locked into a particular vendor's products and services, which had been the case prior to open systems.

13.4   Client-server

Client-server technology is the result of advances in hardware and software. It has become a popular strategy for companies while they try to minimise costs and improve control and customer services. As shown in Figure 13.1, client-server applications have three elements, these are:

- *Client:* which is responsible for managing user interactions and in so doing hides the server from the user providing transparency of location of the application.
- *Server:* which serves several clients by passively waiting for requests for services and then carries out the appropriate tasks.
- *Network:* which facilitates the client-server communication.

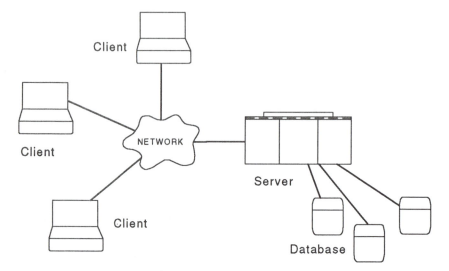

Fig. 13.1: Client-server system

In the 1970s the most important technology for organisations was the mainframe. The 'client' element of these environments were 'dumb' terminals which were non-intelligent computer screens and keyboards used for the input and output of data to the mainframe. These terminals were not very user friendly. In the 1980s the minicomputer became very popular for running business applications. These were either proprietary systems or open-systems based. Again, connection to the system was via a dumb terminal of some kind.

The next era of computing was that of the personal computer. Since the late 1980s and early 1990s, personal computing has become an important computer resource in virtually all sizes of organisation. Personal computers have been able to present a challenge to both mini and mainframe computing technology due to their advantageous price/performance ratio. Their original use was very much as stand-alone, non-network connected machines. They tended to be largely used for personal productivity applications such as word processing and spreadsheet packages. However, personal computers have played an important role in the client-server model of computing. The client workstation is the system at which the user sits and works and the machine on which the client applications and tools run. Typically this will be a personal computer on which there is a graphical user interface (GUI). The client workstation controls the flow of the application and issues requests for data from the server. It is also responsible for putting the output data into an appropriate format.

A server can be any computer that is used to provide services to other computers on a network. These services might be file sharing, database access, peripherals, network bridging or application processing. The server will typically be running a relational database management system and provide data access services. It responds to requests from clients, will process SQL queries and will return results to the client.

One advantage of client-server technology is that the distribution of tasks across multiple platforms is optimised. Clients are the means by which the user uses the system and they therefore need to provide an appropriate user interface and applications logic. The server must be concerned with issues such as concurrency, security and integrity, and has to have a high capacity.

Another advantage of client-server technology is that there is an opportunity for interoperation of different client tools with servers, that is, a 'mix-and-match' approach is possible. Since the major components, user interface, business logic and database are separated, there is an opportunity to use different products and not be tied to one product. There is an opportunity to provide new types of application and better access to data while reducing hardware costs and improving control of personal computers. Another benefit of client-server computing is that it is highly scalable, with additional components being added as appropriate.

The risks are that the technology is still relatively immature, there is a skills shortage in the area, very few standards exist and there are hidden costs associated with the technology. However, if organisations use a considered approach in moving towards this technology these risks can be reduced and their effect minimised. Organisations need to consider introducing it in a relatively small, simple area where returns can be maximised. Any move to new technology needs to be done in a learning culture. Suppliers and technologies should be limited to the small number that the organisation can deal with effectively. Care should be taken in integrating existing information systems development styles with any new ones.

13.5 Object-oriented systems

Object-oriented concepts are important in the information systems world. Object technology is used in analysis, design and programming as well as in database design. The ideas originated in programming, with the invention of object-oriented programming languages. This resulted in work being done on object-oriented design followed by developments in object-oriented analysis. Early object-oriented languages were Simula and Smalltalk.

The ideas underlying object orientation are concerned with abstraction at a different level compared to conventional approaches. Traditionally in programming there has been a deliberate separation of data and the code which processes that data. Object-oriented languages bring the two together into an object. The description of an object contains information about the structure of the data of that object and also information about the behaviour of the object. This behaviour is the code part of the object description. This code part is referred to as **methods**. Objects are grouped into **classes** according to a sharing of common data and methods. Access to objects is limited to the predefined methods. Each object has an **interface** and an **implementation**. The interface is public and access to the object is via this interface, since it is visible to other objects and users of the system. The implementation of an object is private. Other objects and users have no access to this part of the object. This concept is called **data abstraction** and **encapsulation**.

Another important concept in object technology is that of **object identity**. All objects are identified by a system generated and maintained identifier, which is independent of any of the values of its attributes including key attributes. The effect of this is that the values of any of an object's attributes can be altered without impacting on the object's identity.

Object orientation includes a very powerful mechanism referred to as **inheritance,** where object classes can be organised into type hierarchies in which a subclass inherits both attributes and methods from its superclasses in the hierarchy. **Complex objects** are possible due to the fact that an object can have an internal structure which is of arbitrary complexity, that is, consists of sub-objects, which in turn consist of sub-sub-objects and so on. Communication and operations are carried out in object-oriented systems by **message passing**. Typically a message consists of an object followed by a method to be applied to it.

Another feature of object-oriented systems is **operator overloading**, which allows the same operation (or method) name to refer to different operations dependent on the object to which it is being applied. Determination of the actual operation to be carried out is done when the object to which it is supplied is provided. An example of this could be an operation to 'invert' a shape, which will be different when applied to a 2D object compared to a 3D object.

The approach described in this text involves analysing and modelling information systems from a data perspective using techniques such as entity-relationship modelling, and from a process perspective using techniques such as data flow diagrams. There has been a deliberate emphasis on separating the two perspectives in order to deal with the complexity of information systems development. In object-oriented systems we encapsulate into an object, both its data and the functions which operate on that data. To avoid the awkwardness that can result from mapping the analysis using traditional structured analysis approaches to an object-oriented design, object-oriented analysis is used. This involves identifying objects and their attributes and also identifying the functions to be applied to each object. The interface each object presents to other objects must also be determined.

Object technology has been used in developing graphical user interfaces incorporating menus, icons and windows. It has also been found useful in video and voice databases. The advantage of object technology is that it allows expansion of features in a modular way, maintaining a common interface and language for all aspects of the system, and by isolating the effects of change.

13.6   AI technologies

There are a number of technologies which are **artificial intelligence** (AI) based which are likely to have impact on some aspects of information systems. These are data mining, expert systems and neural networks. Use of all these is being made by organisations in order to support decision-making.

Data mining is closely connected with the idea of data warehousing (described later in this chapter). The idea is to combine these technologies to enable organisations to make better use of their data. Data mining tools use new techniques, such as neural networks, to explore data and identify patterns in the data which is in the organisation's data warehouse. Organisations hope to gain competitive advantage by extracting information from the data enabling them to acquire customer knowledge in order to both improve service to existing customers and attract new customers. Data mining is very important to large systems as it attempts to find information in large data sets that organisations do not necessarily know exist. Data mining is used to find relationships and make forecasts. Within these categories data mining can produce the following information types:

- *Classifications:* This is information about classes with shared characteristics, for example, what percentage of customers of a bank have more than one account but no tax-free savings plan?

- *Clusters:* This is information about a subset of a class, that consists of patterns or relationships that have not been predefined. Such relationships could be valuable when discovered. For example, on mining a set of data, it might be found that 85% of men with store cards use them mainly for purchases from the menswear department while 60% of women use them for purchases in the children's department.
- *Associations:* This is information which is event driven, such that there is an association between the occurrence of one event and the occurrence of another event. For example, it might be found that for a particular retail store, 65% of the occasions when a case of dog food is purchased, customers also buy a can opener.
- *Sequences:* These are similar to associations in that they are linked to events, but are over a period of time, and therefore describe trends. For example, it might be found that store card holders who have recently requested an increase in their credit limit will usually make purchases which take them to that limit within a week of the new limit being agreed.
- *Forecasts:* These involve making forecasts about the future using current data. Forecasts can be applied to virtually all organisational situations. For example, they might be used to predict sales of products to assist with purchasing of materials. Data mining provides support in this area on the basis of having identified patterns and trends.

Applications of data mining are many and in a variety of fields. Dilly (1996) identifies the following applications of data mining:

Retail and marketing
- Identify buying patterns of customers
- Find relationship between customer demographic characteristics
- Predict response to mailing campaigns
- Market basket analysis.

Banking
- Detect patterns of fraudulent credit card use
- Identify 'loyal' customers
- Predict customers likely to change their credit card affiliation
- Determine patterns in credit card spending by different customer groups
- Find hidden correlation between different financial indicators
- Identify stock trading rules from historical market data.

Insurance and health care
- Claims analysis
- Predict which customers buy new policies
- Identify behaviour patterns of risky customers
- Identify fraudulent behaviour.

Transportation
- Determine the distribution schedule among outlets
- Analyse loading patterns.

Medicine
- Characterise patient behaviour to predict surgery visits
- Identify successful medical therapies for different illnesses.

Expert systems software supports users in their tasks by incorporating the knowledge of an expert or experts in the system. A definition of an expert is someone who has special knowledge or training and so is particularly effective in a specific domain. This expert knowledge forms a knowledge base in the expert system. An inference engine is the component which applies the knowledge to a particular problem. Expert systems can play a useful role in organisational decision support. They are commonly used for credit checking, medical diagnosis, urban planning and design, chemical analysis, consulting, controlling and legislation. Expert systems software can be purchased or developed and while there are benefits to using expert systems, such as the replication and availability of a certain expertise, it should be remembered that they are of limited applicability in many situations.

STRATEGIC	Unstructured decisions Potentially suitable for neural network technology Planning New sites New products
TACTICAL	New markets Selecting and purchasing hardware Personnel recruitment
OPERATIONAL	Approval of loans and credit Selection and purchase of software

Fig. 13.2: Neural network technology for decision making

Neural network software is an attempt to imitate human learning and knowledge acquisition by 'learning' from experience. Such software creates a model based on its input and output. It processes data in order to recognise patterns and relationships in the data. Once its learning about the patterns and relationships between data is complete, the software can make its own decisions on new cases. While neural networks are not a new technology, they have only recently been applied to business, for example, medical diagnostics, forecasting, approval of loans and analysing price and volume patterns in stock trading. This technology has been relatively successful, but one difficulty is that such systems are not able to explain how a solution was arrived at. In terms of the three-level management architecture previously described in section 2.4, neural networks have potential to provide support for decision making at all levels of the architecture: strategic, tactical and operational, where the decisions being made are unstructured (see Figure 13.2). As we have seen, data mining is another area in which neural networks are used to great effect.

13.7   Multimedia and virtual reality systems

Multimedia is the use of different representational forms, that is, data, text, sound, still images and motion video. The term multimedia is often used synonomously with hypermedia. Hypermedia systems are essentially multimedia systems with link-based navigation. The main applications of multimedia systems are in the area of information presentation, education and computer-based games. Multimedia systems provide convenient access to a combination of various types of information, all of which is stored in a digital form.

Virtual reality is a new style of computer interface. It creates the illusion of being in an artificial computer-created world. Interaction with a virtual reality system is carried out by the user wearing a pair of special goggles which provide 3D vision, via individual computer screens for each eye. Earphones are also used so as to enhance the illusion, using sound. 'Data gloves' are used to give a more realistic ability to 'feel' computer-produced objects. The term **cyberspace** is used to refer to the virtual world which is computer-produced. The virtual reality user moves around and manipulates objects in this virtual world.

Virtual reality systems have resulted from the advances in computer speed and power combined with advances in image processing, tracking mechanisms and human-to-computer communication (Larijani, 1994). Virtual reality is concerned with the idea of human presence in a computer-generated space.

Complex processes can benefit from the use of this technology. For example, designing automobiles and aircraft can involve the use of virtual reality to explore how users interact with different designs. The technology is still relatively new and unexplored, and confusion and debate still exists in the area with regard to what constitutes a virtual environment. Other applications are in the training of surgeons for carrying out surgery and the training of fire-fighters, where virtual reality is used to simulate the presence of the fire-fighter in a burning building.

13.8   Workflow computing

This is concerned with document management technology. Workflow is part of a larger category of computer applications called **computer supported co-operative work** (CSCW). This field is also known as computer supported collaboration, groupware or group decision support systems (GDSS). There is currently considerable interest in CSCW and workflow with organisations such as Lotus, Novell and Hewlett-Packard all marketing software in this area.

Workflow applications contain instructions for directing documents so that they are automatically routed from one user to another as they are completed. The whole approach is streamlined, similar to that of a more modern process rather than a function-oriented view of organisations. **Structured workflow** systems are found in predictable and repetitive environments. **Unstructured workflow** is used in environments where procedures are non-sequential, *ad-hoc,* collaborative and subject to change. A **workflow engine** is the core of a centrally-controlled workflow system which governs the process and monitors each step performed by clients. **Active workflow engines** monitor the state of the workflow system and determine what to do next. When a workflow client completes an action, the information is sent back to the workflow engine where a decision about the next action is taken. **Passive workflow engines** do not directly manage the workflow but rely on the clients to process each piece of the process and send the data on to the next participant in the process.

Workflow technology was initially tied in with expensive document imaging equipment. Amongst the first companies to use workflow technology were insurance companies, where inefficiency often led to the misplacement of files. This technology represented a solution to these problems. Workflow and imaging technology were used together to automate repetitive procedures normally associated with this type of clerical work. Typical applications of this technology are the processing of customer correspondence, and the automation of expense claims processing.

The fact that workflow computing was largely associated with (expensive) imaging meant that it was largely isolated into niche markets. To use the technology, massive investment in document scanners, high resolution displays and mass storage had to be justified. However there was no valid underlying reason why workflow technology should not have been applied to all the electronic documents that the organisation used. A difficulty encountered was that such documents had to be printed out from business computers and then scanned into the workflow systems. More recently, workflow is being decoupled from imaging, which means that it is easier to integrate into existing systems. Workflow technology can be used to improve both customer service and internal business processes.

It should be noted that workflow computing is not a substitute for an inefficient system and can only be optimised if companies understand their own business processes and how they interface. It is becoming recognised that the Internet (described in section 13.9) is a useful platform for workflow applications. It can be used to enable customers to initiate and follow through business processes. One example is that of a bank which already has a workflow system in place for processing mortgage applications. Adding a web browser means that customers can fill out loan application forms on-line and go back periodically to get reports on how their application is progressing. Workflow computing is a powerful lever for improving productivity. There are a number of organisations using workflow technology and a variety of products on the market. Examples of workflow packages are Lotus Notes, JetForm and HP AdminFlow.

13.9   Internet

The early Internet was not user friendly, and it was the advent of the World Wide Web (commonly referred to as the **Web**), a graphical user interface, hypertext-based linking system, which led to easy access and the explosive growth in its use. The Internet is made up of thousands of interconnecting networks. Communication is through computers and individuals, and organisations can communicate directly with one another regardless of where they are or when they wish to communicate. The Web consists of an enormous collection of documents called **pages** which are located at a variety of sites. Web pages are created using a relatively simple programming language called **HTML** (hypertext mark-up language). These pages are accessed by a unique address called a **URL** (universal remote locator). Each page may contain **links** to other related pages anywhere in the world. A link may be followed by the user clicking on it. This would take the user to that page. This process can be repeated any number of times, enabling traversal of hundreds of linked pages.

Web sites may be accessed and viewed through web browser software or using a **search engine** to search the web for a specific topic or keyword(s). The browser is software which retrieves the requested page, interprets the text and formatting commands contained within the document and displays the page appropriately formatted onto the screen. Web browsers use a variety of buttons and features to make it easier to navigate the Web, for example, common buttons are for going to the previous page or to the relevant home page. Web pages typically consist of ordinary text (not underlined) and hypertext (underlined and therefore clickable to link with other pages), plus icons, line drawings, maps and photographs which can all be linked to another web page. As we have seen, hypermedia integrates text and other media such as audio tracks and video clips. Appropriate browser software would be required for such web pages. Berghel (1996) compares the features provided by a number of different browser software packages.

With the phenomenal growth of the Internet, a new electronic market-place is evolving. Bhimani (1996) argues that the phenomenal growth of the Internet has largely been fuelled by the prospect of performing business on-line. Organisations anticipate many business benefits from using the Internet, including:

- Potential access to a huge number of people. In particular access to people actively choosing to visit the organisation's site.
- Expansion of the organisation's market place beyond current boundaries, such as sales in countries.
- Interaction with customers so that queries and orders can be placed and dealt with over the Internet.
- Cost-effective advertising, in that any advertisements exists continuously unlike, for example, a newspaper advert which is valid only until the next issue.
- Support of other existing advertising and marketing.
- Potential competitive advantage due to 24 hour daily availability and access to international markets.
- Ease of updating Internet material compared to other sources.
- Increased efficiency and potential for reduction in workload of departments providing customer support and repetitive information.

From the viewpoint of information systems development, it is very likely that many future information systems will be Internet-based. Indeed many organisations are currently developing systems for use over the Internet. Information systems developers need an understanding of issues currently of concern in the Internet arena.

Due to the size of the Internet, and hence the size of the target potential audience, increasing numbers of companies are using it for communication, advertisement and commercial purposes. Internet security issues are of increasing concern due to its potential for business use. Since the Internet has previously been used largely by the academic community, security was not a major concern. Now issues regarding an individual's financial and personal privacy are raised. For example, information about a person's credit card may be passed through the Internet. Internet security is a vital issue for organisations using or wishing to use the Internet for business activities as the increased connectivity contains an inherent security risk.

There are a number of approaches to providing security on the Internet, however one method or piece of software is unlikely to be sufficient. A consistent overall approach to security which encompasses a number of methods should be utilised. To aid this, the administration and monitoring of security should be performed from a centralised source as this ensures consistency and accountability. It is important to ensure that the security policy adopted guards against both internal and external attack. Steps should be taken to counter viruses. Physical access to systems should be secure, as many breaches to security take place from within the organisation rather than outside it.

Approaches for ensuring the security of the Internet include the use of **firewalls** and **encryption**. A firewall is the first line of defence for a system. It enforces access control between the company's internal network and the Internet. The firewall can be thought of as being the security checkpoint at the only entrance/exit to a building. All traffic into and out of the building is via the firewall, so security measures can be focused here. Encryption is the transformation of data into some unreadable form. Its purpose is to keep the information hidden from those for whom it is not intended, even if they have access to the encrypted form.

Internet technologies have lead to the provision of the following technological benefits (Levitt, 1996):

- Connected computers which enable the sharing and transfer of information.
- Connected computers that are heterogeneous, in that they run different operating systems, use different hardware and are from a variety of different suppliers.

- Common user applications, such as e-mail and web browsers are available across a number of different platforms.
- Hypertext links which simplify navigation and information retrieval.

Use of the Internet is increasing at a rapid rate. New users are finding it useful for all sorts of purposes. Reengineering of business processes (James, 1996) and groupware (Varney, 1996) are two examples. Web browsing software has become a universal interface to all kinds of information and web servers have become the source of a variety of information. Several hundred thousand web servers provide simple point-and-click access to an incredible range of information sources (Levitt, 1996).

13.10 Intranets

The success of the Internet has quickly led to the recognition that it can be applied to corporate information to make it more readily available. Intranets enable organisations to provide an effective, up-to-date and extensible means for corporate communications. The intranet can be the source of all information for the organisation, its various regional, distributed offices and their employees, as well as customers, partners and suppliers.

Levitt (1996) has identified the following advantages of the intranet.

- Inexpensive to start, requires little investment either in monetary terms or in terms of infrastructure
- Significantly more up to date and less expensive than traditional paper-based information delivery
- Distributed computing strategy uses computer resources more effectively
- Users who are familiar with the Internet are familiar with the underlying concepts of the intranet
- Open platform architecture means large (and increasing) numbers of add-on applications are available.

It is expected that in future, the growth of intranets will be four times that of the Internet itself. Large software organisations have focused on the commercial potential of intranets as well as on the Internet. There are three main stages in which organisations are using intranets. These are:

- *Publishing:* Organisations have recognised the effectiveness of the use of intranets to publish and distribute organisational information. For example, instead of e-mailing everyone a copy of the company newsletter, it can be placed on the Web server so that anyone in the company can access it. This results in a reduction in network traffic and disk space since the only copy of the information is held on the server and only those who are interested in it will access it. Document control is made easier since updated versions of documents simply replace previous versions on the server. Next time anyone accesses a particular document they will access the latest version.

- *Document management:* It is often the case that in the early stages of using an intranet for document publication, little consideration is given to how that information is to be managed. With increasing amounts of information being stored on unstructured servers, manual maintenance of their content is problematic. It is at this stage that there is the realisation that the intranet is a corporate level tool and needs to be managed as such. In managing the intranet there are both technical and organisational considerations. Technical considerations include the selection and/or development of systems to manage the contents of the intranet. These systems often use a database for information rather than store Web pages, the data in the database being converted into appropriate Web pages when required. Different strategies can be used for constructing Web pages. For example, they could be constructed dynamically by the server using the information in the database when a user request for those pages is made. Alternatively, they could be held on the server having been built up or updated by the server when the data is changed periodically or in an *ad-hoc* manner. The appropriateness of a particular strategy depends on the nature of the information. Organisational considerations include document management issues, such as who has responsibility for a server or information on a server.

- *Client-server applications:* The advent of Java has made Web-based applications possible. Java is an object-oriented programming language. Java code can be compiled into 'byte-code', this is then interpreted by a 'Java Virtual Machine' which can be a piece of software or hardware. Latest versions of most Web browsing software support Java, and Java 'applets' can be embedded into Web pages. This means that applications developed in Java can reside on a Web server and be downloaded and interpreted on a browser giving functionality well in excess of standard Web pages.

Undoubtedly, as with many new technologies, there has been a considerable amount of 'hype' about intranets. However, many organisations have now seen through this hype and while wishing to take advantage of the opportunities offered by the technology, realise that there are a number of important information management issues that they have to address. It is the opportunity for distributing applications (as well as data) which is likely to be of most interest to organisations in the near future.

13.11   Data warehouses

In recent years, many organisations have begun implementing data warehouses. A data warehouse is an architecture rather than a specific product and usually comprises a number of software components. It is the technique used to structure and store data for subsequent analytical processing. The data collected into the data warehouse is intended to support management decision making. The requirement for data warehousing has arisen due to the fact that the organisation's data arises from a number of unintegrated, heterogeneous and disparate systems often referred to as legacy systems. Organisations have a huge amount of valuable information locked away in the data of their information systems. The data has arisen from the day-to-day transactions of organisations, such as point-of-sale transactions, automated teller machine transactions, credit card transactions and so on. Businesses have recognised that this raw data can be turned into valuable information that can be used for their business strategy. Strategic decision making requires access both to internal and external information, such as share prices, exchange rates, market research, economic forecasts, demographic data, industry trends and financial and business articles. A data warehouse would integrate and store both types of information.

Data mining, described in section 13.6, is an approach which aims to discover something new from the facts recorded in a database, and the use of a data warehouse can make this more effective.

There are two main schools of thought in the database warehouse arena. The first advocates that data should be put into a warehouse to provide organisations with strategic information. The belief is that large organisations have their data dispersed across a number of different databases, which means that these organisations cannot get a corporate view of their activities. By putting all their data into a data warehouse, they can get this wider and much more strategic view. In addition, many organisations have **legacy applications**. Inmon (1996) considers these to be applications which:

- Have no shared information, only private data
- Are typically mainframe applications designed to do a specific job, for example commitment accounting
- Are relatively old
- Have been hand-crafted.

Legacy applications tend to be difficult to modify due to their complexity and the lack of external support. Inmon describes them as 'data rich, information poor'. Such applications are difficult to reengineer (that is transformed into up-to-date standards and requirements), to allow shared data access, and they are difficult to interface with other software. Given that legacy applications often have many thousands of lines of code, attempts to reengineer them is likely to introduce errors.

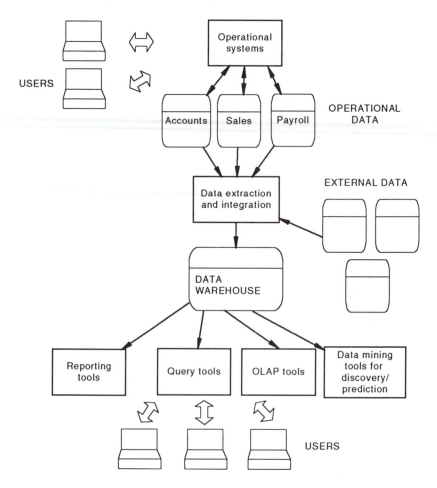

Fig. 13.3: Data warehousing environment

The other school of thought is that the data warehouse is a separate store of organisational data which is useful for querying, but is quite distinct from the organisation's operational data stored by its operational processing programs, more commonly known as **on-line transaction processing** (OLTP). The basis of this view is that database technology developed into relational databases which were very flexible but rather slow for transaction type processing, proving themselves to be most useful for query-intensive applications. Vendors saw this as a problem and tried to modify them for typical on-line processing type applications. They were trying to use relational databases to meet all of the organisation's business needs. Increasingly it was found that data organised for *ad-hoc* querying had to be organised differently for transaction processing. More recently, it has been recognised that current data is probably best organised for transaction processing while the remaining data should be organised into a data warehouse for query purposes to support decision support systems. Figure 13.3 shows an overview of the data warehouse environment.

Inmon (1996) describes 'the architected environment' to provide both OLTP and organisation decision support. In the architected environment there are four levels as shown in Figure 13.4:

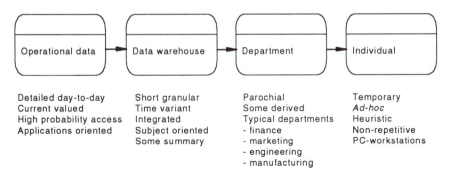

Fig. 13.4: Four-level architectural environment (after Inmon, 1996)

- *Operational level:* stores day-to-day detailed, application-oriented data (that is, concerned with the tasks of the business: for example, an insurance company has applications for car insurance, life assurance and so on).
- *Data warehouse level:* stores time variant, lightly summarised and subject oriented data (concerned with the entities that are affected by those tasks, for example, an insurance company is concerned with customers, premiums claims and so on).

- *Departmental level:* stores information that is usually derived and highly summarised, relevant to departments of the organisation.
- *Individual level:* stores data temporarily when accessed from the other three levels, this is when it is transformed into decision-support information.

It has been estimated that some 80% of organisations are looking at or are actually doing data warehousing. The size of the databases that we are talking about are huge, in the order of 8-10 terrabytes, typically extending over hundreds of disk drives. Databases of this size have many difficulties associated with them.

Data warehousing is a technology that is currently receiving a lot of attention. This is vendor-driven, since there is considerable financial gain if such technology is taken up by users. Extra software licenses are sold and additional hardware is required. There have been examples of failed data warehousing projects which have had huge sums of money invested in them. These failures have resulted in a more conservative approach by users.

An example of such an approach is a **data mart** which is a data warehouse aimed at one organisational area or department. For example, a data mart could be developed for the finance department. The organisation might try a larger scale project if the data mart succeeds. An organisation is likely to have a number of data marts.

Due to the amount of data being processed in a data warehouse, response times can be 3-4 hours or even days. Data in the warehouse is usually replicated at all appropriate sites. Replicating the data has additional costs associated with it in terms of purchasing and licensing replication tools. These are still relatively expensive. There are still many unresolved problems. Data organisation is still problematic due to the fact that on-line transaction processing needs indexes to data, whereas decision support systems, management information systems and executive information systems do not.

The huge amounts of data present in data warehouses have given rise to a new breed of tools called OLAP tools. **OLAP** stands for **On-Line Analytical Processing**, and tools to support these are more than simple query processing tools. These deal with multidimensional data. Dimensions are coexistent identifiers of the measures of aspects of the organisation that we are interested in. Dimensions are also referred to as factors, perspectives, keys, identifiers and subject areas. For example, in a retail organisation we will be interested in how many products have been sold, over time, in different regions and by different sales people. The dimensions are products, time and outlet. The type of query might be 'What products have been sold by Salesman A in area B by the end of last year?' Such a query can take hours of processing to resolve.

OLAP tools optimise such queries by preparing data before the query. *Ad-hoc* queries are usually determined by the results of previous queries and the tool attempts to ensure that relevant data are prepared in advance. Techniques such as 'slicing and dicing' are used to produce a 'cube' of related data. In the 'slice and dice' approach, related data is grouped one way and analysed, then grouped another way and analysed and so on. To do this we need to be able to 'drill down' data, that is, we start at a particular summarisation of data and break that summary into a succession of finer summaries.

There are an increasing number of publications in the database warehousing area. Devlin (1996) emphasises data management issues from an enterprise-wide view and gives a detailed description of a conceptual data warehouse architecture. Kimball (1996) gives practical advice on how to model and build a data warehouse. Mattison (1996) provides a comprehensive and pragmatic coverage of this area. Meredith and Khader (1996) looks at partitioning and aggregation techniques appropriate for the design of data warehouses. Inmon *et al.* (1997) give practical techniques for monitoring operations and performance and administrating data.

13.12 Summary

Organisations are experiencing many new and exciting technological advances, which they hope will help them towards their business objectives. The technologies mentioned above have a part to play in this. Networking will be the enabler of potentially transparent distribution of data and applications, and the means of access to resources are potentially limitless and boundaryless. Data warehousing is becoming increasingly popular, enabling organisational decision making and also providing a rich source of information for data mining technology. The data warehouses of the future will contain structured data and audio, video and spatial multimedia data. It is possible that workflow will be integrated into data warehousing technology, enabling automatic distribution of reports. AI-based technologies will initiate workflow through the identification of certain situations indicated by data in the data warehouse or the scheduling and delivery of reports to particular managers at specific times The Internet has a major part to play allowing access to a wealth of diverse yet accessible information and commercial opportunities.

For the information systems developer these technologies indicate the complex new environment for information systems and they represent a challenge as well as an opportunity. The pace of change is extraordinary, and the proliferation of tools and software is potentially overwhelming.

References

Berghel , H. L. (1996) The client side of the web, *Communications of the ACM*, **39**, pp. 33-40.

Bhimani, A. (1996) Securing the commercial Internet, *Communications of the ACM*, **39**, 6, pp. 29-35.

Devlin, B. (1996) *Data Warehouse: From Architecture to Implementation*, Addison-Wesley, Reading, Ma.

Dilly, R. (1995) *Data Mining: An Introduction*
http://www.pcc.qub.ac.uk/tec/courses/datamining/datamining

Inmon, W. H. (1996) *Building the Data Warehouse*, 2nd Edition, Wiley, New York, NY.

Inmon, W. H., Welch, J. D. & Glassey, K. L. (1997) *Managing the Data Warehouse*, Wiley, New York, NY.

Isaak, J., Lewis, K., Thompson, K. & Straub, R. (1994) *Open Systems Handbook: A Guide to building open systems*, IEEE.

Kimball, R. (1996) *The Data Warehouse Toolkit: Practical Techniques for Building Dimensional Data Warehouses*, Wiley, New York, NY.

Larijani, L. C. (1994) *The Virtual Reality Primer*, McGraw-Hill, New York, NY.

Laudon, K. C. (1995) Ethical concepts and information technology, *Communications of the ACM*, **38**, 1995, pp. 33-39.

Levitt, L. (1996) *Intranets, Internet Technologies Deployed behind the Firewall for Corporate Productivity*
http:www.process.com/intranets/wp2.htp

Mattison, R. (1996) *Data Warehousing: Strategies, Tools and Techniques*, McGraw-Hill, New York, NY.

Meredith, M. E. & Khader, A. (1996) Divide and aggregate: designing large warehouses, *Database Programming & Design*, June 1996, pp. 24-30.

Parsaye, K. (1996), Data mines for data warehouses, *Database Programming and Design (Supplement)*, pp. S6-S11.

Tanenbaum, A. S. (1996) *Computer Networks*, Prentice-Hall, Englewood Cliffs, NJ.

Varney, S. E. (1996) Will Intranets lay waste to groupware?, *Datamation,* Dec. 1996, pp. 72-80.

All the above provide further detail on aspects of the technology which have been introduced very briefly in this chapter. Further references are provided in the bibliography.

Questions

1. What is a computer network?
2. What are the main reasons for organisations using computer-based networks? How do they contrast with home-based networks?
3. Explain the terms open and closed networks. Explain how open systems contribute to the notion of portability.
4. What are the specific benefits of open systems?
5. What are the three elements of client-server computing?
6. What are the advantages and risks of client-server technology?
7. What are the main concepts of object technology? List each with a brief description.
8. What is data mining used for? What are the information types that it can produce? Distinguish between data warehousing and data mining.
9. Distinguish between expert systems and neural networks.
10. What are multimedia systems? How can they support virtual reality?
11. Explain the term workflow computing. Include in your answer the distinction between structured and unstructured workflow.
12. Distinguish between the Internet and World Wide Web. How are Web documents created and accessed?
13. Identify the main potential business application benefits from using the Internet.
14. Describe the use of Intranets by organisations and their advantages.
15. What are legacy systems?
16. Explain the terms OLTP and OLAP.

Areas to debate

1. Client-server computing involves decisions about distribution. Identify the components that can be distributed and the alternative distribution strategies that might be adopted.

2. For each of the technologies identified in this chapter, explore the literature to identify the main topics of concern about them. Produce a report discussing these.
3. Explore the literature on workflow computing and groupware. What methods and tools are available and needed for organisations to introduce such technologies?
4. Discuss the significance to the information systems developer of the various technologies described in this chapter?

CASE STUDY

What technology described in this chapter might be relevant to Asifiori Salons? Describe how it may fit into the organisation. Would more aspects be relevant if the organisation was much bigger?

BIBLIOGRAPHY

Ackoff, R. (1967) Management misinformation systems, *Management Science*, **14**, 4, pp. 147-56.

Ahituv, N., Neumann, S. & Riley, N. H. (1994) *Principles of Information Systems for Management*, 4th edition, B&E Tech, New York.

Alavi, M. & Weiss, I. R. (1985) Managing the risks associated with end-user computing, *Journal of Management Information Systems* **2**, 3, pp. 5-20.

Amoroso, D. L. & Cheney, P. H. (1987) A report on the state of end-user computing in large North American insurance firms, *Journal of Information Management*, **8**, 2, pp. 39-48.

Amoroso, D. L. & Cheney P. H. (1992) Quality end-user developed applications: some essential ingredients, *Data Base*, **23**, pp. 1-11.

Avison, D. E. & Shah, H. U. (1994) From third generation to fourth generation applications development: a case study, *Information Technology and People*, **6**, 4, pp. 233-248.

Avison, D. E. (1992) *Information Systems Development: A Database Approach* 2nd edition, McGraw-Hill, Maidenhead.

Avison, D. E. & Fitzgerald, G. (1995) *Information Systems Development: Methodologies Techniques and Tools*, 2nd edition, McGraw-Hill, Maidenhead.

Avison, D. E. & Taylor, V. (1997) Information systems development methodologies: a classification according to problem situation, *Journal of Information Technology*, **12**, 1, pp. 73-81.

Ballantine, J. A., Stray, S. J. & Galliers, R. D. (1996) Information systems/technology evaluation practice: evidence from UK organisations, *Journal of Information Technology*, **11**, pp. 129-141.

Barnatt, C. (1996) *Management Strategy and Information Technology Text and Readings*, Thomson, London.

Batra, D. & Marakas, G. M. (1995) Conceptual data modelling in theory and practice, *European Journal of Information Systems*, **4**, pp. 184-193.

Bento, A. M. (1994) Systems analysis: a decision approach, *Information and Management*, **27**, 3, pp. 185-194.

Benyon, D. & Skidmore, S. (1987) Towards a tool kit for the systems analyst, *Computer Journal*, **30**, 1, pp. 2-7.

Berghel, H. L. (1996) The client side of the web, *Communications of the ACM*, **39**, pp. 33-40.

Bernard, R. (1996) *The Corporate Intranet*, Wiley, New York, NY.

Beynon-Davies, P. (1995) Information systems 'failure': the case of the London Ambulance Service's computer aided despatch project, *European Journal of Information Systems*, **4**, pp. 171-184.

Bhimani, A. (1996) Securing the commercial internet, *Communications of the ACM*, **39**, 6, pp. 29-35.

Bigus, J. P. (1996) *Data Mining with Neural Networks*, McGraw-Hill, Maidenhead.

Booch, G. (1994) *Object-Oriented Design with Applications*, Benjamin/Cummings, Redwood City, Ca.

Borenstein, N. S. (1996) Perils and pitfalls of practical cyberspace, *Communications of the ACM*, **39**, 6, pp. 36-44.

Bosco, M. F. & Gibelli, M. (1991) Extending entity-relationship systems to support hypotheses, constraints, versions and documents, *Information and Software Technology*, **33**, 8, pp. 538-546.

Brachman, R., Khabaza, T., Kloesgen, W., Simoudis, E. & Pratetsky-Shapiro, G. (1996). Mining business data, *Communications of the ACM*, **39**, 11, pp. 42-48.

Brancheau, J. C., Janz, B. D. & Wetherbe, J. C. (1996) Key issues in information systems management: 1994-95 SIM Delphi results, *MIS Quarterly*, **20**, 2, pp. 225-242.

Bruno, L. (1996) Internet security: how much is enough?, *Data Communications*, April 1996, pp. 60-72.

Bullen, C. V. & Rockart, J. F. (1984) *A Primer on Critical Success Factors*, Information Systems Working Paper (No. 69), Sloan School of Management, MIT.

Burger, J. (1993) *The Desktop Multimedia Bible*, Addison-Wesley, Reading, Ma.

Buzan, T. (1993) *The Mind Map Book*, BBC Books, London.

CACM (1997), Special feature on the debugging scandal & what to do about it, *Communications of the ACM*, **40**, 4.

Chatzoglou, P. D. & Macaulay, L. (1996) Requirements capture and IS methodologies, *Information Systems Journal*, **6**, pp. 209-225.

Chau, P. Y. C. (1994) Selection of packaged software in small businesses, *European Journal of Information Systems*, **3**, 4, pp. 292-302.

Chen, P. P. S. (1976) The entity-relationship model - towards a unified view of data, *ACM Transactions on Database Systems*, **1**, 2, pp. 9-36.

Clifton, H. D. & Sutcliffe, A. G. (1994) *Business Information Systems*, 5th edition, Prentice-Hall, Chichester.

Coad, P. & Yourdon, E. (1991) *Object-Oriented Analysis*, Prentice-Hall, Englewood Cliffs, NJ.

Codd, E. F. (1972) A relational model of data for large shared data banks, *Communications of the ACM*, **13**, 6, pp. 377-387.

Coleman, D., Arnold, P., Bodoff, S., Dollin, C., Gilcrist, H., Hayes. F. & Jeremaes, P. (1994) *Object-Oriented Development: the Fusion Method*, Prentice-Hall, Englewood Cliffs, NJ.

Comer, D. E. (1995) *The Internet Book*, Prentice Hall, Englewood Cliffs, NJ.

Computing (1996) Workflow computing, *Computing*, 25th July 1996, pp. 21-22.

Corey, M. & Abbey, M. (1996) *Oracle Data Warehousing*, McGraw-Hill, New York, NY.

Coupe, R. T. (1994) A critique of the methods for measuring the impact of CASE software, *European Journal of Information Systems*, **3**, 1, pp. 28-36.

Currie, W. L. (1996) Outsourcing in the private and public sectors: an unpredictable IT Strategy, *European Journal of Information Systems*, **4**, pp. 226-236.

Currie, W. L. & Willcocks, L. (1996), The new branch Columbus project at Royal Bank of Scotland: the implementation of large-scale business process re-engineering, *Journal of Strategic Information Systems*, **5**, 3, pp. 213-236.

Curtis, B. (1992) The CASE for Process, In K. E. Kendall., K. Lyytinen. & J. I. DeGross. (eds.), *The Impact of Computer Supported Technologies on Information Systems Development*, North-Holland, Amsterdam.

Curtis, G. (1995) *Business Information Systems: Analysis, Design and Practice*, 2nd edition, Addison-Wesley, Wokingham.

Daniels, C. (1991) *The Management Challenge of Information Technology*, Economist and Business International, London.

DeMarco, T. (1978) *Structured Analysis and System Specification*, Prentice-Hall, Englewood Cliffs, NJ.

Devlin, B. (1996) *Data Warehouse: From Architecture to Implementation*, Addison-Wesley, Reading, Ma.

Dilly, R. (1995) *Data Mining: An Introduction*, http://www.pcc.qub.ac.uk/tec/courses/datamining/datamining

Dingley, S. & Shah, H. U. (1996), Strategic management and soft systems analysis: a convergence, *Systemist*, **18**, 1, pp. 8-27.

Dingley, S. & Shah, H. U. (1996) Uniting strategic learning and soft systems concepts to support the strategic alignment of information systems development, *Business Information Systems 6th Annual Conference,* 1996, Manchester, UK.

Doke, E. R. & Barrier, T. (1994) An assessment of information systems taxonomies: time to re-evaluate?, *Journal of Information Technology,* **9**, pp. 149-157.

Doukidis, G. I., Lybereas, P. & Galliers, R. D. (1996) Information systems planning in small business - a stages of growth analysis, *Journal of Systems and Software,* 33, 2, pp. 189-201.

Downs, E., Clare, P. & Coe, I. (1988) *Structured Systems Analysis and Design Method: Application and Context.* 2nd edition, Prentice-Hall, Hemel Hempstead.

Drummond, H. (1996) The politics of risk, trials and tribulations of the Taurus project, *Journal of Information Technology,* **11**, 4, pp. 347-357.

Earl, M. (1989) *Management Strategies for Information Technology,* Prentice-Hall, Hemel Hempstead.

Earl, M. J. (1992) Putting information technology in its place: a polemic for the nineties, *Journal of Information Technology,* **7**, 2, pp. 100-108.

Earl, M. J. (1993) Experiences in strategic information systems planning, *MIS Quarterly,* **17**, 1, pp. 1-24.

Ein-Dor, P. & Segev, E. (1991) Intensity of end-user computing, *Data Base,* **22**, 1/2, pp. 30-37.

Engels, G., Gogolla, M., Hohenstein, U., Hulsmann, K., Lohr-Richter, P., Saake, G. & Ehrich, H-D. (1992) Conceptual modelling of database applications using an extended entity-relationship model, *Data and Knowledge Engineering,* **9**, 2, pp. 157-204.

Eva, M. (1994) *SSADM Version 4: A User's Guide.* 2nd edition, McGraw-Hill, Maidenhead.

Ewusimensah, K. & Przasnyski, Z. H. (1995) Learning from abandoned information systems development projects, *Journal of Information Technology,* **10**, 1, pp. 3-14.

Farbey, F., Land, F. & Targett, D. (1992) Evaluating investments in information technology, *Journal of Information Technology,* **7**, 2, pp. 109-121.

Farbey, F., Targett, D. & Land, F. (1992) Matching an IT project with an appropriate method of evaluation: a research note on 'Evaluating investments in IT', *Journal of Information Technology,* **9**, pp. 239-243.

Fayad, M. E., Tsai, W. & Fulghum, M. L. (1996) Transition to object-oriented software development, *Communications of the ACM*, **39**, 2, pp. 108-121.

Fayyad, U. & Uthurusamy, R. (1996) Data mining and knowledge discovery in databases, *Communications of the ACM*, **39**, 11, pp. 24-26.

Fidler, C. & Rogerson, S. (1996) *Strategic Management Support Systems*, Pitman, London.

Fitzgerald, B. (1996) Formalised systems development methodologies: a critical perspective, *Information Systems Journal*, **6**, 1, pp. 3-23.

Flynn, D. J. & Hepburn, P. A. (1994) Strategic planning for information systems - a case study of a UK metropolitan council, *European Journal of Information Systems*, **3**, 3, pp. 207-217.

Flynn, D. J. & Arce, E. A. (1995) Theoretical and practical issues in the use of strategic information systems planning (SISP): approaches to integrating business and IT in organisations, *International Journal of Computer Applications in Technology*, **8**, 12, pp. 61-68.

Frenzel, C. W. (1992) *Management of Information Technology*, Boyd & Fraser, Boston, Ma.

Galliers, R. D. (1993), Towards a flexible information architecture: integrating business strategies, information system strategies and business process redesign, *Journal of Information Systems*, **3**, 3, pp. 199-213.

Galliers, R. D., Merali, Y. & Spearing, L. (1994) Coping with information technology? How British executives perceive the key information systems management issues in the mid-1990s, *Journal of Information Technology*, **9**, 3, pp. 223-238.

Gora, M. (1996) Object-oriented analysis and design: guidelines for applying object modelling and object orientation to your applications, *DBMS*, September, 1996.

Gora, M. (1996) Object-oriented analysis and design: the good, the bad and the ugly of OOAD methodologies and various approaches to using them, *DBMS*, June, 1996.

Gorry, G. A. & Scott Morton, M. (1971) A framework for management information systems, *Sloan Management Review*, **13**, 1, pp. 55-70.

Hammer, M. & Champy, J. (1993) *Reengineering the Corporation: A Manifesto for Business Revolution*. Harper Business, New York.

Hammergren, T. C. (1996) *Data Warehousing: Building the Corporate Knowledge Base*, Thomson, London.

Hicks, J. O. (1993) *Management Information Systems: A User Perspective*, West, Minneapolis.

Huff, S. L., Munro, M. C. & Marcolin, B. (1992) Modelling and measuring end user sophistication, *Proceedings of ACM SIGCPR Conference*, April 1992, Cincinnati, Ohio.

Iivari, J. & Hirschheim, R. (1996) Analysing information systems development: a comparison and analysis of eight IS development approaches, *Information Systems Journal*, **21**, 7, pp. 551-575.

Iivari, J. (1995), Factors affecting the perceptions of CASE effectiveness, *European Journal of Information Systems*, **4**, pp. 143-158.

Iivari, J. (1996) Why are CASE tools not used?, *Communications of the ACM*, **39**, 10, pp. 94-103.

Iivari, J. (1994) Object-oriented information analysis - a comparison of 6 object-oriented analysis methods, *Proceedings of the IFIP WG8.1 Working Conference on Methods and associated tools for the information systems life cycle*, Maastricht, Netherlands 26-28 Sept 1994, **55**, pp. 85-110.

Inmon, W. H. (1996), *Building the Data Warehouse*, 2nd edition, Wiley, New York, NY.

Inmon, W. H., Welch, J. D. & Glassey, K. L. (1997) *Managing the Data Warehouse*, Wiley, New York, NY.

Isaak, J., Lewis, K., Thompson, K. & Straub, R. (1994), *Open Systems Handbook: A Guide to building open systems*, IEEE.

Jackson, M. A. (1983) *Systems Development*. Prentice Hall, Hemel Hempstead.

Jacobson, I. (1992) *Object-Oriented Systems Engineering*, Addison-Wesley, Reading, Ma.

James, G. (1996), Intranets rescue reengineering, *Datamation*, Dec. 1996, pp. 38-45.

Joshi, K. (1992) Interpersonal skills for cooperative user-analyst relationships: some research issues, *Data Base*, **23**, 1, pp. 23-25.

Kappelman, L. A. & McLean, E. R. (1994) User engagement in the development, implementation, and use of information technologies, *Proceedings of 27th Hawaii International Conference on System Sciences*, volume 3, pp. 512-521.

Khan, E. H. (1992) The effects of information centres on the growth of end-user computing, *Information and Management*, **23**, 5, pp. 279-289.

Kimball, R. (1996) *The Data Warehouse Toolkit: Practical Techniques for Building Dimensional Data Warehouses*, Wiley, New York, NY.

King, M. & Macaulay, L. (1997) Information technology investment evaluation: evidence and interpretation, *Journal of Information Technology*, **12**, 2, pp. 131-143.

Larijani, L. C. (1994) *The Virtual Reality Primer*, McGraw-Hill, New York, NY.

Laudon, K. C. (1995) Ethical concepts and information technology, *Communications of the ACM*, **38**, pp. 33-39.

Lawrence, D. & Shah, H. U. (1994), Tools for supporting user development of information systems, *Third Conference on Information Technology and its Applications (ITA '94)*, 2-3 April 1994, Leicester, UK.

Lawrence, D. R., Shah, H. U. & Golder, P. A. (1996) Business users and the information system development process: a need to know basis, *IFIP W. G. 3.4 conference 8-12th July (The Place of Information Technology in Management Education)*, Melbourne, Australia.

Lawrence, D., Shah, H. U. & Golder P. A. (1997) End user computing - how an organisation can maximise potential, *STEP '97*, 14-18th July 1997, London.

Lawrence, D. R., Shah, H. U. & Golder, P. A. (1996) Business user development - success factor development, *Proceedings of PRIISM '96*, 1-3 Jan 1996, Maui, pp. 33-37.

Lazarevic, B. & Misic, V. (1991) Extending the entity-relationship model to capture dynamic behaviour, *European Journal of Information Systems*, **1**, 2, pp. 95-106.

Lederer, A. L. & Salmela (1996) Toward a theory of strategic information systems planning, *Journal of Strategic Information Systems*, **5**, 3, pp. 237-253.

Levitt, L. (1996) *Intranets, Internet Technologies Deployed behind the Firewall for Corporate Productivity*, http:www.process.com/intranets/wp2.htp

Linthicum, D. S. (1996) Selecting a client/server application development tool, *DBMS*, July 1996.

Linthicum, D. S. (1996) Tool time: taking stock of the available development tools and what may work for you. *Internet Systems*, October 1996.

Linthicum, D. S. (1997) Driving development: a look at the reasoning behind today's application development tools, *DBMS*, April 1997.

Macintosh (1987) *Human Interface Guidelines: The Apple Desktop Interface*, Addison-Wesley, Reading, Ma.

Martin, J. (1985), *Fourth Generation Languages - Volume I: Principles*, Prentice Hall, Englewood Cliffs, NJ.

Mason, D. & Willcocks, L. (1994) *Systems Analysis, Systems Design*, McGraw-Hill, Maidenhead.

Mathiassen, L. & Sorensen, C. (1996), The capability maturity model and CASE, *Information Systems Journal*, **6**, pp. 195-208.

Mattison, R. (1996) *Data Warehousing: Strategies, Tools and Techniques*, McGraw-Hill, New York, NY.

Meredith, M. E. & Khader, A. (1996) Divide and aggregate: designing large warehouses, *Database Programming & Design*, June 1996, pp. 24-30.

Miter, N. N. (1996) Convergence and divergence in information systems and knowledge based systems development methodologies: a case for integrated strategic planning, *European Journal of Information Systems*, **4**, pp. 237-247.

Monteiro, L. & Macdonald, S. (1996) From efficiency to flexibility: the strategic use of information in the airline industry, *Journal of Strategic Information Systems*, **5**, 3, pp. 169-188.

NCC (1995) *SSADM 4+: Version 4.2*. Volumes 1 and 2, NCC Blackwell, Oxford.

Nelson, R. R. & Cheney, P. H. (1987), Training end users: an exploratory study, *MIS Quarterly*, **11**, 4, pp. 547-559.

O'Brien, J. A. (1991) *Introduction to Information Systems*, Irwin, Boston, Ma.

Parsaye, K. (1996) Data mines for data warehouses, *Database Programming and Design (Supplement)*, Sept 1996, pp. S6-S11.

Poe, V. (1996) *Building a Data Warehouse for Decision Support*, Prentice Hall, Englewood Cliffs, NJ.

Porter, M. (1985) *Competitive Advantage*, Free Press, London.

Poulymenakou, A. & Holmes, A. (1996) A contingency framework for the investigation of information systems failures, *European Journal of Information Systems*, **5**, pp. 34-46.

Powell, P. L. & Klein, J. H. (1996) Risk management for information systems development, *Journal of Information Technology*, **11**, 4, pp. 309-319.

Price Waterhouse *IT Review* (annually), Price Waterhouse, London.

PRINCE 2 (1996a) *PRINCE Version 2 Reference Manual*, Stationary Office, London.

PRINCE 2 (1996b) http://www.open.gov.uk:80/CCTA/prince

Rai, A. (1995) External information source and channel effectiveness and the diffusion of CASE innovations: an empirical study, *European Journal of Information Systems*, **4**, pp. 93-102.

Renaud, P. (1993) *Introduction to Client/Server Systems: A Guide for the Systems Professional*, Wiley, New York, NY.

Reynolds, G. W. (1992) *Information Systems for Managers*, 2nd edition, West, Minnesota.

Rockhart, J. F. & Flannery, L. S. (1983), The management of end-user computing, *Communications of the ACM*, **26**, 10, pp. 776-784.

Rumbaugh, J. (1991) *Object-Oriented Modelling and Design*, Prentice-Hall, Englewood Cliffs, NJ.

Schneiderman, B. (1987), *Designing the User Interface: Strategies for Effective Human-Computer Interaction*, Addison-Wesley, Reading, Ma.

Shah, H. U., Dingley, S. & Golder, P. A. (1994) Managing systems development - bridging the culture gap between users and developers, *Journal of Systems Management*, **45**, 4, pp. 18-21.

Shah, H. U. & Lawrence, D. (1996) A study of end-user computing and the provision of tool support to advance end user empowerment, *Journal of End-User Computing*, **8**, 1, pp. 13-21.

Shimberg, D. (1995) Following a client/server database methodology, *DBMS*, May 1995.

Shlaer, S. & Mellor, S. J. (1988) *Object-Oriented Systems Analysis - Modeling the World in Data*, Prentice-Hall, Englewood Cliffs, NJ.

Shlaer, S. & Mellor, S. J. (1992) *Object Lifecycles: Modeling the World in States*, Prentice-Hall, Englewood Cliffs, NJ.

Tanenbaum, A. S. (1996), *Computer Networks*, Prentice Hall, Englewood Cliffs, NJ.

Taylor, M., Moynihan, E. & Wood- Harper, T. (1997) Knowledge for Software Maintenance, *Journal of Information Technology*, **12**, 2, pp. 155-166.

Van Dam, A. (1997), CACM the next 50 years, *Communications of the ACM*, **40**, 2, pp. 63-69.

Van Wegen, B. & De Hoog, R. (1996) Measuring the economic value of information systems, *Journal of Information Technology*, **11**, pp. 247-260.

Varney, S. E. (1996) Will Intranets lay waste to groupware?, *Datamation*, Dec. 1996, pp. 72-80.

Vidgen, R. (1997) Stakeholders, soft systems and technology: separation and mediation in the analysis of information systems requirements, *Information Systems Journal*, **7**, 1, pp. 21-46.

Ward, J., Taylor, P. & Bond, P. (1996) Evaluation and realisation of IS/IT benefits: an empirical study of current practice, *European Journal of Information Systems*, **4**, pp. 214-225.

Ward, J. & Griffiths, P. (1996) *Strategic Planning for Information Systems*, 2nd edition, Wiley, Chichester.

Watt, J. (1985) *Applied Fourth Generation Languages*, Sigma, Wilmslow.

Weaver, P. L. (1993*) Practical SSADM Version 4: A Complete Tutorial Guide*. Pitman, London.

Whitten, J. L., Bentley, L. D. & Barlow, V. M. (1994) *Systems Analysis and Design Methods*, Irwin, Boston, Ma.

Willcocks, L. (1992) Evaluating information technology investments: research findings and reappraisal. *Journal of Information Systems*, **2**, 4, pp. 243-268.

Willcocks, L., Fitzgerald, G. & Lacity, M. (1996) To outsource IT or not?: recent research on economics and evaluation practice, *European Journal of Information Systems*, **5**, pp. 143-160.

Wood-Harper, A. T., Corder, S., Wood, J. R. G. & Watson, H. (1996) How we profess: the ethical systems analyst, *Communications of the ACM*, **39**, 3, pp. 69-77.

Wu, S. Y. & Wu, M. S. (1994) *Systems Analysis and Design*, West, Minneapolis.

Wynekoop, J. L. & Russo, N. L. (1997) Studying system development methodologies: an examination of research methods. *Information Systems Journal*, **7**, pp. 47-65.

Yeates, D., Shields, M. & Helmy, D. (1994) *Systems Analysis and Design*, Pitman, London.

Zinatelli, N., Crass, P. B. & Cavaye, A. I. M. (1996) End user computing sophistication and success in small firms, *European Journal of Information Systems*, **5**, pp. 172-181.

INDEX

Items in *italic* refer to names of cited authors (see also Bibliography), companies, and products. Page numbers in **bold** indicate principal references.